SETON HALL UNIVERSITY

MAIN

S0-BNA-713

3 3073 00260104 3

DATE DUE	
MAR 1 6 1999	
APR 1 3 1999	
MAY 2 4 2003	
GAYLORD	PRINTED IN U.S.A.

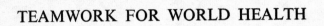

TEAMWORK FOR WORLD HEALTH

Florence Nightingale, O.M., 1820–1910.

Bronze cast from a bust by Sir John Steell, 1862. Photograph reproduced by kind permission of the National Portrait Gallery, London.

Teamwork for World Health

A Ciba Foundation Symposium
In honour of Professor S. Artunkal

Edited by
GORDON WOLSTENHOLME
and
MAEVE O'CONNOR

SETON HALL UNIVERSITY
SCIENCE LIBRARY
SOUTH ORANGE, N. J.

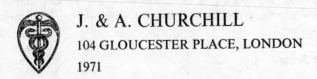
J. & A. CHURCHILL
104 GLOUCESTER PLACE, LONDON
1971

First published 1971

With 5 plates

International Standard Book Number 0.7000.1497.7

SCIENCE
LIBRARY

Sci. Lib

RA
442
T43

© *Longman Group Ltd.*, 1971

All rights reserved, no part of this publication may be reproduced, stored in a retrieval system, or transmitted, in any form or by any means, electronic, mechanical, photocopying, recording or otherwise, without the prior permission of the copyright owner.

Printed in Great Britain

Contents

Membership

Symposium on Teamwork for World Health
held at the Tarabya Grand Hotel, Istanbul, 8th–12th June 1970

R. V. Christie (Chairman)	Emeritus Professor of Medicine; Office of the Dean, Faculty of Medicine, McGill University, McIntyre Medical Sciences Building, 3655 Drummond Street, Montreal 110, Quebec, Canada
S. Artunkal	Professor of Pharmacology and Therapeutics, University of Istanbul; Moda, Devriye sokak 2/1, Kadiköy, Istanbul, Turkey
T. D. Baker	Professor of International Health, Dept of International Health, School of Hygiene and Public Health, The Johns Hopkins University, 615 North Wolfe Street, Baltimore, Maryland 21205, U.S.A.
A. L. Banks	Professor of Human Ecology, University of Cambridge, England; from 1971 at World Health Organization, Avenue Appia, 1211 Geneva, Switzerland
G. J. Barbero	Chairman, Dept of Pediatrics, Hahnemann Medical College and Hospital of Philadelphia, 230 North Broad Street, Philadelphia, Pennsylvania 19102, U.S.A.
E. Braga	Director, Division of Education and Training, World Health Organization, Avenue Appia, 1211 Geneva, Switzerland
H. Bridger	The Tavistock Institute of Human Relations, The Tavistock Centre, Belsize Lane, London N.W.3, England
M. Dadgar	Director-General, Health Corps Organization, Ministry of Health, Teheran, Iran
A. G. Dickson	Honorary Director, Community Service Volunteers, Toynbee Hall, 28 Commercial Road, London E.1, England

MEMBERSHIP

I. Dogramaci — President, and Professor of Paediatrics, Hacettepe University, Ankara, Turkey

N. H. Fişek — Professor of Community Studies, Institute of Population Studies, Hacettepe University, Ankara, Turkey

Yvonne Hentsch — Director, Nursing Bureau, League of Red Cross Societies, 1211 Geneva 19, Switzerland

K. R. Hill — Professor of Pathology, Pathology Unit, Royal Free Hospital, Gray's Inn Road, London W.C.1, England

Lisbeth Hockey — Nursing Research Officer, Queen's Institute of District Nursing, 57 Lower Belgrave Street, London S.W.1, England

J. S. Horn — Lecturer, Dept of Anatomy, London Hospital Medical College, Turner Street, London E.1, England; 1954–1969, Professor of Orthopaedics and Traumatology, Peking

Sarah Israel — Medical Officer in Charge, Government of India Family Planning Training and Research Centre, 332 Sardar, Vallabhbhai Patel Road, Bombay 4, India

M. H. King — Professor of Social Medicine, Dept of Social Medicine, University of Zambia, P.O. Box 2379, Lusaka, Zambia

Docia A. N. Kisseih — Chief Nursing Officer, Ministry of Health, Nursing Division, P.O. Box M. 44, Accra, Ghana

J. A. C. de Kock van Leeuwen — Professor, and Director, Nederlands Instituut voor Praeventieve Geneeskunde, Wassenaarseweg 56, Leiden, Holland

A. Ordoñez-Plaja — Former Minister of Public Health, Carrera 7 Bis, 94–65, Bogotá D.E., Colombia; 1970–71: Milbank Faculty Fellow, Dept of Epidemiology and Public Health, Yale University School of Medicine, 60 College Street, New Haven, Connecticut 06510, U.S.A.

viii

M. Rebhun	Associate Professor of Sanitary Engineering, Sanitary Engineering Laboratories, Technion-Israel Institute of Technology, Haifa, Israel
H. B. L. Russell	Senior Lecturer in Tropical and Preventive Medicine, Dept of Social Medicine, University of Edinburgh, Usher Institute, Warrender Park Road, Edinburgh 9, Scotland
B. L. Salmon	Deputy Chairman, Messrs J. Lyons & Co. Ltd, Cadby Hall, London W.14, England
Fahrünnisa Seden	Tutor, Public Health Nursing, Zeynep-Kamil Nursing College, Istanbul; 35/4 Sakayik Sok, Teşvikiye, Istanbul, Turkey
G. E. W. Wolstenholme	Director, Ciba Foundation, 41 Portland Place, London W1N 4BN, England
F. G. Young	Professor of Biochemistry, and Master of Darwin College; Dept of Biochemistry, University of Cambridge, Tennis Court Road, Cambridge CB2 1QW, England

Observers

General Professor Dr N. Ayanoğlu,
Gülhane Askeri Tip Akadenisi
   Komutani,
Ankara

Dr B. Berkarda,
Assistant Professor,
University of Istanbul,
Tedavi Klinigi,
Istanbul

General M. A. Büyükçakmak,
M.S.B. Saglik Başkani,
Ankara

Miss Esman Deniz,
Blok Apt. 9/2 Bal Mumcu,
Besiktas,
Istanbul

Professor Dr E. S. Egeli,
Former Rector,
University of Istanbul,
Yazi Iseri Müdürlüğü,
Istanbul

Dr J. Gallagher,
Education and Training Officer,
WHO Regional Office for Europe,
Scherfigsveg 8,
Copenhagen, Denmark

Dr R. Heybeli,
Assistant Under Secretary,
Ministry of Health and Social
   Assistance,
Saglik ve Sosyal Yardim Bakanliği,
Müstasar Muarini,
Ankara

Dr S. Hubbard,
Editor,
CIBA Journal;
CIBA-GEIGY Ltd,
CH4002 Basle, Switzerland

Professor Dr D. Karan,
Professor of Psychiatry,
Faculty of Medicine,
Hacettepe University,
Ankara

Professor Dr S. Karatay,
Faculty of Medicine,
University of Istanbul,
Istanbul

Professor Dr Ilhan Kerse,
Dean,
Faculty of Medicine,
Hacettepe University,
Ankara

Dr E. de Oliveira,
World Health Organization,
WR/Turkey,
P.K. 235-Yenisehir,
Ankara

Professor Dr E. Sabar,
Atatürk Üniversitesi Tip Fak,
Dekani,
Erzurum

Professor Dr N. Terzioğlu,
Rector,
University of Istanbul,
Beyazit Şehir,
Istanbul

Miss Asuman Türer,
Kizilay Üzel Hemşirelik Koleji,
Aksaray,
Istanbul

Dr I. Urgancioğlu,
University of Istanbul,
Tedavi Klinigi,
Haseki Hastanesi,
Istanbul

Mrs Perihan Velioğlu,
Director,
Florence Nightingale Yüsek Hemşire,
Okulu Müdürlüğü,
Sişli,
Istanbul

Mr C. A. W. Williamson,
Regional Director of the British
   Council,
Miralay Şefik Bey Sokak,
Reşat Bey Apt. No. 1/2–3
Ayazpaşa, Istanbul

Preface

At the Ciba Foundation's symposium on *Health of Mankind* in 1967 the disturbing imbalance between the urgent need for medical care in most parts of the world and the lack of manpower in the health services was made very clear. At that symposium I put forward an idea for a World Health Service which I hoped would help to make members of the health professions, in particular, more aware of the priorities in medical care and of the vital necessity of employing all members of the health team in the most humane and economic manner possible.

The symposium on *Teamwork for World Health* recorded here grew out of that meeting, and out of the increasing uneasiness many people have expressed about international inequalities in health care. The 150th anniversary of the birth of Florence Nightingale, who first provided a team of skilled nurses to assist doctors at Scutari during the Crimean War, prompted the Foundation to hold this symposium in Istanbul, to examine ways in which the concept of teamwork could lead to more effective national and international use of medical resources.

The symposium was held in honour of Professor S. Artunkal, for many years a good friend and valued representative for Turkey on the Ciba Foundation's Scientific Advisory Panel. In addition to the members of the meeting it was a great pleasure to welcome other representatives of Turkish medicine and nursing as observers at the symposium. Their presence added much to the value of the many discussions outside the conference room which were characteristic of the week.

The meeting was held in the Tarabya Grand Hotel on the shores of the Bosphorus, but through the courtesy of the Prefect, the Hon. Dr Fahri Atabey, we were privileged in being able to hold the opening session in the City Hall, Istanbul, and in having the present Rector of Istanbul University, Professor N. Terzioğlu, as chairman there; the previous Rector, Professor S. Egeli, kindly acted as chairman of the closing session at the hotel. The Foundation is also greatly indebted to Professor R. V. Christie for coming from Montreal to take the chair at the rest of the meeting with his characteristically vigorous and friendly authority.

Dr Katherine Elliott, Assistant Medical Director at the Foundation, played a large part in organizing this symposium. We owe much to the chairman of our Executive Council, Professor F. G. Young, for his summary of the proceedings, prepared as the symposium progressed; and we gratefully record our warmest appreciation of the continuing teamwork of all contributors in the preparation of this volume.

G. E. W. WOLSTENHOLME

The Ciba Foundation

The Ciba Foundation was opened in 1949 to promote international cooperation in medical and chemical research. It owes its existence to the generosity of CIBA Ltd, Basle (now CIBA-GEIGY Ltd), who, recognizing the obstacles to scientific communication created by war, man's natural secretiveness, disciplinary divisions, academic prejudices, distance, and differences of language, decided to set up a philanthropic institution whose aim would be to overcome such barriers. London was chosen as its site for reasons dictated by the special advantages of English charitable trust law (ensuring the independence of its actions), as well as those of language and geography.

The Foundation's house at 41 Portland Place, London, has become well known to workers in many fields of science. Every year the Foundation organizes six to ten three-day symposia and three to four shorter study groups, all of which are published in book form. Many other scientific meetings are held, organized either by the Foundation or by other groups in need of a meeting place. Accommodation is also provided for scientists visiting London, whether or not they are attending a meeting in the house.

The Foundation's many activities are controlled by a small group of distinguished trustees. Within the general framework of biological science, interpreted in its broadest sense, these activities are well summed up by the motto of the Ciba Foundation: *Consocient Gentes*—let the peoples come together.

SPEECH BY PROFESSOR NÂZIM TERZIOĞLU

Rector of the University of Istanbul

ON the occasion of the 150th anniversary of the birth of Florence Nightingale, the Ciba Foundation has very appropriately chosen Istanbul for the symposium on *Teamwork for World Health*. The name Florence Nightingale has been, and will always be, a symbol of benevolence, affection, courage and bravery in world history. We are very proud of the fact that this great woman will again be commemorated in our country, where she so affectionately and skilfully took care of the wounded during the Crimean War. On behalf of Istanbul University, I therefore take the liberty of thanking and expressing our gratitude to the Ciba Foundation for organizing the symposium in our city. I would also like to let you know that the University is ready to do all it can for the success of this most important symposium.

I believe that cultural and scientific relations are more important than diplomacy for the development of mutual understanding between nations, and contribute more to the progress of civilization. Political events play a minor role where sound international understanding is achieved through cultural and scientific means.

I wish the best of success to the symposium on *Teamwork for World Health* and welcome its distinguished members to our University and our city.

1

SPEECH BY PROFESSOR R. V. CHRISTIE

Emeritus Professor of Medicine, McGill University, Montreal
Chairman of the Symposium on Teamwork for World Health

FIRST, Mr Rector, I would like to congratulate the Ciba Foundation on its wisdom and good taste in choosing this beautiful city for the scene of our deliberations. This is not my first visit, but Istanbul with its natural and architectural beauty and its history is, like Rome and Athens, a city which should never be visited only once.

There are 26 members of this symposium, drawn from 13 different countries, including representatives from the World Health Organization and the League of Red Cross Societies, which must be the two largest and most successful organizations contributing to world health. We are here to discuss the various ways in which teamwork, or organized cooperation, can contribute to man's health.

Teamwork in preventive medicine has been with us for a long time, having received its first impetus when Edward Jenner discovered vaccination for smallpox in 1796. I, like any other visitor to Turkey, carry an international certificate of vaccination against smallpox, which is a fine example of teamwork on an international basis but, as will no doubt emerge from our discussions, this kind of international cooperation should be carried much further if the interests of mankind are to be served.

Teamwork in hospitals has also been with us for a long time, but it was Florence Nightingale, more than a hundred years ago, who taught us how hospitals should be organized and conducted. Today, with teams for cardiac surgery, for renal dialysis, for resuscitation and for the many laboratory and other procedures which have become part of medical routine, our hospitals have become very much more complicated and more expensive. New problems of management and support have arisen which have not yet been solved.

It is with the practising physician, who is the hard core of any medical service, that the need for teamwork has appeared most recently. When I graduated in 1925 it was said that all the physician needed in his office was two chairs, one for himself and one for the patient, and if he had forgotten to bring his stethoscope he could always put his ear to the patient's chest. Today the practitioner of medicine working in isolation is fast disappearing in most countries. In the towns the general practitioner has at his elbow the large hospitals, the laboratory services and the advice of specialists, all of which he needs if he is to render good service. In small towns the trend in many countries is towards the form-

2

ation of group practices, each containing the variety of knowledge and experience which allows the group to operate as a team with the support of a local hospital and its laboratory services.

It is in rural areas that the greatest difficulty arises in providing the patient with the variety of expertise his condition may demand. Unless this problem is solved I believe there will be increasing difficulty in recruiting practitioners to work in rural areas, because a good doctor is not content to practise second-class medicine even if he is well paid for it. One part of the solution is the provision of a team of nurses and social workers. Under these circumstances the public will be better served and the practitioner may be able to practise in a way that gives him satisfaction.

In the first part of our meeting we will discuss and criticize examples of team service which are now in operation, while during the second part we will define the direction in which events are leading us and the types of teamwork which should be planned for the future. It is a complicated and controversial subject but in this symposium we have a wide range of expertise and I am confident we will make a worthwhile contribution. On behalf of my colleagues, I thank the Rector for the encouragement of his generous welcome.

1: Florence Nightingale—Handmaid of Civilization*

G. E. W. WOLSTENHOLME

When Health is absent
Wisdom cannot reveal itself
Art cannot become manifest,
Strength cannot fight,
Wealth becomes useless
And Intelligence cannot be applied

HEROPHILUS, *c.* 300 B.C.

IN many parts of the world this year (1970) services and meetings are being held, lectures and exhibitions arranged, commemorative stamps issued, to remind us of the birth 150 years ago, on 12 May 1820, of one of the world's most remarkable women, Florence Nightingale.

We have the privilege of gathering together in Istanbul within sight of the Selimiye barracks, across the Bosphorus, in which for 20 months between 1854 and 1856 Florence Nightingale went through the severe experience which made her for the next 50 years the world's greatest authority on nursing; and we are met to discuss a subject—Teamwork for World Health—which was originally inspired by the role which Miss Nightingale's nurses played in support of the medical doctors attending the thousands of sick and wounded near this great city, at the crossroads of the world.

Florence Nightingale believed that at the age of 16 she had a direct call to God's service. She became acutely aware of the artificiality and frivolity of the conventional life expected of women in society in the mid-nineteenth century. Apart from those to whom marriage offered little scope for their talents, there were in Britain at that time about $2\frac{1}{2}$ million unmarried women, widows or spinsters, many with some education. Josephine Butler in 1866 said of them: "These women cannot teach because they are so ill-educated and again they are so ill-educated they can do nothing but teach." They were without any outlets for creative responsibility other than the role of a children's governess or a little charitable visiting of the sick and the poor. It was in calling upon the poor villagers near her home that Florence Nightingale became certain

* Introductory Lecture in Belediye Sarayinda, Istanbul.

5

that her lifelong duty lay in creating opportunities for respectable women to work as nurses, both in hospitals and in the poorer urban and rural districts. Despite her own strong affections she turned down offers of marriage in order to devote herself to her chosen task, and perhaps in this hard self-denial we can see the origins of her long life as a neurotic recluse and invalid after her return from the Crimean War. In a matter of months she had become a legendary figure. Although on her return to England she avoided all public demonstrations of adulation, from her perpetual lonely sickroom she used every ounce of her public influence to secure the reforms on which she had set her heart—reforms not only in nursing but also in hospital construction, sanitation, army welfare, and the advancement of the lives and prospects of the millions of inhabitants of India.

I have written elsewhere[6] of the perceptive and revolutionary views of this wise and passionate woman, but I should like to give you a few illustrations from her own writings[1] to demonstrate her exceptional qualities. Clearly I must begin with nursing.

"Nursing is putting us in the best possible condition for nature to restore or preserve health. Health is not only to be well, but to be able to use well every power we have to use." "Nursing must be treated like an Art in its relation to Medicine, Surgery and Hygiene; it is almost co-extensive with them." ". . . and the Art is nursing *the sick*; *not* nursing sickness."

A hit at the doctors, perhaps even nearer the mark 100 years later: "It is quite surprising how many men (some women do it too) practically behave as if the scientific end were the only one in view, or as if the sick body were but a reservoir for stowing medicines into, and the surgical disease only a curious case the sufferer has made for the attendant's special information."

Miss Nightingale wrote endlessly on hospitals, about anything from the composition of the walls and floors, to ventilation, to the provision of chutes for dirty linen. I give only two short general quotations: "It may seem a strange principle to enunciate as the very first requirement in a hospital that it should do the sick no harm." And: "Hospitals were made for patients—not patients for hospitals."

Facts, accurate facts, were ceaselessly demanded by Florence Nightingale and they came pouring into her lonely room from all parts of the world. She was a pioneer in the use of statistics and graphic representation, and in the recording of trustworthy figures for mortality and morbidity. More than 100 years ago she asked: ". . . mothers of families,—do you know that one in every seven infants in this civilized land of England perishes before it is one year old? That in London, two in every five die before they are five years old? and, in the great cities of England nearly one out of two? . . ."

The knowledge of health—correct feeding, clothing, cleanliness, space, ventilation—was to be taken into every home, and this form of nursing she regarded as superior to that done in hospitals: "A District Nurse . . . must be of a yet higher class and of a yet fuller training than a hospital nurse, because she has no hospital appliances at hand at all; and because she has to take notes of the case for the doctor, who has no one but her to report to him. She is his staff of clinical clerks, dressers, and nurses." The work made demands on heart, mind and body: ". . . the love that springs from the sympathy of a close and accurate knowledge of the ways, habits, the lives of the poor is not a mere sentiment, but an active and fruitful enthusiasm."

Florence Nightingale is famous, I might say notorious, for imposing discipline on nurses. This was to make it possible for respectable women to take up the work, but it was self-discipline, not authoritarianism, which she sought. "True loyalty to orders cannot be without the independent sense or energy of responsibility." And: "No one was ever able to govern who was not able to obey."

Miss Nightingale was no feminist; rather, she saw everybody doing all the tasks of which they were capable, regardless of sex. She wrote: "Women cannot stand alone (though, for that matter, still less can men)." Also: "There can be no freedom or progress without representation. And we must give women true education to deserve being represented. *Men* as well as women are not so well endowed with that preparation at present and if the persons represented are not worth much, of course the representatives will not be worth much."

Just as she regarded war between the sexes as irrelevant and distracting, so Florence Nightingale felt about prejudices in regard to class, colour, creed or race. Each rough soldier was an individual of dignity and value. Every Indian was her "fellow countryman or countrywoman". It was one world, in which the interests of one people were of importance to all. In 1873 she wrote: "This great essential work of regulation of the water of India is perhaps at this moment the most important question in the world." "There are, at this moment, at least 100 000 horse water power available and made no use of in the great irrigation canals. The canals will convey the goods to and from the manufactories, the irrigation will set free millions from agricultural labour for such work . . . with cheap labour, cheap power, cheap carriage, cheap food, India will have the very highest advantages for manufacture, for civilisation and also for life, and all that makes life worth living. . . ." But long before most people, Florence Nightingale recognized that "A people cannot really be helped except through itself. . . ." "A people is its own soil and its own water. Others may plant, but it must *grow* its own produce." And she commented shrewdly: "If all England could set their face against the Suez Canal, we must not be surprised if there are people

7

almost as stolid. Another nation had to cut the Canal for us and thus force upon us an incalculable benefit."

Her inspired theorizing in her ivory tower was not enough. She wrote passionately: "The want is nearly as old as the world, nearly as large as the world, as pressing as life and death . . ." "My mind is absorbed with the idea of the sufferings of man, I can hardly see anything else and all that the poets sing of the glories of this world seems to me untrue. All the people I see are eaten up with care or poverty or disease." And she can remind us today that: ". . . while we are choked with the flood of Sanitary books, pamphlets, publications, and lectures of all sorts . . . we have remained a book and a pen. We have not become a voice and a hand." ". . . it takes long, long years of patient, steady, persevering endeavour to bring any work to perfection, and still, O still must it be watered every day with care . . ."

Florence Nightingale had opinions which are worth hearing on a great many other matters, but these illustrations are enough for my present purpose.

And what is this purpose? I want to draw on these references, references to surplus and frustrated women, to the "simple, stern necessity" of nursing, to the needs of poorer nations and races who are all our 'countrymen', to the relationship between education and responsibility, and to Florence Nightingale's call for patience and perseverance.

The relief of the worst poverty, and the eradication or diminution of diseases which in the last 25 years have so immensely increased the number of people who live to middle and old age, still leave us with a world of gross, and indeed increasing, inequalities; inequalities which are being thrown into higher relief by the unprecedented tidal wave of population, which is only the first of bigger and bigger waves speeding towards us.

Some people may think that the dramatic lowering of mortality rates, and the vast increase in the number of people living to reproductive age and beyond, indicate that the great efforts of the World Health Organization (WHO) are already sufficiently successful—perhaps even too successful for the comfort of those blessed with a high and secure standard of living. Complacency is evident in the more developed countries, as was shown by the Report of the Pearson Commission on International Development,[3] published recently, which briefly notes the conquest of disease and ignores health as a factor in further economical and social development. Apparently we must remind ourselves that we live in a world where, for example, many hundreds of millions of people suffer so severely and continuously from chronic infestations and infections that they never learn what is meant by normal health or vigour, physical or mental; where, despite all the eradication campaigns, probably 25 million people a year still contract malaria; where there are between 15 and 30 million people still infected with tuberculosis; where 100 million each year suffer from a disease such as measles, carrying a mortality in some areas as high as 7 per cent; a world where one hospital bed in four is occupied by someone ill from infected water; where, if you look for them, you could find about 12 million affected by leprosy, and 10 to 12 millions who are blind; where between 300 and 500 million are undernourished; where in the technically advanced countries just about half of all the people consulting their doctors do so because of mental or emotional problems; a world where each year the number of cases of the common cold exceeds the whole world population.

How does the whole profession of medicine—doctors, nurses, midwives, dentists, veterinarians, sanitary engineers, pharmacists, health inspectors, radiographers, laboratory technicians, physiotherapists, and so on—respond to this physical, mental and social sickness of the world? So far, apparently, we have the situation quoted in the Bible: "Unto everyone that hath shall be given, and he shall have abundance; but from him that hath not shall be taken away even that which he hath."

The most privileged developed countries seduce more and more doctors and nurses away from the underprivileged countries; the towns entice them from the rural agricultural areas. The U.S.A. is said to employ 25 000 doctors from developing countries; in Britain there are 10 000 doctors from Asia and Africa, while probably not more than 1500 British doctors are working in developing countries.

The World Health Organization in 1963 proposed that one doctor for 10 000 people should be regarded as a minimum throughout the world. On this basis, Britain and the United States already have 12 to 16 times the minimum, compared with half the minimum in Nigeria, one-fifth the minimum in Malawi, and something like one-tenth the minimum in Ethiopia.[4] It is in England that: "Immigrant doctors meet dire need", according to a recent headline in *The Times*. Australia, Canada, France, Germany, Switzerland join in this draining of skill from countries at all times infinitely worse off than themselves. The number of medical graduates moving from one country to another each year is a minimum of 40000 and may well be as high as 100000.[2] When the first class of doctors graduated in one underdeveloped country a few years ago, practically the whole class went off together in a chartered plane to the United States.

What is true for doctors is true also for qualified paramedical professionals; for example in 1962/63, 7000 West Indian girls were training as nurses in the United Kingdom, compared with a total of 9000 qualified nurses and midwives on the register at that time throughout the West Indies; and experience shows that two-thirds of these nurses remain, after qualification, to work in England and Wales.

The favoured nations and regions represented by the U.S.A., the Soviet

Union, Europe, Canada, Australasia and Japan account for nearly 1000 million (that is rather less than one-third) of the world's population; excluding China, for which we have no figures, this one-third of the world possesses three-quarters of the world's doctors. It is also this third of the world where the population increase is at the perhaps manageable level of 1 per cent per year, i.e. a doubling of the population in every 70 years. The remaining 2300 million people increase at the rate of about 2·4 per cent per year, a doubling in numbers every 30 years.

If the world's population were stable, and doctors were distributed in strictly correct proportion to the population (again excluding China), there would be one doctor for about 1500 people. In Ethiopia at present it is doubtful whether there is even one doctor for 100000 people and this pitifully small proportion of doctors are nearly all to be found in a few main cities.

We are faced, not only with unfair distribution, but also with the rapidly disproportionate increase of population in the areas inadequately provided with medical care. And even the most privileged countries are beginning to be aware that they face a period of comparative starvation of trained medical staff—whether they encourage the return of doctors and nurses to their own countries or not.

The answer to the shortage of medical manpower in all countries is in four related parts: first, the further development of training to the highest professional levels of doctors and paramedical personnel; second, the fully economic use of such people on the jobs, and only on those jobs, in which they have become skilled; thirdly, a far wider employment of auxiliaries in support of all the medical and paramedical professional workers; and fourthly, the deployment of mixed teams which will enable doctors and nurses to care for much greater numbers of patients.

Even if some of the shortages of medical manpower can be tided over for a time, the world imbalance remains grossly immoral and contrary to the concern of every doctor and nurse for people regardless of their nationality, race, colour and creed.

About three years ago, in an earlier conference of the Ciba Foundation on *The Health of Mankind*,[5] I ventured to suggest the formation of an international medical service, a World Health Service (WHS) in extension of the splendid work of WHO and of the International Red Cross and Red Crescent. I envisaged a world-wide organization obtaining its money from non-political sources. It would have to be a supranational organization, to which all countries would be able to make some contribution of manpower; an organization with international headquarters separate but not far removed from that of WHO in Geneva; it might also have regional administrative and training centres sited close to the existing Regional Centres of WHO, namely, Washington, Copenhagen, Alexandria, Brazzaville, New Delhi and Manila. It would be essential that any such Service should be professional in the highest sense of efficiency. It would need the simplicity and accuracy of the most sophisticated techniques for recording and analysing geographical variations in morbidity and mortality, the health needs of large regions and small localities, and the resources in manpower, hospitals, health centres, equipment and transport. It would require a career structure with world equivalence of qualifications and pay. To be accepted to work in such a Service would be an international hallmark of personal quality and skill. The Service could be a major factor in raising standards of medical and paramedical education throughout the world to the highest levels, encouraging reciprocity in recognition of entrance requirements, intermediate examinations, and general and specialized qualifications, and facilitating greater mobility of staff and students between institutions, both nationally and internationally. I see such a Service using coordinated teams, very flexible in constitution according to the circumstances, operating on a priority basis. In natural disasters such as earthquakes, which Turkey knows too well and too sadly, the teams (in collaboration with the Red Cross and Red Crescent) would stay in any one area long enough not only to provide emergency care and to institute preventive measures against the occurrence of disease, but would also, if necessary, leave appropriate members of the team for a longer term to give the fundamentals of health education and train local people in basic medicine, however primitive.

I believe that such a World Health Service could be organized and financed. Its greatest virtue might well be to provide a network of international cooperation of an indisputably humane and peaceful nature. It might also give opportunities for great numbers of young people of both sexes to spend one or two years serving their fellow men, modestly or entirely unpaid, as auxiliary health workers—clerks, dressers, simple technicians, drivers, and so on. In this way, the young of each generation would play a real part in international cooperation, prevention and relief of suffering, and multiracial understanding. In time this shared experience might also go a long way towards making each generation more comprehensible to the one immediately before and after it.

Florence Nightingale recognized the potentiality behind the frustration of millions of women of her time, and today we have our own frustrated millions in every country. They are of both sexes and from young to old ages, the young with their high energy of idealism being at present employed, mostly destructively, in working *against* the policies and actions of governments, institutions, classes, and the older generation. But women today also present an increasing and special challenge, since for the first time in history millions of them throughout the world can plan to have modest families to which they need to devote themselves for only a few of the many years they can now expect to live. Waste of ability and

11

boredom face many of them. Yet consider what their combined energies might achieve internationally for the good of mankind; the possibility has been suggested that women alone could successfully 'man' the sort of Service I have outlined. But it is men, unless we get the power to pre-determine sex, who will soon be 'surplus' in the sense of being in excess of marriageable women.

These largely personal views are behind the preparation of this symposium on *Teamwork for World Health*. I hope that the widely experienced contributors from many different countries will draw inspiration from what was achieved in Selimiye barracks 115 years ago, and also from two further closing quotations from Florence Nightingale herself: ". . . if we can transform by a few years' quiet persistent work the habits of centuries, the process will not have been slow, but amazingly rapid"; and "It would be a noble beginning to the new order of things to use hygiene as the handmaid of civilization."

2: Response to Emergencies, National and International

Y. HENTSCH

It is a very great privilege to have the opportunity to introduce in the present symposium the subject of response to emergencies from as broad an international viewpoint as that afforded by the Red Cross. It is an additional privilege for a nurse to do so, since it implies recognition by the organizers of the preponderant place the nurse occupies today in teamwork for world health. This privilege is appreciated.

In the following remarks I shall attempt to describe some of the ways in which the Red Cross ideal, based on the principle of humanity, inspires world-wide team action today towards meeting at all times the health needs of people everywhere. I shall further endeavour to highlight how nursing is involved in that action.

EMERGENCIES

The *Oxford English Dictionary* defines 'emergency' as a "sudden juncture demanding immediate action". We shall here be concerned only with those emergencies which involve human suffering, and thereby affect the health of individuals or groups. Health is understood here as defined by the World Health Organization—"a state of complete physical, mental and social well-being, not merely the absence of disease or infirmity".[13] There are emergencies, known as natural disasters, which are caused by the disruption of the forces of nature: fire, floods, earthquakes, etc. There are those due to the outbreak of communicable diseases, and others originating in conflict between peoples or in inadequate social and economic conditions.

RESPONSE TO EMERGENCIES

Basically, it is the responsibility of the public authorities in each country to assist the victims of calamities occurring on their territory. On the one hand, however, it is unrealistic in practice to expect the authorities alone to provide immediately all the help required. On the other hand, today's society as a whole has an obligation to protect and ensure the health of its members. This obligation, therefore, rests also with the individual members of society. In fact, I submit that psychologically it is essential for members of any community to have some opportunity of giving assistance voluntarily to their fellow men in need. Poor indeed

13

would be the people of any country where such a possibility did not exist!

A few basic concepts underlie the attitude of society today in regard to emergencies.

First, it is generally accepted that it is essential to be prepared for giving service and that the more sudden and urgent the need for assistance, the better prepared one must be if one is to meet it effectively. It is fitting to recall here that this philosophy was common to both Florence Nightingale, the founder of modern nursing, and Henry Dunant, the founder of the Red Cross. Henry Dunant, in his *Memory of Solferino* first published in 1862, suggested the possibility ". . . in time of peace and quiet, to form relief societies for the purpose of having care given to the wounded in war-time by zealous, devoted and *thoroughly qualified* volunteers".[2] Florence Nightingale, at approximately the same time, when she founded in London the school for nurses which bears her name and thereby set the principles of nursing education, based her whole undertaking on the belief that "goodwill must be educated". The concept was new at the time.

Another basic concept is that emergencies can often be avoided or rendered less disastrous through preventive measures. There again, Florence Nightingale and Henry Dunant were of one mind not only in recommending the preparation of qualified personnel whose services, they said, would render wars less inhuman, but also in advocating preventive health measures as a means of putting a check on, for example, disease and poverty.

A third important concept is that the planned joint effort of many is essential for an effective response to emergencies, especially when these affect more than one person at a time. In other words, such a response stands or falls with teamwork. The word 'team' is accepted here as defined in the *Oxford English Dictionary* as being "a set of persons working together". At the same time, what a team is able to achieve in response to emergencies is both more effective and more satisfying to all concerned than anything that could be undertaken by individual persons assigned to fragmented tasks. Further, early involvement in their own relief of the people affected by an emergency is basic to effective teamwork intended to meet any such emergency.[8]

General acceptance of these concepts, through time, by society is demonstrated today by some recent decisions taken at top international level.

The *United Nations* (U.N.) General Assembly at their twenty-third regular session (December 1968)[11] adopted unanimously a Resolution (No. 2435) inviting governments, *inter alia*, to make preparations to meet natural disasters, to promote scientific research regarding their causes and to encourage preventive and protective measures.

The XXIst *International Conference of the Red Cross* (September 1969)[6] unanimously approved a new compendium of principles and rules governing international disaster relief actions and resolved that these be published and disseminated. This has since been done.[9] These principles and rules will in time be embodied in a handbook of guidelines for National Red Cross (Red Crescent, Red Lion and Sun) Societies on how to plan disaster relief at national level and how to assist each other in international relief action.

At the Twenty-Third *World Health Assembly* (May 1970) technical discussions were held on the theme 'Education for the Health Professions'.[12, 14] As a result, some 225 participants representing both a great number of countries and most of the health professions emphasized the concept that to ensure both quality and efficiency of service to all segments of the population, a team of health workers was needed and that the education of each category of workers should be adapted to local needs and resources. Although expressed in terms of solving the problem of expanding health services generally, this concept also applies specifically to health aspects of emergency relief plans.

The 2nd *World Food Congress*, meeting in the Hague, Netherlands in June 1970 under the Food and Agriculture Organization (FAO), will bring together statesmen, writers, scientists, farmers, economists, Church representatives and others to seek ways and means of meeting the world emergency situation caused by hunger and malnutrition.

In addition to these decisions, mention should be made of the intense technical assistance provided under the *United Nations Development Programme* (established 1965).[10] Such assistance covers a variety of fields, including health. Moreover, in its attempt to promote the economic and social advancement of all people, it is obvious that the Programme deals in many cases with problems of an emergency nature.

Although reference has only been made to the international field, many national endeavours could be mentioned to illustrate the fact that public authorities, private organizations and individuals everywhere are banded together as never before in a humanitarian effort to establish and implement both short and long-term relief plans. This is encouraging, although we know that there is room for much improvement in the ability of the people involved to pool their skills, experience and personal strengths and weaknesses towards the common aim in a true teamwork approach.

RED CROSS ACTION

Traditionally, the Red Cross—nationally and internationally—plays a leading role in meeting emergency situations. In fact, it has sometimes been referred to as the World Fire Brigade. This role stems from the

15

ideal it has set for itself, namely that whoever needs care must be attended without delay. The Red Cross, however, locally, nationally and internationally also acts as a permanent volunteer auxiliary to public authorities. It supplements official action and often opens the way for the latter, as a pioneer in promoting community health and social welfare generally. Since Henry Dunant over 100 years ago appealed to his contemporaries to join forces internationally in making plans for the relief of war victims, the Red Cross movement has truly become a world-wide practical reality in bringing relief to victims of wars and internal strife, natural calamities, epidemics, hunger and malnutrition and other social ills.

Here, a parenthesis is needed to describe briefly what is understood by the *Red Cross movement*.[3] Let us say that it is an ideal which in the field of mutual aid inspires practical solutions adapted to man's requirements. Its action is guided by the fundamental principles of humanity, impartiality, neutrality, independence, voluntary service, unity, and universality. Referred to as the International Red Cross, it consists of the International Committee of the Red Cross, the League of Red Cross Societies and the 113 recognized National Red Cross, Red Crescent, Red Lion and Sun Societies (hereafter referred to as National Societies). The International Conference of the Red Cross is the supreme deliberative authority of the International Red Cross. It assembles representatives of the Red Cross bodies and the Governments who are parties to the Geneva Conventions. It meets, in principle, every four years.

The *International Committee of the Red Cross* (I.C.R.C.) is the founder organization of the Red Cross (1863), the promoter of the Geneva Conventions and an independent and private organization, politically, ideologically and religiously neutral (it is composed of 25 Swiss citizens); it disseminates humanitarian law and ensures observation of the principles of the Red Cross; and as a neutral intermediary, it intervenes in armed conflicts on behalf of the wounded, sick, prisoners of war and civilians.

The *League of Red Cross Societies* (L.O.R.C.S.) is the federation of the National Societies.[1] Its aims are to facilitate the development of member Societies' activities on the national level; to coordinate their activities on the international level; and to promote the establishment and development of new Societies.

In the field of international disaster relief and in the accomplishment of tasks within the Red Cross Development Programme it plays a fully operational role.

The *National Societies* are voluntary aid societies, duly recognized as such by their governments—and, in the spirit of the founder of the Red Cross, the word 'voluntary' designates service rendered voluntarily, and not necessarily unpaid service. The primary commitment of

National Societies is to assist the military medical services of their country in case of need, and to care for war victims—friend or foe. They have accepted, however, the equally important responsibility of acting as auxiliaries to their public authorities in the improvement of health, the prevention of disease and the mitigation of suffering, both in times of emergency and otherwise.

Red Cross action in bringing relief to war victims is best described by referring to the four international treaties known as the Geneva Conventions of 12 August 1949:

I. For the Amelioration of the Condition of the Wounded and Sick in Armed Forces in the Field.

II. For the Amelioration of the Condition of Wounded, Sick and Shipwrecked Members of the Armed Forces at Sea.

III. Relative to the Treatment of Prisoners of War.

IV. Relative to the Protection of Civilian Persons in Time of War.

Each deals with the protection of well-specified persons not participating or no longer taking part in hostilities, in order to ensure that they receive humane treatment in all circumstances and without delay. On 1 January 1970, 128 sovereign States were parties to the Geneva Conventions.

Red Cross action on behalf of victims of all calamities rests essentially with the National Societies. For the last 50 years, the L.O.R.C.S. has coordinated the work of its member National Societies, gradually building up between them a strong fellowship and team spirit. This is strikingly apparent today when disaster occurs. Within a matter of hours, the National Society of the country in which the disaster has occurred is offered help through the League from sister societies. It is then often no more than a day or so before the first consignments of relief in cash or kind or, if necessary, relief teams reach the scene of disaster. International Red Cross action is then pursued only until such time as the emergency needs are met and other national or international organizations can take over. The decision as to when the phase of emergency ceases rests with the national authorities, and it is also up to them to entrust their National Society with all or part of whatever reconstruction or rehabilitation programmes may be needed.

In this connexion it may be of interest to know that, in 1969 alone, the League assisted in emergency relief operations in 18 countries on behalf of some 50 donor Societies and governments as well as other governmental and non-governmental organizations. From January to May of this year (1970), the L.O.R.C.S. has already intervened in eight new emergency situations besides carrying on with those with which it was involved at the end of 1969.

May it be stressed once again that the effectiveness with which a National Society meets an emergency situation—be it with its own resources only or with the assistance of the League—depends on its degree of preparedness. In all events, such preparedness requires a teamwork approach. On the one hand, the National Society must know exactly what will be its share of responsibility in a given emergency, as related to that of the public authorities and other organizations, national and international. On the other hand, it must prepare its own workers to function as a team among themselves and with workers of other organizations who have come to the rescue. More often than not, the National Society is the coordinating agent of all relief action in time of national emergency. Its ability to establish good teamwork between all concerned will determine the degree of success of the action.

To summarize, today over 220 million people give their time and skills to the Red Cross movement, including 83 million young people between the ages of eight and 18 years.

NURSING

Modern nursing and the Red Cross were born at the same time in the middle of the last century. The Red Cross ideal is also that of the nursing profession and they both function under the same basic principles. There is, therefore, reason enough for them to have been closely associated over the years and for their partnership to be still a reality today. One evidence of this is a clause which was introduced in the Code of Ethics of the International Council of Nurses in 1965, stating that "... it is important that all nurses be aware of the Red Cross principles and of their rights and obligations under the terms of the Geneva Conventions of 1949",[5] remembering that all members of the medical services of the armed forces are subject to these rights and obligations. Moreover, it is a fact that most National Societies today are engaged in some nursing activity.

Some run basic, and a few of them post-basic schools of nursing; several offer specialized courses for nurses; a large number train auxiliary nursing personnel; over half of them conduct a Health in the Home instruction programme and many more give various types of home nursing and other health courses; almost all of them, as auxiliary bodies to the public health authorities, enrol nursing personnel for service in hospitals, homes and other institutions for the physically or mentally handicapped, public health services and disaster relief.

Thus, nurses and nursing auxiliaries are present in most Red Cross action designed to meet emergency situations, be it locally, nationally or internationally. It is today undisputed that, in all cases and like all other Red Cross workers, such personnel must be prepared for the service they

18

are expected to render. Such preparation includes not only the specific nursing skills required, but also an awareness of the place of each member in the health team and a knowledge of what the Red Cross stands for.

With this in mind, and with a view to perfecting the service of nurses in natural disaster relief operations, especially in international operations, the L.O.R.C.S. is at present working on the establishment of a set of guidelines for the use of National Societies. As this work proceeds, it has already become apparent that if relief personnel are to function as a team in the field, they should also come together during their training and learn to function as a team before they ever get into the real situation. This applies to all emergency relief operations, disaster relief and others that require immediate action in order to save lives and relieve distress. Epidemics, malnutrition, displacement of populations are some of them. They all require nursing service. The insufficient number of people qualified to give such service where it is most needed has resulted in a vast mutual aid programme. Whether it be known as technical assistance, a development programme or some other name, whether it be conducted under official or private auspices, the fact remains that a worldwide mutual aid programme is in progress, in which hundreds of nurses are engaged. As members of an independent profession, they are being increasingly better prepared to assume their full share of responsibility in the health team, alongside members of the medical profession, social workers, public health engineers and various non-professional workers.[7] Their contribution to world health is important. It will become even more so, inasmuch as they themselves and the other members of the health and social welfare professions recognize increasingly the need to work as a team and to include in the latter the people whom they serve.

SUMMARY

This paper is concerned with emergencies which involve human suffering, and thereby affect the health of individuals and groups.

Response to such emergencies is basically the responsibility of the public authorities, assisted however by society as a whole. Effective assistance requires preparation, prevention and teamwork. The United Nations, the International Red Cross, the World Health Organization and the Food and Agriculture Organization provide examples of a humanitarian effort undertaken at international level to establish and implement short and long-term relief plans.

Red Cross action in meeting emergency situations is over 100 years old. It is world-wide, and applies to victims of wars as well as of all other calamities.

Nursing service is closely involved in Red Cross action and in all other existing mutual aid programmes. Its contribution to world health is important and will become even more so as the need is increasingly recognized for teamwork between all members of the health and social welfare professions and between them and the people they serve.

* * *

In conclusion, society today is constantly engaged in mutual aid action designed to meet emergencies, national and international. As time goes on, such action is perfected not only through industrial development and progress in medical science, but also through the application to emergency relief operations of a deeper knowledge of human relations and of the potentiality of team work. The Red Cross plays a leading role in this world-wide action, and, in the words of Max Huber ". . . is one of the constructive and positive elements in the contemporary world, a factor of understanding, tolerance and conciliation".[4]

DISCUSSION

Barbero: Could you give more details about the communication network which is so important in this work?

Hentsch: The League of Red Cross Societies (L.O.R.C.S.) in Geneva has a news agency Telex working 24 hours a day. Immediately we are informed of any disaster we send a Telex to the National Society in the affected country asking what is needed. Our first rule is never to rush relief to the place before we know this, and we rely on the people on the spot to carry out the very first relief action. We usually appoint a liaison officer immediately to assist in assessing needs. When these are known the other National Societies are asked to help.

Generally speaking a relief operation comprises three phases. The first is to save lives, the second is to attend to all victims, and the third is rehabilitation. The Red Cross as such is usually concerned mainly with the first two phases. The L.O.R.C.S. as the coordinating agent between National Societies has established seven depots in the world which are placed in the care of the corresponding National Society. When the recent earthquake happened in Peru, for example, we ordered some material to be released from our depot in Santiago, and before 24 hours had passed this material was in Lima ready to be sent into the disaster area. The main difficulty in this case was transport. The L.O.R.C.S. depots are refilled when the time comes with the assistance of National Societies. If there is any money over after the close of an operation, a decision is taken in consultation with the donor National Societies about the use to be made of it. It is often used for rehabilitation programmes.

Barbero: How do the national organizations communicate with each other about the kind of planning they do?

20

Hentsch: They communicate through the central headquarters of the L.O.R.C.S. by the quickest way possible.

Banks: The disaster relief organization of the Red Crescent in Turkey is certainly one of the best in the world. They can be on the way to a disaster, fully organized with a complete team and equipment, and if necessary a hospital, within half an hour of the request arising. That brings out well the point raised on communications, and Miss Hentsch mentioned the knock-for-knock arrangements which arise as a result of such a demand. When the Turkish depot needs more stores it can indent on another depot in Eastern Europe, and so on back and back. But, however perfect the communications and other international arrangements, they are of no use without leadership.

Dogramaci: Sometimes things may not run so smoothly. In Biafra when famine was killing so many people they were reluctant to accept help, and the same happened in North Vietnam. How do you persuade a country to accept the help it needs?

Hentsch: The Red Cross can only try to be as persuasive as possible. We are not interested in why the people may or may not want relief. We try to relieve pain and suffering as much and as far as we can, but people remain masters in their own houses, so we cannot go further than the master of the house will allow us.

Hill: At the end of the Biafran war, two things came out quite clearly. The British armed forces, which are well organized for disaster relief, had their services rejected. The other was that probably many of the volunteers did not know the environment. For example, many of them were horrified at kwashiorkor, yet this was not uncommon in those areas in normal times. They said, too, that the deaths from measles were part of the war, yet measles was already a killer there. So how do we get over this problem? At the XXIst International Conference of the Red Cross in Istanbul in 1969, the 31st resolution was that National Societies should establish in their respective countries, in cooperation with official and private bodies, a pool of health personnel who would be available to the International Committee of the Red Cross (I.C.R.C.). In Britain the government has before it at the moment a proposal for a British Disaster Relief Flying Squad. The proposal includes a feasibility study with a unit which will be headed by a doctor and an administrative officer, with ordnance and non-medical staff, including clerks and typists. If this is successful it is proposed that there should be a permanent secretariat which will liaise with the Red Cross, and so on. The British Red Cross has been kept informed of all this. There will be a permanent Assessment Team for immediate dispatch to any area. But this secretariat will organize a panel of medical and nursing experts in cooperation with the Royal Society of Tropical Medicine and Hygiene. We shall then have people with experience to go to any area. It is proposed

21

to organize civil defence experts, hydraulic engineers, and so on, stock-pile equipment and transport, and put forward a proposal for finances. It is hoped that this will get over the problem by being non-military, as host countries are generally resistant to any form of military aid, no matter how well meant.

Kisseih: In certain countries, the young members of the health professions, especially young nurses and medical officers, do not seem to be as interested in the work of the Red Cross as their seniors.

In my country, for instance, it is easier getting senior nurses and doctors to assist in the training and examination of Red Cross personnel in first aid and home nursing than the younger ones. Every effort is made to incorporate Red Cross activities in the training of nurses, yet somehow or other they do not seem to keep up any interest after qualification. Many young doctors, too, do not seem to be conversant with Red Cross activities.

I wonder whether this is a common problem in many countries, and whether Miss Hentsch is aware of it?

Hentsch: I am aware of this. It seems to me that I spend my life trying to persuade nurses to be interested, and doctors as well. It is mainly a matter of information and the way in which one presents the information.

King: The scope of Red Cross activity needs to be widened in the developing countries, particularly in the field of child welfare and nutrition. In Zambia we have reached the stage where a role that might have been taken by the Red Cross is in fact being taken by other organizations. In the long term it does not perhaps matter who does the work, provided that it is done, but it is a pity that it is not done by the Red Cross. We need to take a particularly careful look at what voluntary workers can do in child welfare work, and particularly in the type of clinic devised in West Africa for the under-fives. Such clinics have been set up extensively in Zambia, and volunteers are starting to work in them, but it looks as if it is going to be through agencies other than the Red Cross. As for teaching the doctors, it is very much our responsibility in the medical schools to acquaint our students with the role of the voluntary agencies and what use can be made of them.

Seden: Has the Red Cross any programme for getting the younger generation more interested in Red Cross work than they are today? I have grandchildren who are less interested in the Red Cross than their mothers were, who in turn were less interested than I was. Of course, the future of every organization depends upon the future generation.

Dickson: Could the concept of training include preparation of governmental minds to accept the services of young people when it is offered? In Britain the emphasis is generally on the training that young people should undergo to be ready in case of emergency, but there is little inclination on the part of the authorities to use young people when the emergencies do arise. This leaves considerable scepticism amongst young people as to why they should go to this trouble. In some of the emergencies in Britain, for example the *Torrey Canyon* oil affair, the Aberfan disaster, the great storm on the West Coast of Scotland in 1968, and the recent catastrophic outbreak of foot-and-mouth disease, the preparation for teamwork at the top was not very evident, although the public was ready to respond. There was a marked reluctance to make use of young people in these cases, and in the Aberdeen typhoid epidemic of some six or seven years ago there was a downright refusal to do so.

Young people respond to emergencies; being young they react to the element of drama and want to be involved personally. If an indication of what could actually be done came from Red Cross Headquarters in Geneva or the disaster area then the readiness to give would be there. But if the only reaction of their own government or relief organization that they hear of publicly is the release of 2000 blankets or the dispatch of a cheque, then their hearts do not beat faster. They want to know if there is action, and if possible action in which they could be personally involved.

Hentsch: This year the League of Red Cross Societies has made special efforts to find new ways by which young people can be associated with the 'adult' Red Cross. We hope to be quite successful. My colleague in charge of that is really trying to find ways and means whereby National Societies could in their turn plan to use young people. The 1968 earthquake in Sicily provided a very good demonstration of what young people could do. They went to Sicily and travelled back with the victims who wanted to join their families in the north of Italy. By talking to the families in the trains they knew exactly whom to refer them to immediately upon arrival in Milan, Rome or Florence and so no time was lost. They did that splendidly. I quite agree with you that they can do much. But they need to be prepared ahead of time, and that is the difficulty.

Israel: I was intrigued by Miss Hentsch's idea that when we talk of emergencies we must think beyond disasters and towards the improvement and maintenance of community health generally, which is also an emergency situation, which has to be prepared for and prevented, and in which we need teamwork. In Bombay the Red Cross and the Bombay Municipal Corporation have together set up a flying maternity squad. This may be something like the disaster relief squad Professor Hill is proposing, though the latter may be a more general thing. In Bombay this flying maternity squad is attached to one of the large obstetric hospitals; it has on its staff a doctor, a nurse and an attendant, who go out to any of the small nursing homes or hospitals, of which there are many in the city, to help with obstetric emergencies before the patient is brought to the large maternity hospital. Unfortunately, this is the only squad of its kind in the whole country and obviously it cannot work beyond a certain

23

radius and for more than a limited number of people. The squad was organized by the Association of Medical Women in India, but now we are informed that it will have to stop functioning because of lack of funds from the local Red Cross. I feel that the continuation and extension of this service is something the International Red Cross could take up, not only in India, but in many other countries. Of course, the essential is that blood bank facilities must be available at the headquarters from which this mobile team functions.

Hentsch: Relations between the government and the Red Cross have to be worked out nationally. If the Red Cross lacks money for a given service it has gradually to persuade the official authorities that this is a worthwhile service, and solicit their support. Until this happens the Red Cross can only rely on itself to find the necessary means. In your case the need is such that it should not be very difficult to persuade the authorities to give assistance. They might even agree to take over this service themselves, which happens very often.

3: The New Priorities in Tropical Medicine

MAURICE KING

IN essence our task as doctors is simple. It is to see disease prevented, and where this is not possible, to see it cured, both in the cities of the wealthy and in the villages of the poor. Medically, a procedure may be comparatively simple; it may perhaps be to put a few drops of what seems to be tasteless water into the mouth of a child to stop him getting polio-myelitis, or to teach his mother how to feed him. But the means of achiev-ing so simple an objective are formidable in their ramifications. In the case of poliomyelitis the technical knowledge for making the vaccine had first to be available, with all that this has meant by way of research and development in the past. To use this knowledge governments have first to raise the money to buy the vaccine—should there be money to raise—and then they must decide to spend it in this particular way. The vaccine must be transported and stored, and trained staff paid to give it. The staff must have a health centre in which to work, and mothers must bring their children to be immunized.

All this is in one sense exceedingly obvious, and at the same time and from another point of view it is immensely complicated. The whole process, which is perhaps best termed 'the epidemiology of medical care', is usefully considered as a web or network of causal and interacting fac-tors which extend outwards further and further from the child being vaccinated. Eventually, some of the factors impinge upon us in the sense that we might at least potentially be able to influence them. These factors are not static, and they change both with time and with place. There was a period when the critical issue was, for example, to invent the vaccines, to explain kwashiorkor, to build roads, to teach people in the developing countries to read and write and to devise the patterns of basic health services. These have now been achieved in large measure, and the factors most critically influencing the preventive and curative process now lie elsewhere. We have to look at the whole epidemiological network as far as medical care is concerned, to discover what the critical factors are and to think about what we can do to influence them favourably. Our analysis must stop at nothing and, as I hope to show, it leads us far be-yond what we are accustomed to think of as medicine. This analysis is what we are here for, and we shall have wasted our time if we end this symposium without some consensus as to what most needs to be done, and with a firm resolve as to how we might better be able to help in doing it. This is so important that I am going to ask you a question—a riddle perhaps: "What today do you think is the most important instrument in tropical medicine in the poorer countries of the world?" Let me give you a clue—it is potentially a major instrument for international teamwork!

Having previously worked in Zambia, my own answer to this question is now strongly conditioned by the experience of writing a brief health plan for Malawi during an eight-week visit there in 1969.[1] The reasons for this are well shown in Table I, which compares the two nations. They

TABLE I

ZAMBIA AND MALAWI COMPARED

	Zambia		Malawi	
Population in millions	4·05		4·6	(1970)
Population growth rate (%)	3·0		3·0	
Gross domestic product ($1 million)	1250	(1967)	213	(1966)
Gross monetary domestic product ($1 million)	1185	(1967)	161*	
GNP ($ per head)	310	(1967)	51	(1966)
Annual minimum wage ($)	417	(1970)	168	
Government recurrent expenditure on health (as % of the gross domestic product)	1·14		1·8	
Percentage of government recurrent expenditure spent on health	5·8 (1967)		8	
Annual government expenditure on health ($ per head)	4·8		0·9	
Persons per doctor	11 000		53 000	
Beds of all kinds per thousand persons	3·58		1·2	
Persons per health unit (dispensaries and above)	7000		20 000	

All figures for 1969, except where stated.[4]
* Estimated figure.

are culturally similar and have an almost identical history, both having been part of the former British Empire and later of the Federation of Rhodesia and Nyasaland, yet economically and in their possibilities for medical care they differ radically. In Zambia, with an annual gross national product of $310 a head, the health services develop rapidly, if not always in the right direction, while in Malawi, with a corresponding GNP of only $51, they are virtually stagnant and may even be deteriorating, so great is the pressure of population increase.

The general situation in Malawi presented a familiar picture. It appears that between 30 and 50 per cent of all children die before they are five years old and that the infant mortality rate is about 160 per 1000. A recent survey showed that 30 per cent of all children under the age of five years suffer from malnutrition, the figure between the ages of 12 and 18 months being 62 per cent, findings which are amongst the worst reported from Africa.

Most of the health units in Malawi date from well before the Second World War, and some even from before the First. The federal regime saw the building of the Queen Elizabeth Hospital in Blantyre and three or four rural hospitals, there being only 1·2 beds per 1000 persons and a doctor-to-population ratio of one to 53000. There are 20000 persons for every health unit and only $0·9 is spent per year by the government on the health of each of its citizens. The dispensaries are small, old, dilapidated and understaffed; many of the district council maternity units are in the gravest danger of falling down and the district hospitals are ancient, ill-equipped and grossly overcrowded, their outpatient departments being particularly congested, poorly designed and badly provided for. Thanks ultimately no doubt to Florence Nightingale, whom we have so rightly honoured, registered nurse training goes well and there is even danger of over-production, so small is the establishment. Enrolled nurse training is comparatively satisfactory but medical assistant training is currently much neglected, both in quality and in quantity.

But even though almost nothing is being done to improve the quantity of medical care, something is being done to improve its quality. A pilot area has been established for the improvement of basic health services, dispensaries are being slowly upgraded into health centres and no less than 180 'Under-Fives Clinics' have already been established.

In face of the acutely strained financial resources of Malawi, and particularly of its Ministry of Health, almost any recommendations I could make were likely to be considered unrealistic. It was decided however to recommend that the first policy objective should be to try to achieve WHO's suggested regional target of one health centre for every 10000 persons. This meant doubling the number of health units per head of the population as well as improving their quality in the face of a 63 per cent increase in the population during the 16 years of the plan period. The second, and associated, policy objective was to increase the skills of the service, both by training new staff members and by retraining old ones. The main means of doing this was to be a large auxiliary training school. Because development cannot take place on all sides with equal intensity at the same time, it was recommended that the development of hospital services should be of such a kind as would only marginally increase their recurrent expenditure. This meant in effect that their development was to be confined to the improvement of their outpatient departments and their general services. It was decided to concentrate on the development of basic health services in this way because basic health services are comparatively cheap compared with hospitals, and because they bring at least some form of health service within range of the villager. Because building costs form such a high proportion of the capital required for health service development, the utmost use was to be made of inexpensive self-help methods of construction, and because salaries form such a large fraction of recurrent costs, measures were recommended that would keep them as low as possible. A carefully phased programme was made out to upgrade existing units and to build new ones, the main limiting factor in the early years of the plan being the availability of newly trained staff.

Then came the time to add up the cost of this very modest development —about $15·5 million over the 16-year-plan period, or about a million dollars a year over this time, with recurrent costs rising from 1·8 per cent of present GNP to 2·3 per cent of that expected by the end of the plan. Informed financial opinion looked upon the long-term recurrent costs as being potentially easier to provide than the capital. Recurrent funds for short-term development are, however, at present as scarce in Malawi as they have ever been, and the service is not this year receiving the annual increment of about a quarter of a million dollars that it needs to cover rising costs, salary increments, etc. The total development capital available to the service—again, about a quarter of a million dollars for all purposes—is less than a quarter of that required for the development of the basic health services alone in the manner suggested.

There is no prospect of diverting money to health from other sectors, for it is already given 8 per cent of the recurrent budget, a share which is second only to education, and it gets more even than agriculture, on which almost the entire economic prospects of the country depend. Taxation is already high, the army tiny, and, with the possible exception of the movement of the capital from Zomba to Lilongwe, expensive and prestigious development projects are conspicuously absent. In effect there is no way in which the country can generate internally sufficient development capital to improve the basic health services in the humble manner proposed.

It is instructive to consider how many other countries in the African region are in the same financial straits as Malawi, and how other countries compare with Zambia, who could easily provide herself with all the basic health services she needs, and who currently congratulates herself on having passed WHO's regional health centre target. This comparison has been made in Table II. It is suggested that with a GNP of less than $75 per head annually it is not possible to provide basic health services on any but the most unsatisfactory and rudimentary scale—a condition into which 12 countries in the region fall, including Malawi. With a GNP of between $76 and $150 a head a reasonable level of basic health services could, it seems, only be provided with great difficulty (15 countries), while above $150 (nine countries) and especially above $250 (six countries) they could be provided increasingly readily. Table II

28

TABLE II

ANNUAL GNP PER HEAD FOR THE COUNTRIES OF THE AFRICAN REGION

Basic health services impossible to provide on any but the most minimal scale—GNP per head less than $75 annually

Burundi	40
Rwanda	40
Upper Volta	49
Malawi	51
Ethiopia	64
Tanzania	69
Somalia	69
Angola	71
Mozambique	71
Portuguese Guinea	71
Mali	75
Dahomey	75

A reasonable level of basic health services only provided with difficulty —GNP per head between $76 and $150 annually

Niger	77
Nigeria	81
Gambia	81
Togo	86
Lesotho	88
Uganda	95
Botswana	96
Sudan	104
Mauritania	107
Central African Republic	113
Madagascar	116
Kenya	117
Congo Democratic Republic	118
Cameroun	120
Sierra Leone	128

Basic health services can be provided increasingly readily—GNP per head between $151 and $250 annually

Swaziland	178
Congo Brazzaville	188
United Arab Republic	189
Morocco	191
Tunisia	208
Liberia	210
Senegal	227
Rhodesia	233
Algeria	245

GNP per head in excess of $250 annually

Ghana	252
Ivory Coast	256
Mauritius	257
Reunion	310
Zambia	310
Gabon	392

shows the wide differences within the region between the richer countries and the poorer ones, differences which are so critically important when it comes to considering what they can do to provide themselves with basic health services. Compared with Zambia, Malawi has in fact done well—with a sixth of the GNP per head she has achieved about a third of the basic health services.

The best reason for aiding the basic health services is of course the humanitarian one, others being their effect on the economy through their effect on the efficiency of the work force and the much more controversial one of their influence on population growth. In the long run, one of the main reasons why basic health services should be aided may paradoxically be that they promise to be the means of reducing population growth. But, in the short run, the provision of basic health services may exacerbate the population problem in that the supply of, say, measles vaccine

29

without the 'pill' can only increase the numbers of children surviving. And yet one of the reasons why mothers in the tropics want large families is to be sure that some of them survive. Mothers have to be convinced that most of their children will live before they are prepared to limit their numbers. Child survival and family limitation may thus be as firmly linked in the mind of such a mother as they should be in the practice of the basic health services.

The risk that by initially providing measles vaccine faster than the 'pill' the improved basic health services will for a time increase population growth, rather than reducing it, is one that will have to be accepted—there is no other way. Unless there are health units—a basic health service—to which a mother can go for her 'pill', or whatever method will replace it perhaps 15 years hence, the population will go on rising. It is not possible, at least in rural Africa at the present time, to consider providing family planning services, either by mobile or static units, which are not part of an integrated basic health service. This is why it is generally accepted that family planning must form part of an integrated service for maternity and child health (MCH). 'MCH services' have in their turn to be an integral part of the basic health services. Basic health services are therefore an essential prerequisite of measures for population control.

Substantial aid for basic health services in which family planning is included might be very welcome in several of the states of sub-Saharan Africa just now. The Kenyan government has accepted family planning as a national policy and is now trying to improve the basic health services. In 1969 the Tanzanian development plan also accepted family planning, but at present there seems little hope of supplying the services. Even in Zambia there is a perceptible shift of opinion towards the need for a population policy. Malawi, in the person of her president, remains adamantly opposed to it, although there is much influential opinion in the government that supports it urgently.

However, even if there was no general acceptance that family planning should be part of them, aid for basic health services would make good population sense. Without these services there is no hope; with them there might be some. Such services take years to develop and the first medical assistant does not start work until at least five, and more probably eight, years after it has been decided to build a school to train him. Political opinion, in East and Central Africa at least, is altering perceptibly on population matters and may well change before the assistant qualifies. Once he and the enrolled nurses who should assist him are available, they can readily be retrained later to give family planning advice, or a specially trained auxiliary can be added to the health centre team. Without such an infrastructure of basic health services, a population policy would be delayed many years.

Compassion apart, it is therefore imperative that, starting with the poorest nations of the world, basic health services be considered urgent subjects for international aid, with, *or for the time being without*, the undertaking that family planning shall form part of them. In the industrial countries health services were developed from motives of altruism, fear of pestilence and economic good sense. In the developing countries these motives still hold good, except that fear of population might be added to them.

Where is the money to come from? Basic health services have never been popular objects for aid, medical aid as a whole is much underrated,[3] and at present there seems little hope of changed opinion. The World Bank has been generous in its loans for education, but has not yet aided health on any substantial scale. WHO provides only expertise, services in strictly limited areas of the direst need, and the wherewithal for narrowly defined projects such as the eradication of smallpox. UNICEF is a valuable although far from sufficient source of equipment for the basic health services, together with grants for training and some drugs. USAID favours major development projects and sometimes builds hospitals. The British Ministry of Overseas Development tops up the salaries of its nationals working in the developing countries and again occasionally builds hospitals. The governments of Sweden, Denmark, France and Russia, although they too have built hospitals, have not yet supported basic health services on any substantial scale, nor have the American foundations. OXFAM, with characteristic flexibility and compassion, has devoted a significant fraction of its limited resources to these services, but its provision is tiny in comparison with need.

Aid is in the doldrums.[2] The prospects of its increase for the moment at least grow dimmer, not brighter. At the end of the 'development decade' few countries have achieved the pledge to give 1 per cent of their GNPs, while 'zero hour'—the point at which receipts in aid by the developing countries will be balanced by the payment of interest and the amortization of loans—is forecast for the early 1970s, after which time there will be a net flow of funds away from the developing world.

Our network of causal factors in the epidemiology of medical care, extending outwards from the child getting his polio vaccine, is thus much bound up with the basic health services and entangles the whole process of aid. In the poorest countries of the world the provision of aid, and particularly medical aid, has now become the critical factor in the provision of the cheapest forms of medical care—basic health services. It is thus no exaggeration to say that, if we want to improve the basic health services of these nations, quite apart from assisting them with their population problems, it will not be by our labours in the field, the laboratory, or even in the classroom or lecture theatre. It will not even be in the developing countries themselves. It will best be by putting our minds to

31

the means whereby the flow of aid can be increased. There was a time when what was wanted in tropical medicine was to find the cause and the cure for cholera and malaria. Later on it was to open up the tropics, to provide the means of communication and education and to start health services. The services have now started, but in many countries besides Malawi they are virtually stagnant at a very low level and substantial aid is required to get them moving. By aid is meant the totality of the means whereby the rich countries assist the poor ones. Where will the aid come from?

We must begin in hope with the premise that the endeavour is not impossible—that nations can be made to change their minds, that we ourselves have a part to play, and that in due course aid can be made to flow. The generation of this aid is surely the most critical issue in tropical medicine at the present time and one of the most important subjects for research in the epidemiology of medical care in the poorer developing countries. What would seem to be required is a massive publicity campaign to 'improve the image of aid', particularly medical aid, in all the richer nations.

As a proper concern for a medical symposium, even as wide-ranging a one as ours, this idea is surely highly unpopular and way out. Yet perhaps this is the very reason why it demands our attention. In the past the novel and the radical was often the least regarded. If we really want to find what needs to be done for 'teamwork for world health', we must peer over the top of the accepted and look round the edges of the conventional.

Means must somehow be found to start a massive public relations campaign on aid, and particularly medical aid, over the mass media of all the donor countries. This is inevitably going to be costly, but it is a quite inescapable investment. Apart from the importance of us all considering it as part of our personal responsibility in our various spheres of action, I have only a few suggestions to make. The first is that it should be a rule that a certain percentage of all aid funds, say 1 per cent or perhaps as much as 3 per cent, should be spent in the donor country explaining aid and preparing the way for more. The fullest use must be made of the mass media and all that goes with them. The medical aid campaign in a donor country must be coordinated by a public relations unit, and institutes of tropical medicine in donor countries should consider it not the least of their functions to explain and promote the case for aid among the general public. The point has probably been reached when an effective department of public relations might be at least as useful to the tropical sick as, say, a department of helminthology.

When substantial medical aid is forthcoming it is on the basic health services of the poorest nations that it should first be spent, whether or not they include family planning services, for it is these that give the greatest value for each dollar spent and provide the rural villager with at least some form of medical care.

We have now come a long way from that child and his polio vaccine, and that network of interacting factors which provide him with basic health services and impinge finally upon us. This network logically analysed has led us far beyond Malawi and the other countries at the bottom of the world's league of wealth. It has led us into regions critical to medicine that we do not properly consider as our concern and has, I hope, shown us that the salvation of the tropical sick at present lies, not so much with the microscopes of tropical laboratories, as once it did, as with the television sets of our affluent societies. As far as the poorer countries of the world are concerned, the television set is, I contend, the most important instrument in tropical medicine at the present time—and hence the answer to my riddle! If the countries of the world are to form a team they must know one another's needs and how they can be met. This is international teamwork and it demands the best possible publicity and the most skilful use of the means of persuasion. Our predecessors used their microscopes well. Our challenge is to use the instruments of our time with equal determination and with equal vision.

DISCUSSION

Dogramaci: We are often told that very poor countries are unable to absorb more than a certain amount of aid. Does that make any sense?

King: I am a doctor, not an economist, but I think the developing countries can make good use of a great deal more aid than they can get. The saturation limit is seldom reached and developing countries as a whole certainly do not get the aid which they might absorb. Just how it is best spent in individual instances is very much a matter for the development economist and varies considerably from country to country.

Kisseih: The developing countries are being advised to place more emphasis on self-help than on 'aid' from the developed countries.

In February 1970, the United Nations Office of Public Information, together with the United Nations Economic Commission for Africa, organized a Regional Conference in Addis Ababa for non-governmental organizations and editors. The objectives of the conference were to mobilize public opinion in support of United Nations development goals in Africa and to highlight the problems of apartheid, racial discrimination and colonialism in Southern Africa.

Throughout the conference the need for the developing African countries to rely more on themselves than on 'aid' from the Big Powers was very much stressed. It was pointed out that the developing countries of Africa had all the resources they needed for their development among themselves. They had surpluses of fuel, fibres, iron ore, copper, bauxite and practically every other raw material. They were also capable of feeding themselves through exchange with each other. By trading more among themselves, they could then as a group sell the surpluses in the world market. Under the present circumstances, however, they all sell independently in the world market where prices are controlled by the Big Powers. These Powers buy at low prices, sell and make huge profits and then hand out about 0·01 per cent of their profit to these poor countries in the form of 'aid'.

At this rate, the poor countries could scarcely be expected to get over their poverty. They were, therefore, being taught not to expect much from outside 'aid' but to form regional trading groups so that they could get more benefit from their own resources than they are getting now. It is admitted that they might require a certain amount of aid even in the form of experts to advise on certain aspects of their economy, but relying mainly on aid for solving local problems is being discouraged.

Foreign aid could also be very complicated. Sometimes the donor countries decide how the aid is to be used. For instance, although a country might regard agricultural development as its priority, the donor country might insist on using the aid for family planning. Even 'foreign experts' have their limitations. Foreign educational programmes were introduced into some of these developing countries, and young men and women graduated from schools without being of any practical use to the community.

Another disadvantage of foreign aid is that it might be spent on certain individuals instead of the overall community it is intended for.

Banks: Miss Kisseih has brought up a very important subject. On an international committee discussing the needs of developing countries some years ago, one of the giants sat up and said "If a country has no resources of its own, I am not prepared to waste time discussing it." It sounded, and it was, a brutal way of putting it, but we should not pour money into small non-viable units. It is better to encourage development on a regional basis, with the grouping of resources.

Fişek: Anything helping to educate the public is most important; I therefore find Dr King's comment on television very interesting. The mere presence of midwives, nurses or medical doctors doesn't make much difference to the health level in a country, especially in the rural areas, but if the people are educated, then the level of health starts to rise. Infant mortality, malnutrition and birth rates decrease steadily.

If we health workers want to do something permanent, we must emphasize education more. We are discussing teamwork in health in this meeting. We have to think of more extensive teamwork in educating the public: teachers, press, radio, television, religious leaders, agricultural extension workers and health workers must come together and educate the people. Otherwise, curing patients and controlling epidemics

34

is like emptying the water from a boat with a hole in it. We cannot prevent the boat from sinking; we have to mend the hole first. To educate the public is a similar action. Television, if it could be made available in the rural areas, is certainly the most effective medium in education.

Horn: I also agree with Miss Kisseih's warning against placing undue emphasis on aid from outside, and I think Dr King has done just that. I disagree with Dr King if he means that television sets in industrially advanced countries are important for expanding health services in poorer countries because they can be used to persuade the inhabitants of the richer country that they should help the poorer. The American aid programme has reached a new all-time low, yet there are plenty of television sets in the United States. The governments of industrially developed countries do not decide their aid policies on the basis of what television viewers think about aid. Undue emphasis has been placed on the role of external aid. Aid from outside has a role, even an important one, but it is not the most important one. The most important task must be the internal development, the self-reliance, self-organization of the countries concerned. Trade between developing countries is important as well and that is part of the self-organization and the self-reliance. Even more important is the way in which the resources of the country are both used and developed. Iran, for example, as Dr Dadgar will describe, provides an excellent illustration of how existing medical services can be utilized to better effect. The answer to the problems we are discussing here lies more in developing new forces inside the country and in using them better than in looking outside. I am reminded very much of China. Dr King's second axiom in his admirable book[1] is that the main determinant of the pattern of medical services in the developing country is poverty; I think this is erroneous. China is still a poor country but it has nevertheless made some striking advances in its medical services, and it has done so by unleashing new forces and by organizing a new orientation within the country.

Rebhun: There is no doubt that there must be some connexion between health services (particularly environmental health services) and the economy of a country or community. From our experience in the development of environmental health services, such as safe water supplies and so on, we have concluded that integral planning of health services within the general development of a community is most efficient. Environmental health factors cannot be separated from the general economic situation. When sanitary engineering projects are being planned in developing countries their integration into agricultural and industrial development provides for their most economical and efficient execution.

Russell: In the last two years I have been through most of south-east Asia, and the problems of these overcrowded countries are very often quite the reverse of those in Africa. They tend to use foreign aid of all kinds as a budget supplement, so that in many cases they are still asking for continued assistance for projects started with UNICEF aid 10 or 12 years ago. Often projects which have been started are not maintained and begin to collapse at the periphery. This is a great pity and I have sometimes felt that large-scale international aid, from whatever source, tempts governments to press their development projects, particularly perhaps in rural health, beyond their own powers to maintain them once they have reached their goal. Tied up with this, of course, is the social attitude of the population in this sort of area. Usually there is a great resistance by doctors, nurses and other health personnel to going to work in rural areas.

King: By aid I mean the whole spectrum of assistance to the developing countries, including such things as the maintenance of just prices for their products, and the absence of import restrictions on their manufactured goods. These are at least as important as its more direct forms, if indeed not more so. What matters is the whole process of assisting the poorer countries of the world, no matter how this is done. I disagree strongly with Professor Banks's 'aid giant' who could casually cast aside a country of four million people just because they were not a viable economic entity. One cannot throw four million people into the wastepaper basket in this way. I entirely agree with Dr Horn that the social processes of the kind that he is going to tell us about are of the greatest importance, and I like to think that I am not quite so naïve as to believe that mere disbursements of cash are the only thing that matters. The whole situation is obviously very complex, but the present falling-off in aid has profound consequences for the sick, particularly in the poorest countries of the world, and we have got to do something about it in whatever way we can. This is surely international teamwork for world health on the grand scale.

4: The Health Corps in Iran: an Approach to the Better Distribution of Health Resources in Remote Areas

M. DADGAR AND G. SAROUKHANIAN

DURING the past two decades the problems involved in the provision of health services have become increasingly complex, not only in developing countries but in the world as a whole. Several reasons contribute to this phenomenon: the increase of medical knowledge and technical know-how, the increase of urbanization, changes in the age composition of the population, and, perhaps the most important of all, the growing belief that everyone has a right to the 'best' health care.

The relevance of attempts to experiment with, and facilitate the delivery of, health services to the people of remote areas can hardly be questioned. This has become an important issue for the countries of the developing world, where the urge to accelerate the rate of development is felt more than ever before.

In this paper we shall attempt to illustrate a new way of using medical manpower for the delivery of health care to the rural communities of Iran. This is a 'revolutionary' attempt to change the pattern of rural health and accelerate the development of rural health services by making military health manpower resources available for civilian use.

The principal aims of this paper are to describe the objectives of the Health Corps Organization and the way it operates in Iran, to present an approach to the better distribution of health resources in remote areas, and to discuss the great educational potential that the Health Corps has for the training of future medical manpower needed for the country.

Since each country should shape its health services according to the nation's history, traditions and economic situation, we shall here review briefly some of the important facts and figures about Iran. This orientation will help you to visualize the country and the stage of its development and conditions when the important change represented by the Health Corps was brought about.

LOCATION AND DESCRIPTION

Iran is a country of great topographic and climatic variety, comprising rocky mountains, arid deserts, lush tropical coastal scenery along the Caspian littoral, and hot flat plains in the south along the Persian Gulf.

The country covers an area of about 1·6 million square kilometres and borders on Turkey and Iraq to the west, on Pakistan and Afghanistan to the east and on the U.S.S.R. to the north.

The Iranian plateau has a history of culture and civilization dating back to 3000 B.C. Basically an agricultural country, Iran is now undergoing a period of rapid industrialization. The reforms instituted by the former Shahenshah have been augmented in recent years by the revolutionary changes introduced by His Imperial Majesty, the Shahenshah Aryamehr, in the political, economic and social life of the country.

Since then networks of roads and communications have been built. More universities and other educational institutions, including a School of Public Health, have been established. Health services have been extended and several industries set up.

POPULATION

According to the 1956 census the population of Iran was about 19 million, 42 per cent of whom were under 15 years of age; 69 per cent of the population at that time lived in rural areas, compared to 31 per cent living in small and large cities.

During the decade following the 1956 census the population of Iran grew on the average 2·6 per cent per year. Other sources, based mostly on sample surveys, have placed the annual growth rate at about 3 per cent.

According to the 1966 census the population of Iran was then over 25 million, with 46 per cent under 15 years of age and 62 per cent living in rural areas.

These and other similar demographic characteristics place Iran among the countries with rapid population growth, a predominantly young population and notable migration from rural to urban areas.

Another important feature of the population of Iran which strongly influences the delivery of health services is its scattered nature. According to the 1966 census, the relative density of population was about 15 per square kilometre. At the same time about 16 million of the rural population were living in about 54000 scattered small and large villages and communities, distributed as shown in Table I.

TABLE I

SIZE OF VILLAGES

Population	No. of villages
2501–5000	256
251–2500	14627
101– 250	15496
Less than 100	23652
	54031

ECONOMICS

Iran is a country riding a high crest of national development. The annual growth rate recently exceeded 10 per cent. Iran nets annually a billion dollars from oil revenues. The income per head shown in Table II has been constantly increasing during the past ten years.

TABLE II

INCREASE IN INCOME PER HEAD OF POPULATION

Year	National income (U.S. $) per head	Annual increase (%)
1959	162 ⎫	
1962	170 ⎭	6·4
1965	197 ⎫	
1968	220 ⎬	9·9
1972*	307 ⎭	

* Estimated figure.

The economic climate in Iran now is such that confidence has been developed among public as well as among private investors, resulting in continued growth and development.

VITAL AND HEALTH STATISTICS (1968)

Due to the lack of an adequate reporting system of vital events, statistics in general are neither reliable nor representative of the country as a whole. Sample surveys and data collected from ten selected cities revealed the statistics shown in Tables III, IV, and V.

TABLE III

VITAL STATISTICS FROM TEN CITIES IN 1968

Birth rate	48–50 per 1000 population
Death rate	16–18 per 1000 population
Growth rate	2·6–3·0 per cent
Infant mortality	86 per 1000 live births
Neonatal mortality	27·5 per 1000 live births
Infant mortality index	26 per cent of total deaths
Death under 5 years	49 per cent of total deaths
Life expectancy	46 years

TABLE IV

THE TEN PRINCIPAL CAUSES OF DEATHS IN TEN SELECTED CITIES IN 1969

(1) Diseases of the circulatory system
(2) Diseases of the digestive system
(3) Diseases of the respiratory system
(4) Infectious and parasitic diseases
(5) Diseases of the genitourinary system
(6) Neoplasms
(7) Accidents, poisoning, violence
(8) Certain causes of perinatal morbidity and mortality
(9) Endocrine, nutritional and metabolic diseases
(10) Diseases of the nervous system and sensory organs

39

TABLE V

THE TEN MAJOR COMMUNICABLE DISEASES REPORTED IN 1968 (PER 100000 POPULATION)

(1)	Grippe and influenza	3525
(2)	Bacillary dysentery and diarrhoeal disease	2812
(3)	Conjunctivitis	841
(4)	Measles	292
(5)	Mumps	224
(6)	Whooping cough	179
(7)	Typhoids (including para A & B)	88
(8)	Food poisoning	70
(9)	Chickenpox	66
(10)	Tuberculosis	65

HEALTH RESOURCES

The distribution of hospital beds in 1968 is shown in Table VI. There are 11·7 hospital beds per 10000 of the population (excluding armed forces hospitals).

TABLE VI

DISTRIBUTION OF HOSPITAL BEDS BY OPERATING AGENCIES (1968)

	No. of beds	% of total
Government and affiliated agencies	19900	64·2
Voluntary organizations	5300	17·1
Social insurance organizations	3000	9·7
Private sector	2800	9·0
	31000	100·00

The Ministry of Health is operating some 810 clinics, mostly in rural areas, in addition to about 400 Health Corps clinics. Another major voluntary organization involved in rural health work is the Imperial Organization for Social Services, which owns and operates some 240 clinics, all in rural areas. It has been estimated that these 1450 clinics cover about 50 per cent of the rural population living within a radius of seven kilometres of a clinic.

MANPOWER

TABLE VII

EXISTING HEALTH MANPOWER AND CAPACITY FOR TRAINING (1969)

Title	Number	No. of graduates annually
Physicians	7800	600
Dentists	1400	80
Nurses	2800	360
Assistant nurses	3600	730
Sanitarian aides	1100	140

The distribution of health manpower is by no means satisfactory. It has been estimated that more than one-third of the physicians are in Teheran, the capital, where only one-tenth of the population lives. Another third of the physicians can be found in large and small cities. And only the remaining third are working in rural areas where more than two-thirds of the population live. This disproportionate distribution is even more serious for nurses and dentists, as well as for hospital beds.

PLANNED DEVELOPMENT OF IRAN

Iran was one of the first countries outside the socialist system to undertake development planning. Although the first attempt in planned development was made in 1937, with the onset of the Second World War the activities came to a halt. Then in 1948 the Plan Organization launched the First Seven-Year Development Plan, which went through the serious financial crisis that followed nationalization of the oil industry and ended by 1955. During this period some hospitals and clinics were built. Very little consideration was given to prevention of disease. However, the Malaria Control Programme was initiated and from the health manpower standpoint three new medical schools were established during that period.

During the Second Seven-Year Plan, which started in 1955 and lasted until 1962, priority was given to control and eradication campaigns directed against major diseases such as malaria and smallpox. However, the Second Plan was considered as a period of maturation and experience in our country for better planning in general, and health planning in particular.

The Third (Five-Year) Plan (1962–1967) should be considered as the beginning of sound planning, where a comprehensive approach was adopted to the development of the National Health Services network and serious consideration was given to the training of a better balance of health personnel. The Third Plan marks a milestone in the socioeconomic development of Iran. It was in this period that the most basic and fundamental reform took place, namely the approval of the Charter of Iran's White Revolution through public referendum. The Charter, among many important social improvements, provided for land reform, with the basic objective of a more equitable distribution of income in favour of the rural population. It was in this general sociopolitical atmosphere that the Health Corps Organization was created to bring medical and health services to the villages.

Thus, with the beginning of the Fourth Five-Year Plan (1968), together with its overall economic development, Iran entered an era of rapid development and expansion of the health services throughout the country.

41

ORGANIZATION OF THE HEALTH CORPS

THE needs of each country should be planned according to local circumstances and prevailing health conditions. The methods of delivery of health services used in developed countries could not be simply transplanted and/or adapted in Iran, which was going through a period of rapid development during the Third Five-Year Plan.

With the special attention and priority given to the growth and development of agriculture and improvement of living conditions of Iranian villagers, it was obvious that immediate measures for the rapid expansion of rural health services were necessary. However, in view of the socioeconomic conditions, and particularly the dispersion of the population in rural areas, it was also obvious that continuous medical care based on the traditional ways of delivering health services was impracticable for at least a good portion of our rural communities.

The need was to mobilize doctors, nurses, sanitarians and other health workers into teams equipped with knowledge and enough facilities to serve the people in remote villages. This need could be met by new graduates of our universities and high schools, who would be drafted according to the law for two years of military service.

So on 21 January 1964, when His Imperial Majesty declared that "all Iranians were to have the benefits of medical care", he also suggested a unique manner of providing this care; thus the Health Corps Organization was founded in the Ministry of Health, on the same general principles as those on which the Literacy Corps had earlier been formed in the Ministry of Education.

The significance of this principle lies in the fact that it meets one of the basic needs of our rural population through a special organizational strategy and approach; that is, military discipline as well as the idealism of our young Iranian cadets are used for the improvement of our rural health.

The underlying methodology of the Health Corps is that graduates of the medical schools and allied professions, together with substantial numbers of high school graduates, on entering the armed forces for their two years of obligatory military service spend 18 months of this period in the villages, providing health and medical care in the most economic and practical manner. In other words, each year about 400 doctors and 1000 high school graduates, who would otherwise spend their entire period of military service in the army hospitals and army medical units, now have their time and skills much better utilized in the Health Corps Organization, looking after the most needy population of our rural communities.

The bill establishing the Health Corps was passed into law on 3 August 1964. By September of that year the first qualifying candidates were inducted and they immediately underwent an intensive four-month course, so that by 1 January 1965 the new Corpsmen were in their field positions. The rapidity with which the Organization progressed from induction to training, and to dynamic action in the field, was the result of extensive planning and careful administration.

The main objective of the Organization is to improve the rural health conditions through relatively well-equipped and semi-mobile health units. Under the 'goals', the law specifies that the Health Corps is to promote rural health, raise the level of health education in the villages, preserve manpower resources, and thus act as an asset to the rural economy through the development of a healthier population.

These goals are to be achieved by:

(1) Treating the sick.
(2) Preventing disease.
(3) Improving sanitary conditions.
(4) Providing maternal and child care and family health.
(5) Improving the nutritional status of the people.
(6) Guiding the people towards a healthier and better way of living.

It may be suitable to mention here some of the important articles from the Health Corps Bill.

"*Article 1.* In order to extend public health and medical care throughout the villages and rural regions of Iran, a Health Corps composed of a Medical Group and a Medical Aid Group will be formed as follows:

(*a*). The Medical Group will be formed of army conscripts who are found professionally qualified to practise in the field of medicine, and public health, comprising—doctors of medicine, dentists, pharmacists, veterinarians, sanitary engineers, and generally speaking, all university graduates whose services would be deemed, by the Ministry of Health, subject to the provisions of the by-laws of this bill, to be approved by the council of ministers.*

(*b*). The Medical Aid Group will be formed of conscripts with a high school education who will be given a special course to fit them for medical aid services."

"*Article 3.* The granting of any type of licence to practise a profession, as well as permission to leave the country for advanced studies, is subject to having rendered military service . . ."

* This article was later amended with the following specification: "Holders of licentiates and higher degrees in the following fields—parasitology, bacteriology, laboratory technique, nursing, nutrition, radiology, health education, social work, environmental sanitation, sociology, statistics and hospital administration."

"Article 4. The budget required to enforce this bill will be provided as follows:

(*a*). During the course of training salaries and advantages out of the budget of the Ministry of War.

(*b*). Training centres required for the training courses will be provided by the Ministry of War and put at the disposal of the Ministry of Health . . .

(*c*). Upon the completion of training, all salaries and advantages, as well as all other expenditures thereof, as to transport facilities, technical equipment, medicine, etc. will be secured from the Development Budget of the Ministry of Health."

"Article 6 (Implementing Statute). Food, lodging, salaries and advantages of the Health Corps will be equivalent in all respects to the conscript officer candidates of the Imperial Armed Forces."

ADMINISTRATION AND FUNCTION

The administrative hierarchy of the Health Corps Organization has the following four levels of staff and line functions (Fig. 1).

  (*a*) Headquarters on the national level.
  (*b*) Regional Offices in each of the 12 provincial health departments.
  (*c*) Base Centres, at present in 30 rural towns.
  (*d*) Health Units, the most dynamic and mobile units of the organization, in about 350 to 400 villages.

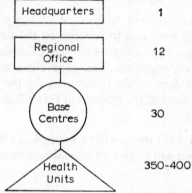

FIG. 1. The administrative hierarchy of the Health Corps Organization.

Headquarters

At the national level, the Health Corps Organization is an autonomous unit of the Ministry of Health, operating under one of the Under-Secretaries. At this level, the overall programme planning, budgeting and some administrative functions, such as the procurement of

44

facilities and drugs and their dispatch to the Regions, are carried out through a small permanent staff, headed by a General Director. Contacts with the Ministry of War in connexion with the selection of new recruits for each year is also done through the Headquarters.

One of the main activities of the Headquarters is the organization and administration of pre-service training programmes, which at first was for four months, later expanded to six months. During the period that Corpsmen are going through this training, they also receive their military training. After the training period the Corpsmen, who until this stage are under the jurisdiction of the Ministry of War, are transferred to the Health Corps Organization.

The curriculum is planned in accordance with the educational backgrounds of new recruits. There is a separate, extensive and concentrated programme (345 hours in 27 subjects), both theoretical and practical, for non-medical groups, stressing such subjects as first aid, vaccination, environmental sanitation and health education. The medical groups receive 257 hours of instruction in 26 subjects, and public health and communicable disease control is stressed, all in the context of rural health. The curriculum includes sociology, nutrition, population dynamics and family planning. The health education section also prepares reports, educational publications and statistics, which are distributed regularly through Regional Offices and Base stations to Health Units. Individually selected Corpsmen attend specialized courses in laboratory work, environmental health, administration, etc., in addition to the general programme.

Finally, another important function of the Headquarters, and maybe the most important of all, is the coordination of the Health Corps activities with other health programmes of the Ministry of Health and other agencies involved in rural health work in Iran.

Regional Offices

At the Regional level, a member of the Provincial Health Department is responsible, with a small staff, for the activities of the Health Corps in that region. His responsibilities are: further coordination, provision of consultation on specialized issues, and facilitating the dispatch of drugs and other necessary items sent from the Headquarters or provided locally.

One of the important functions at the Regional level, which so far has not been fully developed (except in one Region), is the coordination and affiliation of Health Corps activities with the provincial medical schools. This will be referred to again, but here it suffices to say that both Base Centres and Health Units have tremendous teaching and learning opportunities for undergraduate as well as postgraduate medical education.

45

Base Centres

The first functional level of the Health Corps consists of the so-called Base Centres. There are about 30 such bases now in the country, or about two bases for each region. Each base includes:

(*a*) Medical section consisting of one or two specialists available for consultation to the mobile teams when such need arises.

(*b*) Dental section with one dentist and a high school graduate assistant, plus the necessary equipment.

(*c*) Laboratory section with one pharmacist or laboratory technician and a high school graduate Corpsman with adequate training to perform routine diagnostic work for the Health Corps physicians and dentists and also for local medical practitioners.

(*d*) Environmental sanitation section, consisting of three Corpsmen: a plumber, cement layer, and a sanitarian aide. These units are concerned with practical improvements in environmental sanitation in areas requiring them. They may replace immersion baths with showers, help to provide improved sanitary water systems, instal sanitary latrines and build mortuaries. Their work is strictly coordinated with that of the base sanitary engineers.

(*e*) Health education section, consisting of one Corpsman with a social science background and special training in health education. These sections have the task of increasing the health knowledge of the people and facilitating the smooth operation of other sections by explaining the programme to the villagers and inducing them to assist the Corpsmen to improve local health conditions. Audiovisual equipment, posters and publications assist Health Units in presenting their programme.

(*f*) Statistics section, consisting of one university graduate and one high school graduate.

(*g*) Administration, with three medical aides (high school graduates) and a technical clerk in charge of various administrative activities.

(*h*) Transport section in the charge of a high school graduate and three or four drivers, equipped with two or three van-cars and one ambulance for taking the patients to the city hospital.

The base is also equipped with engineering equipment and health education material, and acts as a back-stop for the mobile teams. For example, when a team decides that the environmental sanitation of a certain area should be improved, it contacts the base, which sends out sanitary engineers and the necessary equipment. Likewise, should a team contemplate running a health education programme in a particular village, it informs the base, whereupon the health education officer is dispatched to the village; similar procedures are followed when a disease is suspected, when blood samples have to be collected, when dental care is required, etc.

All Health Corpsmen meet at their home base at the beginning of each month to discuss their problems, exchange ideas and receive new equipment and facilities, as well as their salaries. The provincial director and other administrative officials also take part in these meetings.

Health Units

The Health Units or mobile teams are the most dynamic part of the Health Corps. Each unit is led by a newly-graduated physician who is assisted in his work by two or three high school graduates and a driver. The unit has transportation, medical supplies and living quarters in the largest or most central village in an area, where it serves a population of 10000 to 20000 in some 30 to 40 villages. Although stationed in one village, the team makes regular and scheduled visits to sub-centres in two or three villages, which each have some five to ten other villages within 2 to 10 kilometres. At any time of the day or night the exact whereabouts of the team is well known to every village in this area.

The duties of the Health Unit are not confined purely to medical matters, but also include activities of a preventive nature. They carry out vaccinations on a large scale, assist people in improving their environmental conditions, and above all carry out extensive health education activities. The arrival of a mobile team is announced well in advance. Each team is equipped with a kerosene or electric refrigerator to preserve vaccines, sera and other medicines. Medicines are dispatched by Headquarters once every four months, but each team has funds at its disposal to purchase any additional medicines that might be needed.

Each ten to twelve such units are connected to a Base Centre where, as stated above, there are better diagnostic and curative facilities, together with ambulance services.

The number of units has fluctuated from 350 to 400, depending on the number of medical graduates available to the Health Corps Organization. Since autumn 1964, nine groups of conscripts have completed training at the military centres. They include 1552 physicians, 138 dentists, 240 pharmacists, 11 veterinarians and 201 graduates in social sciences. In the medical aid group, 4444 secondary school graduates have completed training. All these Corpsmen were sent to rural areas in medical teams, laboratory units, dentistry units, health education units, sanitary engineering units and administration units. Since the Health Corps began seven groups of Corpsmen have completed their service. At present there are 392 medical teams, 30 dentistry units, 41 laboratory units, 15 pharmacy units and 30 health education units in the rural areas, ready for any self-sacrifice to meet the needs of their compatriots in the villages.

Since 1969 women, who account for 10 to 15 per cent of all medical school graduates, are also accepted for the Health Corps. This ratio is constantly growing and now there are 725 women doctors and high school graduates in the Health Corps. They are mostly posted to the base stations where living accommodation is better and they concentrate on family planning, maternal and child health, etc.

Thus, with these semi-mobile health teams over six million people living in some 14 323 villages in very remote areas of the country are being provided with minimum medical and health care, and in those areas no village is further than 10 kilometres from a Health Unit.

Since 1965, when the programme was first implemented, some 1800 such mobile units have been organized and sent to various villages, each for a period of 18 months. Some of their major activities are listed in Table VIII.

TABLE VIII

THE WORK OF THE HEALTH UNITS, 1965–1969

Type of activity	Number
Outpatient visits	13 091 703
Hospital referrals	42 216
Laboratory procedures	386 467
Vaccinations	6 148 107
Dental visits	345 659
Health films shown	7615
Health education conferences	24 580
Clinics constructed	216
Water supply made sanitary or newly built	13 409
Slaughterhouses made sanitary or newly built	245

RESULTS AND CONCLUSION

The results obtained from the Health Corps have been remarkable and hopeful. Its importance is not only as a measure to meet the health and medical needs of today, or as a measure that meets a vital need of the new society that is taking shape in our rural communities. It is also a new way of utilization of medical manpower, and a way to distribute it better.

In action, the Health Corps has been met with great enthusiasm by the inhabitants of the rural areas of the country. The national programme has not only significantly altered the health pattern of these people, but has also encouraged them to contribute to and cooperate in the struggle for improvement; with this cooperation the Health Corps has gone a long way towards improving the sanitation and environmental health of the villages.

The Corps is creating a new awakening among the rural population. It has shown new horizons to the farmers of Iran—horizons that have made them work harder for their own future social and economic well-being.

Each year upon completion of their term of service in the Health Corps, several physicians ask to stay for one or two years, in the same place or similar areas. The numbers of such requests are growing considerably. For example, among 400 recruits of two years ago, about 168 have asked if they may continue for another two years. This enables the organization to move into more remote areas each year and leave behind permanent rural Health Units to be operated by the Ministry of Health and staffed by ex-Corpsmen.

The value and the advantages of this phenomenon do not lie only in the expansion of rural health services, which in itself is vitally important for a country such as Iran. There are also several other points to be considered. For example, when a young graduate for one reason or another commits himself for two or more years to rural health work in his country, naturally he reduces the possibilities and eventually gives up the idea of migrating to foreign lands. It is therefore expected that the Health Corps in the long run, along with other national devices, will serve as a means to prevent the 'brain drain', which in recent years has become a serious national problem.

Another inherent advantage in the Health Corps programme is the impact that it has as a teaching laboratory for rural field experience. The undergraduate medical curriculum of our medical schools is lacking in this respect. Practically none of the medical schools so far have been able to develop rural clerkship or even internship programmes. The Health Corps programme in itself is compensating for this deficiency, when for 18 months our young medical graduates are working in ambulatory care and communicable disease control, and participate in several mass campaigns in rural settings.

Finally, while discussing the advantages and effects of the Health Corps in our country, we should consider also the new developments which are taking place in connexion with some medical schools and the School of Public Health. For example the Medical School Faculty of Pahlavi University in Shiraz through its Rural Medical Programme is extending its supervision, technical and professional, over the Health Corps Units which function at the village level and through smaller teaching hospitals located in the region connected to the University Hospitals in Shiraz. This network of medical care will improve the quality of practice in Health Corps Units, will make the job more attractive, and will also secure more extensive medical care for those who need further diagnostic and specialized services. Obviously, this network will create a two-way traffic of knowledge and experience.

As stated earlier (p. 42), the methods for delivery of medical care in each country should be planned within the complex of the socio-economic development as well as the political conditions of that country. The countries of the developing world should try to experiment with ways and means to make better use of their existing facilities, and should find ways to accelerate the rate of their health coverage.

The Health Corps experience of Iran has made a contribution towards the delivery of medical care to the widely scattered rural population. Although the Organization has been developed within the structure of the Ministry of Health and has been purely service oriented, it has grown to be of potential value and interest for medical education.

DISCUSSION

Dogramaci: Your presentation was a most fascinating one, Dr Dadgar. Since the members of the team are all drafted, do they all change at the same time? And do those who continue their service beyond the compulsory period then get a higher salary which makes the extension more attractive?

Dadgar: The members of a team all finish their service at the same time, and they are immediately replaced by another team. But they work in the rural areas for one and a half years of the two years and if there is a gap because of shortage of physicians for replacement we use the physicians that we have recruited for longer employment.

During his two-year term the physician has the same pay as an army second-lieutenant and the aide the same as a sergeant. After the two-year term, we pay them two or three times more, because this is the regular salary for a physician outside. However, before the Health Corps began the doctors would not go to the villages, but now that they are familiar with village life they want to stay and continue their work. Last year we had vacant places for 96 physicians and we received 168 applications.

Dogramaci: Since there is a move to establish people for longer than the two-year period, is there also a plan to build upon this programme a permanent infrastructure for future health services in Iran?

Dadgar: A rural Health Corps clinic created by the Health Corps will be permanent and when it is eventually staffed by the voluntary employees the Health Corps team moves to a more remote area.

Baker: I must congratulate you on this very stimulating and exciting new programme. From which professional groups did the 725 women you mentioned come? You have only 360 nursing graduates per year in Iran.

Dadgar: About 100 of the 725 women are physicians, dentists and chemists. There are only a few nurses because nurses are exempt from military service if they are working in a hospital, since we are very short of nurses in Iran. The other 625 are high-school graduates who receive special training to help the technical staff.

Hill: This is an excellent example of teamwork in medicine, but has the fact of having a Health Corps in community medicine led to any changes in the general curriculum for medical students?

Dadgar: Actually none of the medical schools have changed their curricula for preparing people for work in the Health Corps. However, during the six months of training they receive sufficient information about rural health problems and how to handle them.

Hill: During the six months' training, are the doctors trained with the non-medicals or do they meet them for the first time in the field? That is, are the doctors being trained as team-leaders during these six months?

Dadgar: The two groups are trained at the same time and during the six months of training the doctors receive enough training to lead their team and the high-school graduates learn enough to work as medical aides.

Bridger: A doctor may be a very good doctor in his own right and even the key person in the team, but what happens when he is not always the best administrator or leader in the team? Secondly, what special problems are you meeting now?

Dadgar: As I said, the doctors get enough training to lead their teams and to understand the plan of their work in the villages. Our present problem is the shortage of medical groups to answer all the medical needs and requests.

Ordoñez-Plaja: How far do the people accept this new type of medical service?

Dadgar: When we sent our first team to a rural area, it was difficult to find any rooms for them, but after they had worked there for six months the local people, using their own money, built a big dispensary and place for them to live. Now we have many requests for teams to be sent to the villages, which illustrates the acceptance of the programme by people in the rural areas.

Russell: This sounds like an excellent example of the social use of military resources. How exactly do the Corpsmen organize their programme of work when they arrive for the first time in a new area?

Dadgar: They work from a plan prepared by the base, showing how many days they should stay in each place. Each team has a complete file on village conditions, giving information about the population, the health situation, the climate, and so on, and indicating the facilities needed.

Russell: Do the physicians make any surveys of diseases or do other epidemiological work in these areas?

Dadgar: Usually they do. They report communicable diseases to the provincial Health Department and send in samples to the laboratory.

DISCUSSION

Four years ago when we had a cholera epidemic in Iran, the Health Corps did very intensive vaccination and preventive work.

Fişek: This type of team is one of the best ways of using medical manpower. How frequently do the teams visit each village? What do people do when they are sick between visits?

Dadgar: The team works two days of the week at the main centre and one or two days a week in each of the sub-centres. If there is an urgent case of illness in any village in the area the people can ask the physician to visit their patient and if the patient cannot be treated in the village he will be sent to the nearest hospital in the base ambulance. Where a sanitation or vaccination programme is needed the team goes to the village and analyses local requirements before asking the base for help.

Fişek: What kind of cooperation exists between the provincial health organization and the mobile army teams?

Dadgar: The Health Corps teams are all under the supervision of the Provincial Health Departments, and the director of the Health Corps in the province is under the supervision of the Health Department, not the army. Only the six months' training is in the army training centre; after that, all the work is under the Ministry of Health, and the Provincial Health Department staff take all the necessary steps in cooperating with the team.

Fişek: Are there any published statistics on how this service has affected the level of health in the rural population? Have communicable diseases, infant mortality and the crude death rate decreased?

Dadgar: Where we carried out vaccination programmes, the death rate was certainly reduced. Five teams are at present evaluating the results throughout the country. For this evaluation random areas where Health Corps Units are working are being compared with other parts which have no facilities (Table I, Fig. 1).

TABLE I (Dadgar)
VITAL STATISTICS FROM RANDOM AREAS (1969)

	Areas where Health Corps units are working	Other areas without facilities
No. of villages	38	38
No. of households	4436	3426
Total population	35834	25292
Family size	5·09	5·10
Birth rate (per 1000 population)	35	38
Crude death rate (per 1000 population)	10·3	14·8
Infant mortality (per 1000 live births)	75	146
Growth rate (%)	2·47	2·32

52

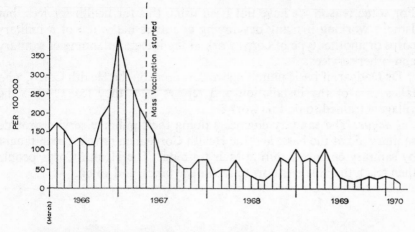

FIG. 1 (Dadgar). Morbidity rate of measles in rural areas of Iran under the jurisdiction of Health Corps teams (from monthly reports of Health Corps teams).

Fişek: Does anyone stay in the villages to follow up the treatment or otherwise cooperate with the team?

Dadgar: No, but where there are serious cases an aide could be assigned to stay. When they are going to prepare a water supply the sanitary engineer stays there to finish the work, of course.

Fişek: If you trained one enlisted soldier from each village in the Health Corps during their military service, you would have some permanent liaison and possibilities for follow-up, because they will return to their own villages after being discharged and live there permanently.

Dadgar: We do this, and we have another programme for recruiting rural midwives in this way. We choose local girls who have had nine years at school, train them for nine months or a year and send them back to the villages as rural midwives.

Hill: Many doctors who enter the Health Corps now volunteer to stay. There are also about 4500 non-medicals who have had two years' training and experience. What has happened to those? Are you going to utilize them at all?

Dadgar: As you know there is no shortage of auxiliary personnel, but mainly of physicians. But the auxiliary personnel go to the sanitary aide school, work as laboratory technicians, and so on, and they are employed in other sections in the medical field if they want.

Bridger: It is pertinent to our main theme to recognize that the planning and thinking that preceded this fascinating and exciting work were vital to its success.

Rebhun: In Israel we have experience in the field of using military service for social benefit, particularly for teaching and engineering work.

53

For some reason we have not been using this for health services, but Israelis working in many developing countries make use of a military corps or another type of corps work in the integral planning of sanitary and other services.

Dr Dadgar, if basic plumbing work is done by the Health Corps, who takes care of the installation and repairs after they leave? Are the villagers trained to do this work?

Dadgar: The sanitary engineers doing their military service provide sanitary aid at the base, and the Health Corps men have all been taught by sanitary engineers during their training. The Health Corps people then teach the villagers how to repair the pipes, and so on.

5: An Example of an Integrated Approach to Health Care: The Turkish National Health Services

NUSRET H. FIŞEK

THE Turkish Government, especially since the First World War, has taken an active part in rendering health services—both preventive and curative—to its citizens.[9, 10] In 1960[1] a new system of Turkish National Health Service, called the 'socialized health services', was formulated and accepted by Parliament. This marked a milestone in the history of health services in Turkey.

The design of the Turkish National Health Services is based on team work and cooperation. The characteristics of the Turkish National Health Services, the status of the health services before nationalization and the results of a field study on the National Health Services are given and discussed in this paper.

THE STATUS OF HEALTH SERVICES IN 1960

(1) *Health organization*

The main official agency administering the Health Services in Turkey is the Ministry of Health and Social Welfare. Patient care is also provided by other Ministries, State economic enterprises, the Workers' Insurance Administration and the private sector, but their activities are not extensive compared to the work of the Ministry of Health.

The health service as a whole is inefficient because of lack of cooperation and coordination among various agencies and departments.

(2) *Hospitals*

The total number of hospital beds—excluding hospitals of the armed forces—was about 49000 (19 per 10000 persons) in 1960. Ninety-two per cent of hospital beds are in the public sector. Patient care in the hospitals is free of charge for those who are poor. Payments are made only by those who can afford to meet the hospital and treatment charges, though even these payments fall short of the actual costs incurred.

(3) *Local health organization*

The local health organization is a part of the general provincial administration (see Fig. 1). Coordination of the different activities of the various units is far from being satisfactory at the provincial level. The

55

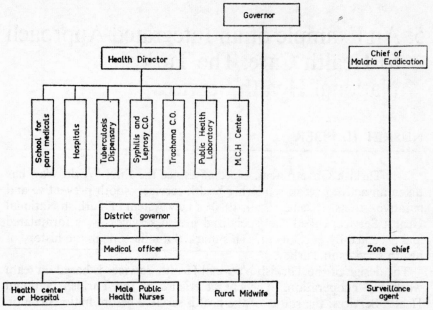

FIG. 1. Organization of health services in a province (old pattern).

burden of the health services is on the shoulders of district medical officers who each serve an average population of 50000. Each officer has two male public health nurses and six to ten rural midwives to aid him. The health centre or hospital, if it exists, in the district centre has a limited function.

The medical officer has several duties to perform, such as preventive services and judicial and administrative duties. In addition, he also attends his private patients. This makes heavy demands on his time. In consequence, health services suffer to a great extent. The rural midwives are usually responsible for groups of eight to ten villages. These midwives live in villages located more or less in the centre of the group. Their primary task is to assist at deliveries, but they are usually called to distant villages only in cases of difficult deliveries.

(4) *Health manpower*

TABLE I

HEALTH MANPOWER IN TURKEY

	1960 (population 27 million)		1969 (population 34 million)	
	Number	Ratio	Number	Ratio
Medical doctor	10260	2700	12389	2744
Nurse	1195	22594	3927	8658
Nursing aide	856	31542	3499	9717
Male public health nurse	3035	8896	6494	5236
Midwife	3182	8485	6676	5093

Turkey had a shortage of health personnel, especially of paramedical workers, in 1960 (see Table I). The uneven distribution of health personnel made this problem more critical. In 1960, 44 per cent of practising physicians were in the city of Istanbul. Only 18 per cent of the physicians were practising in communities with populations of less than 25000, although 80 per cent of the population live in such communities.

(5) *Schools for health personnel*

Medical education in Turkey goes as far back as 1206, when a medical school was established in Kayseri. The schools established by the Turks in Anatolia during the Middle Ages were the most prominent and advanced centres of medical education and practice in the world at that time. Following the Renaissance movement—especially in the seventeenth and eighteenth centuries—medicine advanced by leaps and bounds in Europe, while theory and practice lagged behind in the medical schools of Turkey. As a result, the necessity for reform in medical education began to be felt deeply in the nineteenth century. The Western system of medical education was adopted in Turkey in 1827, with the establishment of a medical school in Istanbul. The second Faculty of Medicine was established 119 years later in Ankara (1946) and the third in Izmir (1954).

As for the training of the paramedical workers, the Turkish Government attached little importance to this problem before 1961. With the exception of the school for nurses established by the Turkish Red Crescent Society, the school for midwives of the Istanbul Faculty of Medicine and two schools established by the Ministry of Health and Social Assistance, no other training facilities existed. In the early 1940s an attempt was made to train more nurses and midwives. Two schools of rural midwifery and one school of nursing were established, but the level of training in the schools was inadequate. The numbers of schools for health personnel and their graduates between 1940 and 1969 are given in Table II.

TABLE II

NUMBERS OF SCHOOLS AND OF GRADUATES (1940–1969)

	Number of schools			Number of graduates		
Years	*Medicine*	*Basic nursing*	*Rural midwifery*	*Medicine*	*Basic nursing*	*Rural midwifery*
1940	1	2	2	190	30	55
1945	1	1	2	424	28	89
1950	2	6	2	409	191	142
1955	3	11	7	567	188	87
1960	3	9	14	495	245	415
1965	5	23	24	681	522	433
1969	7	27	29	718	860	1160

(6) *The use of health services by the public*

The use of available health services by the public was quite limited, for several reasons: low standards of education, especially health education; poor economic conditions; long distances between villages and towns where the health establishment was located; and the widespread practice of folk medicine.

THE HEALTH PLAN AND ITS ACHIEVEMENTS

In 1960, the Turkish Goverment started to design an overall plan for socioeconomic development, and the health services were accepted as an integral part of this plan. The details of the Health Plan in Turkey have been given elsewhere.[2,3] Reorganization of health services and training of health workers are given high priority in the plan, as outlined below:

(1) *Reorganization*

The health services will be nationalized and the services of the public sector—except the armed forces—will be under the direction of the Ministry of Health. The main features of the National Health Services are as follows:

(*a*) Medical doctors and health personnel are free to choose either private practice or the National Health Services. If they choose the National Health Services, they receive a fixed salary and do not have the right to engage in private practice.

(*b*) Individuals are free to choose their doctor or hospital, if they are prepared to pay for their services. General practitioner and visiting nurse's services, life-saving drugs, hospital care and all preventive work, including periodical check-ups, are free of charge to every resident who wishes to use the facilities of the National Health Services according to the regulations.

(*c*) Doctors and other health personnel in the hospitals and in the community units are members of a large team responsible for both curative and preventive services.

(*d*) Because of the insufficiency of health personnel, the reorganization will be carried out stepwise and will be completed within 15 years, nationalizing health services in three to five provinces every year.

The nationalization of health services was started in the Province of Muş in 1963.[5] The number of provinces in which health services had been nationalized reached 25 in 1970 and the population covered was nine million, which is 26 per cent of the population of Turkey. There are 840 health units, 1314 health stations and 82 hospitals with a total of 9821 hospital beds. Eighty-nine per cent of rural midwifery posts, 59 per cent of nursing posts, 41 per cent of medical officer posts, and 20 per cent of the specialist posts were filled in 1969.[8]

(2) *Training of health personnel*

(a) *Medical doctors.* It was decided that five new medical schools should be established within the period of the Plan. Four new schools in Ankara (Hacettepe Medical School), Erzurum, Istanbul (Cerrah Paşa Medical School) and Diyarbakir were established between 1963 and 1969. The number of graduates each year increased to 700 (see Table II). It is also indicated in the Plan that more emphasis must be given to teaching the community aspects of health and patient care to students at all levels of medical education. Training in the field of public health is also emphasized.

(b) *Nurses and midwives.* Teaching staff and facilities were very limited before 1960. The schools and dormitories are usually housed in the hospital buildings. It was decided that 41 new school buildings with dormitories housing 150 to 200 students each would be built. Education for nurses and midwives at the university level was also planned and the curricula for nursing and midwifery were revised.

The implementation of this Plan was very successful and surpassed the targets. Fifty-six new school buildings were built between 1963 and 1969. In 1970, 2623 students are expected to graduate from the nursing and midwifery schools in Turkey (see Table II).

Rural midwives are given three years' professional training, in public health nursing as well as midwifery, after their primary education.

The duration of training in the basic nursing schools is four years after completing junior high school. Nursing schools admit male students who are trained in public health nursing.

Higher education in nursing lasts for three to four years after high school training or basic nursing education.

(c) *Other paramedical workers.* Schools for physiotherapists, dieticians, medical technologists, sanitary inspectors and laboratory technicians were planned and opened during the period of the Plan, but they are still inadequate in meeting the needs of the country. Training in public health engineering is only just beginning in Turkey.

THE HEALTH TEAM IN THE NATIONAL HEALTH SERVICES

(1) *Organization*

The organization at ministerial level has not been changed, except that a new general directorate has been established for the National Health Services.

In the provinces where health services have been nationalized (see Fig. 2), coordination and cooperation between different units of the health organization have been established. The health director is the top official. He plans, directs and supervises health activities in the provinces.

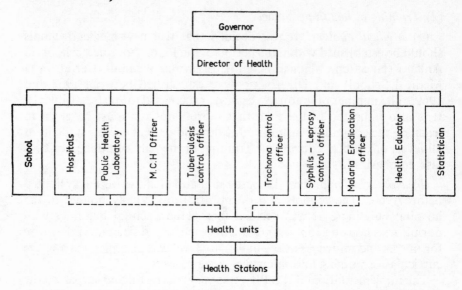

Fig. 2. Organization of the National Health Services in a province
(new pattern).

The main organizational unit of the Turkish National Health Services is the 'Health Unit'. A rural Health Unit is staffed by one medical officer, two nurses and four district rural midwives who also function as district nurses. They serve an average population of 7000 persons. In cities and towns, two to four units are combined in one unit, and the staff is increased accordingly.

The medical officer and his paramedical workers are responsible for ambulatory work and home care, for all preventive work, for the control of chronic and degenerative diseases and for the improvement of nutritional standards. The activities of the Health Units are supported and complemented by the hospitals, dispensaries and public health specialists of the provinces.

In patient care, patients are examined first by a medical officer, and those who need further examination or hospitalization are referred to the district or provincial hospital. Chronic cases are followed up by both a specialist in the hospital and the medical officer in the unit. This helps considerably in reducing the cost of medical care and the need for hospital services.

Free medical care, the establishment of medical practice in the rural areas and emphasis on health education create a better environment for changing the health behaviour and practices of the people.

When the organization of the health services is examined from the standpoint of modern trends in health administration, it will be seen that it creates the most favourable conditions for (*a*) integration of home care and hospital care, (*b*) integration of medical care and prevention of diseases, (*c*) the possibility of the follow-up of every person—sick or healthy—from his birth until his death, (*d*) the consideration of the individual in his environment as a whole, and (*e*) overcoming all barriers in order to satisfy the human right of people to obtain better health and medical services.

(2) *The Health Unit*

The health team consists of:

(*a*) *Medical officer.* He is the leader of the team and is responsible for examining and treating patients, for directing and supervising all preventive work which is carried out by his staff, for the in-service training of the staff, and for health education of the public; as a responsible member of the community he is expected to motivate the people for community development. Medical officers do not function only in their offices, but also visit health stations and other villages regularly.

(*b*) *Rural midwives.* They are the most important members of the team in preventive work. They spend most of their time visiting villages and houses regularly. The responsibilities of rural midwives are as follows:

(i) Maternal health: antenatal and postnatal care, family planning education of the women, assisting the medical officer in advising those women who may have difficult deliveries to get admitted to a hospital when their labour starts, and assisting in deliveries at home.

(ii) Child care: following-up the development of children between birth and six years of age, educating mothers in child care and nutrition and vaccinating children against diphtheria, whooping cough, tetanus, poliomyelitis and smallpox.

(iii) The surveillance of communicable diseases.

(iv) Health education.

(v) Patient care: the care of chronic diseases such as tuberculosis, and parenteral injections for other patients.

(vi) Reporting births, deaths and migrations.

(vii) Motivating people in community development.

(*c*) *Public health nurses.* There are two public health nurses in each unit. One of them is responsible for supervising the work of the rural midwives and training them in service. She also gives BCG vaccination to infants and gives group training to others.

The second nurse, a man, is responsible for rural sanitation and the school health programme, and he makes the biannual census of population in order to correct the records of residents, if there is any mistake. He is responsible for health education for the men. In outbreaks of communicable diseases, he takes part in the efforts to control them.

61

(d) *Medical secretary.* He is in charge of the routine secretarial work. In addition, he keeps the archives, the household forms and the individual health forms. He tabulates the statistical data, prepares the monthly report and keeps accounts of expenditure and drugs.

(3) *The hospital*

In addition to the routine hospital services rendered, the specialists are expected to visit Health Units regularly for consultation and in-service training. The medical officers meet in the hospital at least once a month, and in some places every week. They discuss administrative and professional matters at these meetings.

The hospital laboratory provides help not only for specialists dealing with hospital cases but also for medical officers in the diagnosis of the patients attending the clinics of the unit.

(4) *The Office of the Health Director*

Public health specialists in the Office of the Health Director or at the district level are responsible for planning, supervising and evaluating public health activities. They also take part in the training of staff in service. Public health specialists or units attached to them assist the work of the units in some special cases, such as health education, spraying insecticides and control of tuberculosis.

The Health Director is the top health official in the province. He, with the assistance of his staff, carries out all the planning, and coordinates and directs the work of the public health specialists, hospitals and units.

A MODEL FOR NATIONAL HEALTH SERVICES: ETIMESGUT RURAL HEALTH DISTRICT

Certain difficulties and setbacks in the expansion and implementation of the National Health Services and in the attainment of certain standards have been discussed elsewhere.[4] The work in the Etimesgut Rural Health District since 1967, however, serves as an example of the successful implementation of the reorganization programme based on teamwork and coordination.[7]

(1) *The District*

The Etimesgut Rural District was established by the Ministry of Health in 1965. The Ministry of Health and Hacettepe University signed an agreement to run the services in this district together and for it to be used by the University for research and training. One of the research projects in the District is in the field of health administration.

The District is located west of the city of Ankara. It covers 83 villages and two towns. The surface area of the District is 640 square miles and it has a population of 55000. The estimated annual income of farmers in the area is 12000 lira (800 U.S. dollars) per family of six persons.

The health organization consists of seven Health Units, 30 health stations and a 50-bed rural hospital under the direction of the district health officer. The total number of professional and service workers is 150, which includes 14 medical doctors, 32 nurses and 27 rural midwives.

(2) *Health services and the prevalence of diseases*

The activities of the health services are given in the Annual Report of the District. The results of the work on mother and child care and on patient care carried out in 1969 are given below.

(*a*) *Child care*. The average number of periodic examinations of infants and of children between one and six years of age was $12\cdot2$ and $4\cdot3$ per year, respectively, in 1969. Infants were vaccinated systematically against tuberculosis, whooping-cough, tetanus, diphtheria, poliomyelitis and smallpox. Children over three years of age were also vaccinated against typhoid fever. Ninety-five per cent of the susceptible population were immunized against the common infectious diseases.

(*b*) *Maternal care*. The average number of antenatal examinations per pregnant woman was $4\cdot3$ in 1969. The total number of deliveries was 1961. Of these, 845 cases (43 per cent) were assisted by midwives and 475 cases (24 per cent) went to the hospital. Thirty-three per cent of deliveries had no professional assistance, as against 55 per cent with no assistance in 1967.

(*c*) *Patient care*. The number of patients examined in the units in 1969 was 47946; 2244 were sent to hospital and examined by specialists. Another 3414 patients were examined by specialists in the hospital without being sent by one of the units. The number of patients hospitalized was 1762.

Infectious diseases are no longer a major health problem. Pneumonia is the major cause of death, followed by heart diseases, the largest number of deaths due to pneumonia being among young children.

(*d*) *Infectious diseases*. There were 19 deaths due to infectious diseases in 1969. Of these, 11 were due to tuberculosis and six to measles. The total number of cases of tuberculosis was 183 in 1969. Streptococcal infections accounted for 379 cases, bacillary dysentery for 70, infectious hepatitis for 51, whooping-cough for 27 and enteric fever for 18. There were no cases of diphtheria, tetanus, poliomyelitis, malaria or syphilis.

(*e*) Epidemiological studies carried out in the District show that the rate of confirmed heart diseases is $1\cdot3$ per cent. The hypertension prevalence rate is 15 per cent for the population over 30 years of age. The rate of lung cancer is $2\cdot3$ per 10000.

(3) *Demographic information*

The changes in demographic values within three years, in comparison with the national average and with the city of Ankara, are given in Table III. As this table shows, there has been a steady decline in death rate and

TABLE III

DEMOGRAPHIC INFORMATION ABOUT THE ETIMESGUT RURAL HEALTH DISTRICT AND ITS COMPARISON
WITH THE CITY OF ANKARA AND THE NATION

Rates	Etimesgut			City of Ankara 1967*	Turkey 1967*
	1967	1968	1969		
Crude birth rate (per 1000)	35·1	34·7	35·4	31·0	40·0
Fertility rate (per 1000)	169	168	167	?	?
Crude death rate (per 1000)	10·3	9·57	8·8	9·0	15·0
Infant mortality rate (per 1000)	142	121	111	101	153
Neonatal mortality rate (per 1000)	36·0	39·3	28·5	?	?
Death under 5 years of age (per 100)	59·0	51·5	52·9	40·5	53·6
Death over 50 years of age (per 100)	29·9	35·3	31·8	36·6	31·1
Maternal mortality rate (per 10000)		5·4†		?	15·0‡
Life expectancy at birth (male)	55·9	57·1	62·80	56·85	55·84§
Life expectancy at birth (female)	57·7	63·6	63·80	58·17	58·49§
Life expectancy at 5 years (male)	63·3	62·6	67·52	60·45	61·85§
Life expectancy at 6 years (female)	66·4	66·8	68·12	62·99	64·40§

* Source of information: Turkish Demographic Survey.[6]
† There were four maternal deaths between 1967 and 1969. The given rate is the average for 3 years.
‡ Only cities and towns.
§ Eastern Anatolia is not included.

infant mortality rate. The figures for the District are lower than the average for Turkey and similar to those for the city of Ankara. The infant mortality rate in the two towns of the District is 71 per 1000, which is the lowest figure in Turkey and much lower than the rate for the city of Ankara, which is otherwise the lowest (see Fig. 3). The maternal death

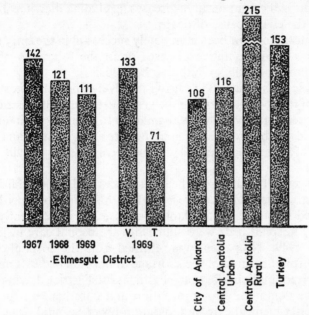

FIG. 3. Infant mortality rates in the Etimesgut Health District (per 1000).

rate is 5 per 10 000 live births, which is in the range of the developed countries. The maternal mortality rate in the cities of Turkey is three to four times higher than the rate in Etimesgut District.

(4) *Investment and expenditure*

The total capital investment in the District is 6 300 000 TL ($420 000). The total expenditure was 2 978 000 TL ($199 000) in 1969. The largest proportion of this (67 per cent) goes towards the payment of salaries. The expenditure per head of population was 54 TL (equivalent to $3·6) in 1969. Nearly half of this was spent on hospital care.

CONCLUSIONS

Results obtained in the Etimesgut project, and observations made in the provinces where health services are nationalized, lead us to the following conclusions:

(1) The team of medical and paramedical workers in Etimesgut District has succeeded in decreasing the crude death rate, infant mortality rate and maternal mortality rate (see Table III). The trend of the decline

65

is very encouraging for the future. If we take the infant mortality rate as the index of the health level, we may deduce that the level of health is improving in this district and is already higher than in the cities, being almost equal to that of metropolitan areas.

(2) Communicable diseases are no longer a major problem for Etimesgut District. All communicable diseases (excluding diarrhoeal diseases) ranked as the eighth cause of death.

(3) The team has not been completely successful in the early detection of chronic and degenerative diseases or in the follow-up of chronic cases and home nursing, excluding tuberculosis.

(4) The success achieved in raising the level of health is mostly due to the work of the so-called rural midwives, who are actually district nurses. If the number of midwives were augmented to bring the ratio of population per midwife below 1000, then home care and screening and the early detection of some chronic and degenerative diseases would be more successful.

(5) The overall planning of health services and the establishment of health teams have led to a decrease in health service costs per head and have helped to utilize the available manpower more efficiently.

(6) Fifty hospital beds were sufficient for hospital care in Etimesgut District in 1969. No patient was returned from the hospital or sent to another hospital because of the shortage of hospital beds. It means that in a young population like that of Etimesgut District, having a health team in the community for prevention and cure makes it possible to provide better medical care and maintain fewer hospital beds.

(7) The success of the health team depends largely on good administration and leadership.

(8) The health service is a part of the whole public service. The shortcomings and failures in one sector affect the others, and *vice versa*. Therefore, all the persons who provide services for the community should cooperate and support each other, and act as members of a large team.

(9) If the health services are organized by governments as a whole in the developing countries, this is more likely to fulfil the goal set in the Universal Declaration of Human Rights of the United Nations and the Constitution of the World Health Organization: "The enjoyment of the highest attainable standard of health is one of the fundamental rights of every human being without distinction of race, religion, political belief, economic or social condition."

(10) The Turkish National Health Service as planned is a feasible project in terms of financial and manpower requirements, because government expenditure in 1969 was only 700 TL ($46·5) per head and the ratio of medical doctors to population was 1:2700 in the area. The number of paramedical workers is increasing rapidly and the shortages will be made good in the near future.

A comparison of the performance of the health services in Turkey before nationalization and the results obtained in Etimesgut Health District after nationalization indicates that a well-designed and carefully implemented system of national health services with an emphasis on teamwork will open new vistas of public and individual health.

DISCUSSION

Banks: In 1962 Professor Fişek was the permanent head of the Ministry of Health and he has in fact described the plans which he had in mind then. Very few men can have gone on to test their own plans in the field and come out nearly ten years later with the results.

Do the midwives actually supervise all communicable diseases, or are they used to follow up contacts, or something of that kind?

Fişek: I used the word 'surveillance', to mean "detecting and reporting suspected cases to a medical officer".

Hockey: Is a midwife who comes in contact with a streptococcal infection taken off midwifery? There is risk of infection.

Fişek: Certainly there is a risk of streptococcal infection, especially if the midwife is careless. The three-year average of maternal mortality rate in our area is 5 per 10000 live births and there is no puerperal infection. So it seems that our midwives care properly for both infectious diseases and deliveries.

Hill: Doctors all over the world jealously regard the powers of prescribing and diagnosis as their own inalienable right. Do you delegate any responsibility down the line, other than in maternity work, for prescribing and diagnosing, or have you any other intermediate personnel who see the patient, make a diagnosis and prescribe?

Fişek: Only doctors make a diagnosis and prescribe. The rural midwife and the nurses are responsible only for screening. For instance, in ante-natal care the rural midwife knows how to examine a pregnant woman and decide on normal and abnormal cases; if she suspects anything she has to refer the woman to the medical officer. Another example: all nurses know how to take blood pressure. They refer all persons having a diastolic blood pressure of over 100 mm Hg to the medical officer. They do not diagnose or treat patients by themselves.

Rebhun: Is environmental health taken care of in these units?

Fişek: The male public health nurse in the unit is responsible for rural sanitation, for school health and for the health education of the men in the community. There is also one sanitary inspector in the office of the Health District. He supervises the work of male public health nurses in the community and gives on-the-job training and assistance.

Russell: Permanent control of many communicable diseases requires the amelioration of the environment, and essentially this needs a multi-disciplinary approach. Is the rural health service in Turkey part of a programme of general community development?

Fişek: In urban areas the construction of the water supply system and improvement of sanitary facilities are not the direct responsibility of the Minister of Health but of the municipal government. Medical officers in cities and towns are responsible for the overall supervision of the work of officers in municipal governments. In rural areas, it is the responsibility of the health personnel to teach people how to make latrines or how to improve their water resources. The government also has an extensive programme for constructing a safe piped water supply for each village.

King: Your data are excellent, Professor Fişek. We very much want to institute effective mechanisms for reporting births and deaths in Zambia. How long has this been done in Turkey, and what particular mechanisms do you use?

Fişek: We register all household members residing in the Etimesgut Health District. The rural midwives follow up cases of birth, death and migration while visiting houses. The population census is also carried out every six months in order to correct any misreporting.

In developing countries the nation-wide registration is very poor. It is the same in Turkey. However, the Ministry of Health started a demographic sampling survey five years ago and we now have quite dependable figures for Turkey. The rates which I gave you are taken from the results of that survey. The infant mortality rate in Turkey seems much higher than in many developing countries, but I understand that what we report is near the correct figure and that if other developing countries improved their reporting systems they would have similar results. An infant mortality rate lower than 80 per 1000 births is an impossible figure for a developing country.

Kisseih: What kind of preparation is given to this type of midwife?

Fişek: We have three levels of education for paramedical workers. The rural midwives are mostly girls from a rural area. After five years of primary education in their villages, they have three years' professional training in midwifery and public health nursing. I should say the in-service training is more important than the school training. Most of them learn while doing, and the supervising nurses of the unit and the district give them on-the-job training. So it is not limited to the three years' schooling but is a continuous education after schooling. For nurses the professional training is four years after junior high school. The university level of nursing education is four years after senior high school. In addition to the basic professional training they also study psychology, statistics and other advanced subjects.

Horn: Are all rural midwives women, or do you include men as well? Do they live in the villages? Who pays them?

68

Fişek: All the rural midwives are women and they live and work in the villages. The medical doctors also live permanently in the villages. One doctor is responsible for 10 or 12 villages. He visits them according to a schedule, but spends the nights in his own village—that is, the centre of the unit. The medical officer and female public health nurse see each midwife at least once a week. Medical officers meet monthly or weekly in the community hospital to discuss problems. In our study area they meet once a week, because it is quite a compact area.

The government employs the midwives, nurses and doctors on a fixed salary basis. None of them is entitled to get any money, even a gift, from the persons they serve. The service is free for the people, and the health workers get quite a good salary by Turkish standards. The rural midwives receive about 1000 lira a month, which is approximately equivalent to $67.

Barbero: Is the cost per head an all-inclusive cost, including hospitalization and any other expenditures, in addition to the primary health team?

Fişek: Yes, it is.

Barbero: As the preventive programme in certain areas begins to diminish or ameliorate those particular communicable diseases, are new problems emerging that may change the future pattern and type of health care that will be needed? Some of the illnesses that at present have a low priority will probably need much more time than the preventive work that can be done now on a mass basis.

Fişek: A programme should always be regarded as a living body and has to be changed as conditions and possibilities are changed. What I have talked about here is the right programme for Turkey at the present time. For the time being a 50-bed hospital is enough for the area. No patient is refused because of the shortage of hospital beds. The rate of occupancy is 75 per cent. Since we now have better control of communicable diseases the expectation of life will go up and then the chronic and degenerative diseases will be more important. We have already started a chronic disease control programme and we now realize that one rural midwife for four villages is not enough to carry out this programme. Such work needs really good home service, and one rural midwife will be needed in every village to make the programme more successful for chronic diseases. We also know that 50-bed hospitals will not be enough in future. In coming years we plan to increase the number of rural midwife-public health nurses to make the services more complete.

Young: A world-wide problem is that doctors tend to congregate in urban areas at the expense of the rural ones. Have you solved this problem under your National Health Service in Turkey by powers of direction, or do you have other inducements for the doctors to serve the rural areas where otherwise they might be reluctant to live?

69

Fişek: That is the main problem of the Ministry of Health in carrying out this programme. Every government has to find the best way of solving this problem in its own country. In Turkey the most important reason hindering the even distribution of medical manpower is the part-time employment policy of the government. A doctor in a government hospital is allowed to have a surgery after 2 p.m. Even medical officers have private surgeries. This is one of the main reasons for congregating in urban areas. If the government suspends the right to have free practice, the doctors will be much better distributed. After all, they would still be free to choose government service or a completely private practice, so their professional freedom would be protected.

Hockey: How much does the health director at the centre direct the medical officer at the periphery? Has the health director had more training than the medical officer, and has the medical officer's curriculum included leadership and health education?

Fişek: In our team the health director is the only one making final decisions, especially if there is a conflict of opinion among the staff at different levels. He has public health advisers for supervision and evaluation. For instance, a head nurse of the district who supervises mother and child health work and home delivery services on behalf of the director has no right to give orders to midwives or nurses in the units, because the medical officer is the team leader in the Health Unit. The head nurse has to cooperate with the medical officer at unit level or report to the director if necessary. The medical officers are general practitioners given short courses in preventive work. They also learn while working. The visits of public health advisers and the monthly or weekly meetings are a kind of course for the medical officers. In our medical schools we teach the students how to work in a community. We send them to the rural units to work with the rural midwives, the nurses and the doctors.

Israel: I would like to present very briefly some of the important public health facets of our programme of family planning in India.

Although India has only 2·4 per cent of the world's land she has 14 per cent of the world's population; that is, one out of every seven persons in the world is an Indian. Although our population has taken about 5000 years to reach the present stage of about 500 million (the estimated figure this year is 554 million), it will double itself in only 28 years from now. This is because the very high birth rate and the lowered death rate due to better public health measures result in a tremendous gap which adds about 13 million people every year. A baby is born in India every one and a half seconds. This means that we have to provide for the development of jobs, education, health facilities, and so on, and it seems quite an impossible task at times for us to keep pace with the population. Although the country's income may be increasing, the income per head has not increased enough. Although there are more educational facilities there are still many millions of children who cannot have education, and certainly the health facilities are very far from perfect.

Our target in the family planning programme, which began at the time of the first Five Year Plan in 1951, is to reach the 100 million couples in the total population who are within the reproductive age group and to bring down the birth rate from its present rate of about 40 per thousand to 23 per thousand by 1978–79. This seems an impossible task but we are attempting to achieve it. Our programme consists of organization and administration, a training programme for all categories of personnel, and educational activities, with a big propaganda machine. The great red triangle has become a symbol of family planning not only in our country but even in other countries, and it is seen everywhere—on the telephone directories, on the backs of the rickshaws, on the billboards, on the houses in the villages, and so on. It cannot fail to have an impact not only on the adult population but even on the younger generation who are the future parents. We also have a very extensive service programme, on which we concentrated a great deal in the early years. But we found that merely providing the services at the clinics was not sufficient. It was necessary to extend the programme to the community, and therefore, in the Third Plan particularly, great emphasis was laid on educational activities, with involvement of village leaders, involvement of the community and working along with the village leaders for implementation of the programme, training these village leaders to eventually carry out the programme on their own. Finally, there is a small allocation for research, but naturally we have to concentrate more on applied research than on basic research because this is our priority.

At the centre of the organization for family planning is the Minister for Health, Family Planning, Urban Development and Works and Housing who has two departments under him, the Department of Health and the Department of Family Planning, the latter headed by a Commissioner. The Health Department is concerned with the national health programmes, hospital facilities, and so on, whereas the Department of Family Planning is concerned with the different aspects of the family planning programme: the service aspect, including the intrauterine device (IUD), oral contraceptives and sterilization, the stores and supplies, the training aspects, including training of maternal and child health workers, the evaluation of the programme, and finally the educational aspect. At the State level we have the State Department of Health headed by the Minister for Health with the State Directorate of Health Services under him, and the State Family Planning Bureau. Under this Bureau we have the various District Bureaus for family planning, of which there are about 315 in the whole country. At each District Bureau there is a

71

District Family Planning Officer, and under him there is an educational department manned by district extension educators, the education and information division, and also the field operations division with the mobile units for sterilization and IUD. At the district level the District Medical Officer is in charge of the several blocks in his district, while each block has a primary health centre with a block medical officer looking after this peripheral unit. Under the block medical officer are the block extension educators, who each look after about 80000 people; then there are the health assistants for family planning, four to each block extension educator, each looking after 20000 people. There are also the health visitors who supervise the auxiliary nurse-midwives (ANMs). These girls are really the people on whom the whole programme pivots. They are the ones who go out into the remote areas, often under very difficult conditions, and each of them looks after a population of 10000.

In our own training centre we have tried to integrate family planning with other activities, because we feel that family planning in isolation cannot have the required effect. Integration with other health services and other educational activities is of extreme importance. We train the paramedical personnel by giving the extension educators from the district level a course for 30 working days in which the main focus is on community work. They go through all the steps that they will be required to take when they go back to their own districts. The service part of the centre's activities includes vasectomy by an honorary surgeon, who also has developed a very good technique of re-anastomosis. It is most important in our programme for people to know that it is possible to recanalize the vas, otherwise many fear that if they want children later on they won't be able to have them. We also have an IUD and an oral contraceptive programme, and conventional contraceptives are distributed. Besides the family planning activities, we also give a gynaecological and infertility service. Papanicolaou smears are taken in all the new cases who come for family planning. We have a well-baby clinic, and until this year we had a child-care centre—a sort of half-day nursery where mothers with large families could bring their small children. Through this centre we involved the mothers in women's meetings at which we spoke to them about child-care and family planning. We also have an intensive educational programme, including a programme for family life education in schools, the objective being to influence the next generation of parents.

Our country has many very beautiful facets and also many which are not so beautiful, and we have a variety of people of different kinds—people of different socioeconomic levels, different religions, different cultures. We have to tackle all these different people according to their own level of literacy and culture. We have many problems, often gigantic.

We are well aware of these problems and we realize how much remains to be done. We are constantly looking out for new methods of grappling with these problems, and I am sure that meetings such as this are very useful in giving us new ideas for our programme.

Russell: In the countries of south-east Asia bordering on the Bay of Bengal, where some 900 million people live, the more conventional type of rural health service has been developed, and the difficulties encountered could possibly be laid exactly at the door of education and training programmes faultily designed and wrongly oriented. My interest in visiting these countries in 1962 and in 1968 was in the development of these rural health services and the training of personnel for them.

In 1968 one of the most disturbing factors was that the rural health team as constituted had been largely ineffective, certainly in the prevention of disease. The accepted pattern of rural health service generally consists of a main centre and a number of subcentres. In the latter are to be found midwives or auxiliary nurse-midwives, while the main health centre may have either a doctor or a medical auxiliary, a health visitor (herself an auxiliary), a midwife or auxiliary nurse-midwife and a sanitarian, plus a few other categories depending on the country and the emphasis placed on certain elements of work, such as family planning, by the health authorities. In many countries the auxiliary nurse-midwife or midwife carries out very few deliveries herself, because for cultural reasons people still prefer to use the indigenous midwife (*dai*) who does a wide range of domestic chores, associated often with problems of ritual pollution, which the trained midwife or auxiliary nurse-midwife will not do. So in some countries the *dais* are given six-month courses in the hygiene of delivery, usually by the health visitor, and a major part of the auxiliary nurse-midwife's function is then to supervise the work of the *dais*. Thus we have an auxiliary supervising an auxiliary supervising an auxiliary. Of course, there is no other way round the problem at present, but it does make nonsense of the theory that an auxiliary can only work under the supervision of a professional. In most of the rural health services in question the midwife or auxiliary nurse-midwife is a substitute for a professional, and we are only bluffing ourselves if we think otherwise.

The same applies in the realm of environmental sanitation. In most countries there is a sanitary inspector in the main rural health centre who is exposed during training to the full range of environmental sanitation, together with other preventive measures such as vaccination, in a course lasting between six months and one year. He is then sent out to work in the rural health service without any technical supervision (except that Thailand and Indonesia are now training a supervisory cadre), and certainly lacking any form of guidance and support. It is therefore not very surprising if he is said to devote most of his time to the lucrative business of persecuting food sellers.

The position regarding sanitation of the environment is very serious in these countries around the Bay of Bengal. The great burden of illness and poor health found there is due almost entirely to a grossly defective sanitary environment. This is true not only for diseases arising from gastrointestinal sources or transmitted through water, food or flies, but also for respiratory infections. For example, in some areas with very active tuberculosis clinics and BCG vaccination programmes, I was told that the reservoir of infection seems actually to be increasing— although where there is a BCG campaign a sharp reduction in the incidence of tuberculous meningitis is always reported.

It seems to me that the sanitary environment could be improved in a developing country, in the sort of context I have described, by having an organization similar to that developed for malaria eradication and indeed perhaps using much of that programme's information. For example, it could be applied to the provision of clean rural water supplies, and could use teams made up of sanitarians from rural health centres who would be given special training courses and the necessary labour force, or preferably local volunteers working under proper public health engineering supervision. There would be a preparatory phase in this sort of programme during which the situation in each area would be assessed, the nature of the work to be done would be established and at the same time training programmes would be carried out. There would be an attack phase during which the work of providing new wells or improving old ones, or whatever it happens to be, would be systematically carried out; and there would be a maintenance phase during which the whole new or renovated system would be kept under supervision until the basic health services were equipped to do the job.

This is only a very sketchy outline of what I mean, but it could probably be applied to other elements of environmental improvement, including housing and new village lay-outs. An essential part of a campaign of this sort would be a very intensive programme of health education as it affected the particular sanitation element being dealt with. Certainly unless some such action is taken it is difficult to see how amelioration of the environment is ever to be effected. Some countries are indeed constructing tube wells, but in most there is no organization to maintain them, and recently I came across one district where two-thirds of 700 tube wells were out of action.

Rebhun: The public health engineer or sanitary engineer in the health team is responsible for the quality of the environment as it affects health. Prevention of diseases transmitted by water or food is of course much more effective than their cure, as well as being cheaper. I shall try to define the problems facing the public health engineer today, based on my personal experience in the so-called developed countries such as the United States, in an intermediate type of country such as Israel, and in the so-called developing countries, which I have not visited, but I have worked on projects carried out by my countrymen in African and Asian countries.

Many of the so-called developing countries still need basic sanitary services, such as a safe water supply and in many places even sufficient water, and also minimum conditions for sanitary disposal of wastes. On the other hand the so-called highly developed countries like the United States or England, because of their highly industrial developments and poor management of environmental resources, are now facing increasing air and water pollution, and noise problems. Perhaps these problems seem exaggerated and should not be brought up in the face of the much poorer conditions in the developing countries, but the oil pollution produced by the *Torrey Canyon* incident, and the many fish killed in the rivers and lakes of the United States, England and Europe, as well as the polluted air in many cities, indicate that these problems exist.

In the 'developed' countries, the present-day public health or sanitary engineer needs a much better knowledge and understanding of non-conventional, advanced methods of pollution control and environment management. This should be based on modern achievements in the physical and chemical sciences and on advanced management methods. Conventional methods are now inadequate.

In the developing countries the task of a sanitary engineer may be even more difficult and demanding. Ingenious methods and adaptation to local conditions are essential. One of the dangers in planning projects in developing countries is the blind translation of methods suitable for a particular developed country to an entirely different technological, economic and social environment. It would be improper to design for a relatively remote area an expensive super-automatic water supply or treatment system equipped with many gadgets which may break down and cause frequent shutdowns because of the unavailability of a part or of technical personnel. Instead, a simple-to-operate but reliable system is required. It may in many cases be easier to design an automatic standard type of plant. However, it is the simple and easy to operate, but at the same time reliable, system that requires ingenuity and good engineering thinking. Better thinking in planning will produce a simple, cheap and reliable system. This should be remembered when giving assistance to developing countries.

The sanitary engineer is faced with teamwork at all levels of his work.

> (*a*) He is a leader of the team in environmental health or environmental control. Environmental health activities are an instance where teamwork is essential. In this area the team must be interdisciplinary and the cooperation of physicians, chemists, biologists and engineers is essential, as well as that of a variety of sanitary technicians (or sanitarians).

75

(*b*) The sanitary engineer is a member of various engineering teams, for example in regional and city planning. His function is to protect the health of the community as it may be affected by engineering projects.

(*c*) He is a member of the health team in district or regional health offices, where he represents the engineering profession.

In all the phases of his work, the sanitary engineer needs the help and understanding of health authorities. The importance of the environment is not always fully appreciated among health officials. However, the public is becoming increasingly aware of the importance of quality control and management of the environment. If health engineering authorities will not adopt new approaches to this topic, environmental management of such problems as water and air pollution may be taken over by other agencies. This has taken place and is continuing in many countries (in the United States, water quality management was transferred from the Department of Health to the Department of the Interior). Whoever wants to control environmental management must allocate sufficient resources for environmental health or (sanitary) engineering.

6: Experiments in Expanding the Rural Health Service in People's China

J. S. HORN

> So many deeds cry out to be done,
> And always urgently;
> The world rolls on,
> Time presses.
> Ten thousand years are too long,
> Seize the day, seize the hour!
> CHAIRMAN MAO TSE-TUNG

CHINA is a highly populous country, which at the time of liberation in 1949 was very poor and backward. There were then probably fewer than 30000 modern-type doctors to care for the health needs of more than 500 million people, and most of them were concentrated in a few coastal towns. In the vast rural areas, where five out of every six Chinese lived, there were virtually no modern-type doctors and only a sprinkling of traditional doctors.

This was the essence of the medical situation which confronted the government of China in 1949. The problem was how to transform this medical poverty into adequacy within a reasonable time. I won't say 'into abundance', for that clearly is something which cannot be achieved so quickly. As to what is meant by a 'reasonable time', that of course is something susceptible of individual and widely varying interpretations. But in New China the emphasis is on speed.

In this presentation I shall try to sketch, very briefly, how the Chinese people 'seized the day and seized the hour' in relation to building a nation-wide health team where none previously existed. I shall refer exclusively to the rural areas, for, as in most, if not all, countries in the world, it was here that the problem was most acute and most difficult to solve.

The principle that the main effort in the medical sphere should be directed towards the countryside was put forward by Mao Tse-tung very soon after liberation, but until the issues involved had been hammered out in a huge nation-wide debate during the Cultural Revolution, it often met with either half-hearted acceptance or disguised opposition. However, by 1964 the policy had been formulated rather concretely, and by 1966 it had become a reality on a very wide scale.

Basically, I think there are only two possible ways of providing a health service for grossly deprived rural areas. One is to redistribute the already existing medical forces and resources in a more equitable manner. This process has already been referred to by a number of speakers at this conference, notably by participants from Iran and Turkey, who have shown that this method has undoubted value, that it is relatively easy to organize on a short-term rotation basis and that up to a point it is effective. However, it also has great limitations, the chief of which is that, after all, a redistribution is only a redistribution and does not in itself expand the overall pool of trained personnel. The second possible method of tackling the problem is to place the main emphasis on training new forces, on enlarging the team capable of safeguarding people's health. This method is, I think, the only one capable of transforming the situation in a fundamental way and of consolidating the advances made.

China has used both methods, and in this paper I shall first describe how existing resources were redistributed, secondly indicate how new forces were created, and thirdly discuss, very hesitantly, what relevance this has for other countries, particularly for what are often referred to as the developing countries.

REDISTRIBUTION

Redistribution was achieved mainly in two ways. An appeal was made for modern-type doctors practising in urban hospitals to leave the cities and settle permanently with their families in the rural areas, including some of the more remote and backward rural areas. Such an appeal if made in a vacuum is very unlikely to meet with a positive response. We have already heard here that even with such incentives as higher salaries and the right to engage in private practice, doctors have been markedly reluctant to uproot themselves and face the rigours and hardships of village life.

But in China the appeal was not made in a vacuum. As you all know, China has its own particular sociopolitical system. It is a Socialist country and a whole generation has grown up imbued with the thinking, values and morals which are considered in China to be essential for the building of a Socialist society. This was the framework within which the appeal was made, and it did not meet with a negative response.

I can vividly recall an event in my own hospital—and here I shall largely be referring to my own personal experience during the 15 years I spent in China,[1] for although one person's experience is inevitably partial and fragmentary and is not necessarily typical of the whole scene, it nevertheless has validity for a certain sector and, when put alongside what he knows or believes to be happening elsewhere, may have a wider significance.

The event which I recall was when we held a meeting in the hospital where I worked to give a send-off to the first 12 doctors who had volunteered to uproot themselves, to leave the modern hospital where they were working, to leave the capital of China with its beautiful boulevards, theatres, shops, museums, art galleries and restaurants, to leave the friends and relatives among whom they had grown up and to settle down with their wives and children in a strange, remote and hard environment. Yet they seemed to be glad to be going. They sat on the platform wearing huge red rosettes; speeches were made about them and they too made speeches explaining why they were going and how they felt about it. We sang songs, ate sweets and chewed sunflower seeds and a very happy and united atmosphere prevailed.

Why had they volunteered to go? It was certainly not because of any material incentive. On the contrary, although initially they would remain on the same salary scale as in Peking, it was anticipated that sooner or later it would probably be appropriate for their salaries to be brought into line with those of the people among whom they would be living.

Neither was there any element of coercion. They really were volunteers.

The incentive was the conviction that they were doing the right thing, that they were responding to the needs of their day and age and that in doing so they were winning the approbation of, and were uniting with, their fellow men; it was a desire to be at one with society, to be part of the inexhaustible dynamic which was moving it forward so visibly and purposefully. They knew that in leaving they were not really cutting themselves off from their hospital, their city, their dear ones, but in a very real sense were cementing these links. They were confident that they would be cared for, helped to solve the problems which loomed ahead, invited back from time to time for refresher courses or to report back at meetings, to 'exchange experiences', as the Chinese put it.

And that indeed is how things worked out.

All have returned to Peking from time to time, and with one exception all have settled down very well and would not change their new life for the old one. The exception could not adapt and has returned to his hospital post in Peking.

This kind of redistribution of manpower cannot, in terms of numbers, make much of an impact on the situation.

The second method of redistribution, since it involved many more people, was more highly organized and had a more clearly defined programme, has proved of greater significance. It involved the dispatch of mobile medical teams from the urban hospitals to the rural areas on a rotation basis.

In order to make my account of the work of the mobile medical teams more concrete, I shall describe what happened in my own hospital, for I was fortunate enough to have been able to join a mobile medical team, and can therefore speak from first-hand experience. However, I would emphasize that what happened in the hospital where I worked was by no means the same as in the other Peking hospitals or in hospitals in other cities and provinces. The pattern varied widely, but there was one thing in common. Every urban hospital of any size in all the big cities of China dispatched mobile medical teams to the countryside with the main objectives of treating existing disease, instituting hygiene, public health and birth control measures and enrolling and training local personnel in the fight for good health.

In 1965 my hospital organized a team of 107 hospital workers to go for one year to an arid mountainous area north of the Great Wall of China. The 107 people were all volunteers and they included doctors of all grades, from the top to the bottom, nurses, dieticians, laboratory workers, cooks, cleaners, administrators—the lot. It was a vertical slice down the hospital staff.

Before we left we underwent a period of six months' training in what to expect in the countryside, not only medically but also socially. We learned that we would not sleep on beds, but on 'kangs'—raised platforms of mud-brick heated by the flue from the cooking stove—and that we would seldom eat rice or wheat, but millet and other coarse grains would be our staple foods. We learned about problems of living and nutrition in the countryside, about agriculture, animal husbandry and side-occupations. We learned what we could about the life and work of the peasants, in order to help us to live harmoniously with them, to facilitate the growth of mutual respect and affection and to enable us to join them in agricultural labour without being too ham-handed and ineffectual.

The nurses who went with us were senior nurses and they were trained to act independently as junior doctors—to prescribe and administer drugs, to diagnose and treat minor diseases, etc.

In the countryside—and I am sure this will cause many eyebrows to be raised—we made no distinction between nurses and doctors. The peasants themselves did not recognize such a distinction; as far as they were concerned we were all members of a team which ministered to their health needs and to those of their wives and children. In fact, doctors and nurses were in essence doing the same job according to the best of their abilities, and their abilities depended as much on their adaptability and sense of responsibility as on the type and duration of the training which they had undergone.

When our team arrived in the area in which we were to work, we split into several groups. The largest group stayed in a central clinic which had been erected a few months previously and which served as a hospital and outpatient department for a number of People's Communes. It was solidly built of mud-brick, had a tiled roof, cement floor and glazed windows. There was no electricity but it was expected that it would be laid on within a few months. There were 25 beds and a more-or-less adequately equipped operating room lit by pressurized oil lamps.

The remainder of the team split into groups of two or three, who went to live in selected villages. These groups, in addition to starting dispensaries in the cottages where they were billeted, were responsible for weekly or biweekly visits to all the villages—some of them very tiny—within a prescribed radius. Communications were bad in this area and usually the only way of getting from one village to another was on foot. Sometimes it was possible to ride a donkey and, rarely, to use a bicycle. Fortunately, however, all the villages were linked by telephone and in case of need doctors could be called anywhere when required.

The activities of mobile team members were many and varied, but unfortunately I cannot give all the details here. We engaged in the sort of therapeutic work that doctors engage in everywhere, but we did so under different and somewhat primitive conditions. We treated illnesses, big and small, handled medical and surgical emergencies, delivered babies and performed operations. At first we performed only minor operations, but when we realized that surgical infection was less of a problem in the countryside, notwithstanding its lack of general hygiene, than in our modern city hospital, we gradually extended the scope of our surgery until we were performing quite major operations in the patients' own cottages.

We engaged in what has been referred to here as 'environmental engineering', although we never thought of it in such grandiose terms. Mostly this meant tracking down the sources of outbreaks of gastro-intestinal infection, such as contaminated wells or impure springs, and, after convincing the peasants of the correctness of our conclusions, putting things right with their help.

We engaged in prophylactic work, vaccinating against smallpox, giving BCG, protecting against diphtheria, measles, poliomyelitis and other infectious diseases.

We carried out propaganda in support of family planning and then showed how to make the desire a reality.

We educated ourselves in the ways of the countryside, learned to understand the peasants, to feel at one with them, to shed some of our deep-rooted feelings of superiority, to understand some of the problems of providing food to feed a quarter of the world's population.

But above all we enrolled new recruits in the fight for health and started them on the road to becoming medical workers of a new type.

That brings me to the second topic of my talk—how China has expanded its resources of trained personnel.

EXPANDING RESOURCES

Ever since liberation there has been a rapid increase in the number and intake of medical schools. In 1962 there were more than 80 modern-type medical schools in China, and the number must be considerably greater now. The student intake of each school is very large, for most city hospitals share the task of training clinical students under the guidance of the teaching hospital. For example, the Zhung Shan Medical College in Canton, by no means the largest in China, has an annual student intake of 350 and a total enrolment of 2200. In 1963 throughout China 25 000 doctors graduated, and I think China must be graduating more modern-type doctors every year than any country in the world.

In addition to this, the training of traditional type doctors has been expanded and regularized. Many new institutes and research centres for traditional medicine have been built and most urban hospitals—such as the one where I worked in Peking—have traditional doctors on the staff working alongside modern doctors.

Similarly, there has been a huge increase in schools for nurses, laboratory technicians, sanitary workers, etc.

But the main source of new health workers, and the source with which I am concerned here, is that which results from the training of peasant/doctors.

The training of peasant/doctors is one of the most important tasks of the mobile medical teams and I shall therefore describe how the team of which I formed a part tackled the job in the inhospitable mountains of Northern Hopei province.

Towards the end of November, when the crops were safely in the granaries, when the rains had ceased until the following spring, when the earth was starting to freeze and farm work was coming to an end, we enrolled our first batch of medical students.

They numbered 32—one from each of the production brigades in the neighbouring People's Communes. All were literate but few had had more than five years' schooling. They were peasants in their early 20s who had been selected by their fellow villagers from a large number of volunteers. They were chosen for their intelligence, their educational level, their keenness to train as peasant/doctors and above all for their overall attitude to the collective of which they formed a part. What counted most was that they should be unselfish and responsible. Other qualities also counted, but they counted for less.

We set up a sort of primitive medical school in the central clinic to which I referred earlier and we, their teachers, members of the mobile team from one of Peking's well-known hospitals, lived there with our students until the following March. We had a little over four months in which to start them on the road to becoming doctors.

First we had a crash course in anatomy and physiology, dissecting pigs and chickens and experimenting on frogs. Then, when patients came to the clinic, we examined them together with the students, demonstrating the physical signs and linking them to the anatomy and physiology which we had been studying. Thus if a patient had a cough, we would review the anatomy and physiology of the lungs, thorax and respiratory passages. If he had jaundice, we would review the anatomy and physiology of the liver.

We did not set our targets too high. We tried to do no more, in this first session, than give the students a rough understanding of the structure and function of the body, to help them diagnose and treat a few commonly seen minor diseases, to grasp the essentials of the spread of disease by food, flies and water and to recognize the danger signs which should tell them to call on someone for help.

Four months is a very short time in which to reach even these relatively low targets, but I was amazed at the speed with which our peasant students grasped the subject. There were, of course, reasons for this.

Although the students had little formal schooling, they were all mature young men who had earned their living for many years. They had been entrusted by their own folk to equip themselves as health workers and they regarded this as a distinction and as a charge on their integrity which they were determined to honour. Moreover, even though our 'medical school' was primitive in its structure and equipment, it also had some advantages compared with better-established and more affluent institutions. Students and teachers lived together on a basis of equality, sharing in the day-to-day chores, with the teachers always available to answer questions and discuss difficulties. We closely linked theory and practice, and avoided the dichotomy which many students in my own country find irksome and frustrating. The textbooks were few and simple, for we had written, duplicated and bound them ourselves. But they concentrated on what was important, avoided padding and verbosity, and were clear and unambiguous.

Our students studied hard and conscientiously, and, since we had no electricity, they often literally burned the midnight oil in their thirst for knowledge.

When spring-time came they were issued with medical bags containing some equipment and a few drugs and returned to their villages to plough the fields and resume their work as peasants. But already they were peasants with a difference. If anyone in the village fell sick he would call out his peasant/doctor. If the peasant/doctor felt that he could treat the case, he did so; if he thought it necessary and the patient was fit to travel, he would arrange for him to go to the nearest clinic; if he was worried he would telephone a mobile team member and ask for advice.

His medical work was unpaid but any losses he incurred as a result of absence from work in the fields were made good from brigade funds. Medicines were charged for at cost price and the money was used to replenish stocks.

At least once a week a member of the mobile medical team would visit the peasant/doctor's village and see with him all who wished for a consultation, and also those whom the peasant/doctor had already seen. They would discuss every case, correct errors, clarify what had been done well and what less well. The peasant/doctor would raise problems which had confronted him, and his doubts, ideas, suggestions. In this way his medical education continued while he still remained a peasant.

The following autumn the same procedure was repeated. All the peasant/doctors in training returned to the 'medical school' for a further four months of full-time study, this time going deeper into the subject and tackling it more systematically. This time, too, there would be a chance to visit Peking and spend a week or so seeing the work carried on in modern hospitals. It would be some years before the peasant/doctor had X-rays, electrocardiographs, a well-stocked pharmacy and a fully equipped operating theatre, but all these would come in time— and judging from the pace of change, that time might not be too long.

The plan is that this cycle will be repeated for three years and that then the peasant/doctors will be regarded as qualified. That, of course, does not mean that their medical education will have come to an end. There is no reason why, if necessary, the course should not be prolonged or the peasant/doctors brought into the city hospitals from time to time for refresher courses or for specialist training, or to rotate with some of the regular hospital doctors.

The pattern and duration of training varies widely in different parts of the country and the whole project is still on an experimental basis.

There are endless possibilities, but they all point in the same direction. That is, that within a few decades China will have a huge army of medical workers deeply rooted in the countryside and will have effectively solved the problem, for the first time in the world, of how a vast, largely rural, technologically backward country can provide a health service for millions of peasants. The size of this medical army in training can be gauged from the fact that there are some 70 000 People's Communes in China, each made up of a number of production brigades which are in turn composed of production teams, and that the first target, which I have no doubt will be reached in the near future, is to train one peasant/doctor for each brigade, one sanitary worker for each team, and enough midwives to ensure that every peasant woman giving birth is helped by a person of some professional competence.

Of course it is possible to say, and I have heard it said, that this is lowering the standards, that the peasant/doctors are not really doctors at all, that they are not registered, that it would be dangerous to permit them to function independently, etc. etc. In my opinion, such viewpoints are unrealistic. The alternative is between an indefinite period of medical poverty with all its attendant sickness and misery, or making a start, breaking new ground and boldly embarking on a programme such as that I have outlined.

It is, of course, true that the peasant/doctors are poorly trained from an orthodox professional point of view. But they also have enormous advantages. They work in the countryside because they belong there. They are not separated from the peasants they serve, because they themselves remain peasants. Neither coercion nor material incentives are necessary to keep them in the countryside, for that is their home, their patients are their kith and kin, and their work gives them immense satisfaction, since they are keenly aware that they are building their country, making it a better place to live in, acting as 'locomotives of history'.

Whatever shortcomings there are in their training, whatever gaps in their knowledge, can be made good in the course of time. Their advantages are real and permanent.

I am sure that the hundreds of thousands of peasant/doctors who are being trained in China will play an invaluable role in safeguarding the health of the Chinese people, and that the same holds for the equally large numbers of midwives and birth-control workers, and for the even larger number of sanitary workers who are being trained along similar lines.

RELEVANCE FOR OTHER COUNTRIES

I must now attempt to answer the question posed in the third topic in my presentation: What relevance has this for other countries?

I must admit that when I first thought about this I came to the conclusion that it did not have much relevance. I thought that since the structure of Chinese society is fundamentally different from that of nearly every other country in the world, it would be impossible to take one facet of it and transplant it to another country. I still think that this is true, but on reflection, and after learning the lessons contained in some of the contributions made at this conference, I am now convinced that the Chinese experience *does* have a relevance for other countries, and especially for the so-called developing countries. I do not mean that any country's experience should be copied slavishly, transferred *en bloc* from one environment to another very different one. I mean that there are certain principles, certain guidelines, which can be adapted to suit widely varying local conditions.

What are these principles? First, there is the principle of relying on the potential talents and enthusiasm and creative ability of ordinary people. I do not intend to go into the question of 'human nature', of whether you can change it, of whether, in fact, there is any such thing. I want merely to state my conviction, which springs from my experience in China, that given the right guidance, the right stimulus, ordinary people are capable of self-sacrificing, voluntary effort which surpasses anything that one

85

would expect. If one relies on the ordinary people, if the obstacles which all too often prevent them from giving effect to their innate initiative and genius are removed, one will find that they are capable of solving all problems, including their health problems.

Secondly, there is the principle of self-reliance on a national scale. No matter how big or well-intentioned an organization may be, no matter how rich, advanced and prestigious a country may be, every nation, rich or poor, large or small, must rely primarily on its own efforts to solve its own problems. Aid from outside may be very useful, and we should support the giving of aid which genuinely benefits the recipient country. But outside aid may also have the effect of damping down the efforts of the recipient country to solve its own problems, may result in economic, scientific or cultural dependence; such aid, in the long term, is harmful and we should oppose it.

Thirdly, there is the principle that the new type of rural health worker should retain deep roots in the village community where he works and lives; that he should remain a peasant and that his medical work should be part-time and voluntary. When the Chinese talk of 'barefoot' doctors they do not mean that such a man has no shoes but that he has no special privileges, that he fully shares the life of the people among whom he works.

Fourthly, there is the principle that the medical education of such rural health workers should closely combine theory and practice at every stage; that it should be carried out in the countryside; that it should be suited to the specific characteristics of the locality and that it should continue, in some form or other, throughout life.

Finally, there is the principle, if one can call it a principle, that we doctors must take a long, cool, detached, self-critical look at ourselves, at our work and at our institutions. The winds of change are blowing and we must change too. Our medical education must change so that we produce doctors who can function effectively in the specific environment in which they work. Our medical research must change so that we primarily pose questions which arise out of the life and suffering of the majority of the people who inhabit our globe.

Our deeply ingrained guild outlook must change. We must be more modest of the achievements of scientific medicine. We must cease to resent the slightest hint of encroachment on our privileges and status but, on the contrary, must be prepared to open the doors wide to all those who can augment the team in the fight for health.

Modern medicine, newborn, began its long period of growth in Turkey, at Pergamon. In Turkey, too, not far from where this conference is taking place, Florence Nightingale tried to instil into her young nurses a sense of responsibility, a love of people, a devotion to patients, a willingness to learn, listen and sacrifice.

We doctors must understand that these are the qualities which are important for us too; that they are more important than our higher qualifications, our technical wizardry, our mastery of medical science.

We in this conference have added our voice to the call that was made by Florence Nightingale, to the call for teamwork in the quest of health.

DISCUSSION

Banks: Did you have any problems in fitting in with the ancient system of medicine and with the indigenous practitioners? And how does the peasant/doctor differ from the Russian *feldsher*?

Horn: In the expansion of the medical forces huge numbers of both traditional and modern doctors are being trained. In 1962 there were some 80 modern-type medical schools in China, in addition to those training traditional doctors. The traditional doctors have a contribution to make. They have a long history of recorded medical observations, some of which may be fallacious while others are valuable and accurate. On the whole, they render a service, and the policy of the government is that traditional medicine should continue and be encouraged, that modern and traditional doctors should learn from each other, trying to absorb what is best in both, and out of this synthesize a new kind of medicine superior to either. This is a very long-term project. In my own hospital and in my own sphere of work, traumatology, we have tried for many years to do precisely that, to synthesize the best of both disciplines, and we have had some success.

Some people call the peasant/doctor a *feldsher*; some call him a medical assistant, or a barefoot doctor or a paramedical worker. As far as I am concerned, he is a peasant/doctor because he is a peasant and he is a doctor. I do not know much about the Russian system but I do know that although the Chinese peasant/doctor may not be a very good doctor today, he will be a very good doctor in three or four years' time. There is no limit to the degree of skill, knowledge and experience that he can acquire. We had them back for refresher courses in my own hospital, which was quite a big modern hospital built in 1956. We showed them electrocardiography, electromyography and other modern techniques because even though they cannot use them now, it gives them a vista of what they are going to become. The *feldsher* in the Soviet Union is, I think, a permanent and exclusive category, whereas in China the peasant/doctor remains a peasant and constantly develops as a doctor. This is very important. He is not divorced from the people who nurtured him. He remains a peasant, but as regards his doctoring the sky is the limit.

Banks: How did the people react to a foreign doctor like yourself? Is there a place for others?

Horn: I would guess there is not much of a place. When I went there in 1954 the needs were very different. I returned to England partly because I felt that I was no longer necessary. Two generations of surgeons had grown up in my own field who are better than I am.

Ordoñez-Plaja: Dr Horn's talk was most relevant and stimulating because what is going on in China is going on all over the world, even if we do not want to realize it. In developing countries we are having simplified medicine, delegation of functions, and so on, but in developed countries this is important too; it is not just a matter of having too many doctors in big cities: even if we could re-locate them, they will not be enough, and we must use other resources.

Dr Horn also raised the question of what is happening to the prestige and stature of the doctor now. We have become more effective with new drugs, etc., but simultaneously we have been losing prestige in the communities. I shall not try to explain this phenomenon here, but it is a fact. The *shamaan* or the local doctor has not lost his prestige, because he is still a human being in front of a human being. When we have a strong weapon to attack a disease we probably neglect the human side of it, and the approach to the patient is more technical and less human. The rural doctors or rural health promoters are gaining status in developing countries, and if that is meaningful for human beings, we are probably in the process of a revolution in medical care, although we have not realized it. It is stimulating to hear what is happening in a country with very different conditions. In my country, you could not call such a man a doctor because he would rush to the capital and start performing gastrectomies and things like that. We have to do it another way, but in the final analysis it is the same thing and it is probably going to be very good for humanity. The positions of the doctor and of the nurse in a society are not determined by the doctor or nurse, but by society; that is what society is demanding now, and even if the medical associations do not want to accept it, it is going to be their last stand.

Horn: I agree with what you say and you remind me of some things I meant to say and did not. One was to give examples of the release of the initiative of the ordinary people and to mention some of the feats which they have accomplished. For example, schistosomiasis is being brought under control, although this is a most extraordinarily difficult disease to control and quite impossible without enlisting the help of literally millions of peasants. Again, the elimination of flies illustrates what can be accomplished by relying on the ordinary people.

Ordoñez-Plaja: I think it was in China that people used to pay the doctor when they were healthy.

Fişek: What I admire in this work, Dr Horn, is the courage to decide for the better instead of for the best. This is what is needed in many developing countries. I have some questions. Is the method of mobile teams going out from a hospital a universal pattern in China? Does a mobile team work permanently in a particular district? Is the peasant/doctor a member of the permanent team in the area, or is he left on his own when the team leaves? Is there any change in teaching medicine in medical schools in China?

Horn: In my area the mobile team went for one year and was then replaced by another team. The peasant/doctors are permanently in their own area but they are always in contact with one or other mobile team. The pattern is not identical all over China. Mobile teams are being sent out in rotation from every big urban hospital in China, but the details of how long they stay, and how they organize their work, are different in different areas. One-third of the hospital staff in my own hospital was always in the countryside, and two-thirds at home, so that within three years everybody in the hospital will have served for one year in the countryside.

Regarding education, the medical curriculum must be changed not only in the developing countries but, I think, in all countries. In China none of this has yet been finalized. The Cultural Revolution has been going on since 1966, and has not yet come to an end. One of the big issues of debate has been education, especially higher education. Although no final decisions have been reached, three principles seem to be emerging for medical education. One is that the courses will be shortened; another is that there will be a much closer fusion of theory and practice at every stage of the course; a third is that there will be more emphasis on the important commonly occurring diseases than on the rarities which occupied so much time when I was a medical student.

King: Another consequence for medical education is the enormous importance of teaching the doctor to be a teacher. We are trying to do this in Zambia, but it is perhaps being done better in Dar es Salaam. If the skills of the auxiliary and paramedical staff are to increase, it is important that the doctor, who is the main repository of medical skills, should be encouraged to replicate and increase them whenever he possibly can. Our graduating doctors must go out from our schools with the idea that they must hand on their skills, and it is not an easy attitude of mind to achieve.

Horn: I agree, but I would add that every doctor must also be a pupil, especially when he goes to the countryside. He has a great deal to learn and he must go there in a modest frame of mind.

Dogramaci: You referred to 12 doctors who volunteered to work in the country. Does volunteering still go on or is there any compulsory dispatch of teams? Does anything happen to those who do not volunteer? You told us that they did not expect that their salary would be raised but that probably it would be lowered. Does this mean that later it was in fact raised?

Horn: They were really volunteers and nothing happens if they do not volunteer. These 12 all came back to participate in the Cultural Revolution. The Cultural Revolution holds a very high place in the estimation of the Chinese people and the Chinese authorities, and is given precedence over everything else. These 12 were still on the staff of our hospital even though they worked hundreds of miles away. They had volunteered to go and it is natural that they should have come back to join in the Cultural Revolution in their parent hospital.

The question of pay is rather complicated. Initially they remained on the same salary that they were getting in the hospital. How rural health services will be financed in future is an open question. One possibility is that doctors who work in People's Communes will be paid in the same way as other commune members, in which case their salaries will come down. When I said they certainly would not get an increase but might have a reduction in pay, it was this possibility I was thinking of. But I have to qualify that, because whereas a commune member gets a low money income, he gets a great deal in addition to money—his food, for example.

Young: In nutrition there is a possible overlap between health education and agricultural matters; so how far did agricultural questions come within the province of your health teams?

Horn: Agricultural matters were very much within their province. Mobile team members were expected to participate in agricultural production, to learn something about agronomy, to investigate the calorie, vitamin and mineral content of the local foods and to discover other existing sources of food, minerals or vitamins.

Young: Did the families of the volunteers accompany them to the rural areas? If not, what provision was made for them, particularly if their salaries were to be lower? There would be problems in relation to schooling of children and so forth.

Horn: If the volunteers were married and had children, either the whole family volunteered to go or none went. Of course it does give rise to problems, because they are leaving a rather comfortable life for one much less comfortable, the schools are less good, and so on. If the husband volunteers to go and the wife does not want to go, probably neither would go, but if the husband insists on going and the wife insists on staying, then her money income would not be allowed to fall. Actually, although money incomes are low in China, the Chinese do not seem to attach much importance to money.

Young: Are sufficient schools available in the remote rural areas?

Horn: Every Chinese child of school age can go to primary school, though possibly for only five or six years. But increasingly there is the possibility of going to the middle schools. The schools are mostly within walking distance, but if not then the children live there and come back at week-ends.

Hill: In the West we seem to put a tremendous emphasis on advancing the frontiers of medicine and by default we forget the actual delivery of medicine. In China you are delivering medicine, but what are you doing about advancing the frontiers? In your book *Away with all Pests*[1] you mention the synthesis of insulin. How did you do that within this structure?

Horn: This is a very knotty point. Where are you to put the emphasis: on popularization, making things more widespread and more freely available, or on raising the levels? I think you have to decide on the priority and the priority in China undoubtedly is on making things available. But that does not mean that you do not simultaneously have to raise the levels. On the contrary it means that you must, because in the course of popularization you get new knowledge which enables you to raise the level. One example has been the reattachment of severed limbs. Probably all of you know that in China something over 100 severed limbs or fingers have been successfully reattached and are functioning well. This is a world advance in surgical science which arose out of what one can call the delivery of medicine. The surgeon who did the first operation had, only a few weeks before, been working in the factory where the accident occurred, as part of the process of the delivery of medicine. So he knew the factory people and respected and admired them, and they also knew him. When the accident occurred, the patient was put into an ambulance and taken to the hospital where this surgeon worked. The worker at the next lathe saw the hand lying on the floor, picked it up and saw it was fairly intact; so he wrapped it up and took it along to the hospital and asked the surgeon "Couldn't you put it back on?" That was the beginning of something which spread all over China, and which resulted in a significant raising of levels. The same thing happened in relation to the treatment of burns, and one could give a number of other examples.

Dogramaci: Is there anything published in English on this work?

Horn: Well, apart from articles in Chinese journals and magazines, there is also my book![1]

Rebhun: The complexity of the problems of health work on the one hand and the shortage of manpower on the other requires teamwork mainly of an interdisciplinary nature. Secondly, priority has to be given to the most pressing problems, but the criteria should be to emphasize those problems whose solution will most efficiently improve health. Environmental health engineering is one of those areas.

The account of the broadening of the base of health workers in China was fascinating. I agree fully that as a temporary or palliative measure it was appropriate to make the decision not to have the best, but it should

4*

be remembered that this is a palliative measure. Perhaps I am prejudiced by the cultural background of my own people who always emphasized learning. "You may drink water and eat just bread, but you must learn always." It seems that this approach has been justified. I appreciate the importance of the peasant/doctor or the less skilled technician. In the USSR it was very clear that the *feldsher* system was a palliative measure. They also invested a lot in a large programme of education of skilled engineers, doctors, etc. Isn't there a danger that the institution of the peasant/doctor would be idealized on account of the greater expense of training more skilled personnel? Both should be done but I do not think that emphasizing one of them would be justified.

Teamwork in health programmes which include people from one country working in another country will not be successful unless it involves people from the country itself. We have had a lot of aid, technical and otherwise, from other countries, but we have solved our problems ourselves, and we know that we have to solve them.

Any work on health improvement should be directly connected with the general programme of community or regional development. If it is not, it will not be successful.

Christie: McGill University has had an exchange professorship with the China Medical College in Peking since 1962. Although they knew that we had no leanings towards Communism, we have been treated with the greatest kindness and with generous hospitality. The quality of their best medical schools, which had a seven- or eight-year course, was as high as in Europe or America and, although these were only four or five in number, making a negligible contribution to the needs of China, they provided a standard of excellence for others to follow. Since the Cultural Revolution in 1966 the policy has been to shorten and simplify the medical course, but before we criticize this as a retrograde step we should remember that before 1966 the output of doctors was a mere trickle compared with what was required, and that this change may greatly accelerate the introduction of modern medicine among the masses.

Rebhun: The Soviet Union has a similar sociopolitical system after all, and although in the beginning they had *feldshers* the emphasis was on the mass production of fully trained doctors. The goal should be better training and not a lower level.

Horn: This antithesis between learning on the one hand and a palliative on the other is not correct. Dr Rebhun says that the people of Israel have a great tradition of learning. So have the Chinese. It is not a question of learning or not learning, but of how to learn. In China we are dealing with some hundreds of thousands of poorly educated peasants who are learning extraordinarily fast. How can one oppose this on the grounds of the defence of learning? The learning process is not one that comes to an end after a three-year course is finished; it is something that goes on throughout life. The training of peasant/doctors fills an urgent need quickly, but it is much more than a palliative or expedient and I think it is going to persist indefinitely, not necessarily in this form but in some other form which we cannot foresee. The higher institutes of medical education are going to coexist with the training of peasant/doctors. There isn't any contradiction between them; they complement each other. We should not think of doctors who graduate from orthodox medical schools as being perfect and necessarily superior to all other kinds of health workers. They have quite a lot of short-comings, including their alienation from the people they work among, especially in the rural areas. The peasant/doctors are very deeply rooted among the people they serve and that, in my opinion, is worth gallons of medicine.

Baker: The information you gave us indicates that there might be one peasant/doctor per 1000–2000 people. This doctor would be working flat out if he took care of all the health services for these people. Does he have time to till his farm, or is he really a full-time doctor?

Horn: There were about 10000 people in the area served by this mobile team, and 32 peasant/doctors were being trained there in the first instance. So 1 to 300 would be about the ratio. Certainly the main occupation of the peasant/doctor is farming, and medicine is subsidiary.

Christie: Of course this is filling a very real need. In 1962 when I was in Peking, I was told that there were not more than 100000 Western-trained doctors in China, and perhaps about 500000 traditional doctors. For a country of 700 million that is nowhere near enough.

7: Backcloth to the National Health Service in England and Wales*

(1) THE National Health Service, which provides a comprehensive personal health service for everyone in Britain, is part of a wider picture of health services in the United Kingdom. The latter would include the public health services, which seek to maintain a healthy environment and clean food, as well as the occupational health and school health services, medical research and professional training for medical and allied professions.

This paper relates only to the Health Service of England and Wales. Similar services, with differences in their administration, operate in Scotland and Northern Ireland. The organization of the National Health Service (N.H.S.) is shown in Fig. 1.

(2) Besides the *objective* of improving the physical and mental health of people, the Service is established to improve the prevention, diagnosis and treatment of illness. The service is available free to all residents in Britain according to their medical needs, except that certain small charges are made for certain items.

(3) *The medical and allied professions* taking part include the great majority of specialists, about 98 per cent of general practitioners (G.P.s), almost all the dentists available for general practice and almost all the retail pharmacies. Only a small number of hospitals remain outside the Service, but many treat N.H.S. patients under contractual arrangements.

(4) *The cost* of the personal health and welfare services in the U.K. in 1966–67 was nearly £1700 millions (U.S. $4080 millions), which represented one-tenth of the total public expenditure and almost $4\frac{1}{2}$ per cent of the gross national product. Payments by patients for certain items referred to in (2) above amount to only 4 per cent of the total cost of the Service.

Expenditure on the N.H.S. rises annually with an increasing population, among whom are large numbers of children and elderly people who make the heaviest demands on it. Purely administrative costs are low, being about 3 per cent of the total cost. Members of hospital boards and committees, executive councils and committees of local authorities serve in a voluntary capacity and are paid only their out-of-pocket expenses.

* Prepared by Lisbeth Hockey, B. L. Salmon and H. Bridger. Source: *Health Services in Britain*.[1]

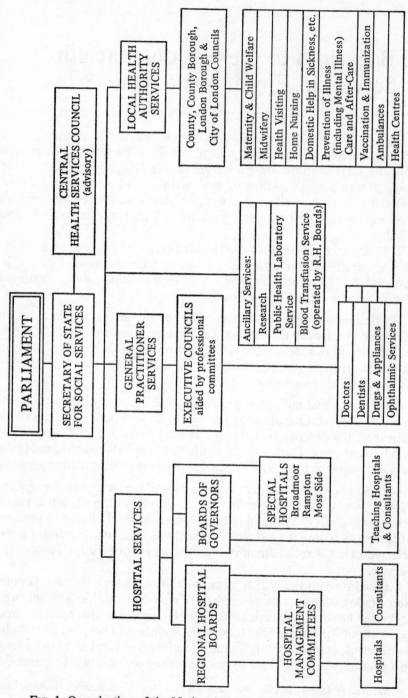

FIG. 1. Organization of the National Health Service in England and Wales.

(5) *Hospitals* are under the management of 15 Regional Hospital Boards, except those designated as 'teaching hospitals' by the Secretary of State to provide facilities for undergraduate and postgraduate clinical teaching. There are 36 teaching hospitals, of which 26 are in London.

Each teaching hospital has its own Board of Governors, which is responsible for its organization and control.

Medical and dental schools are university departments.

The detailed internal administrative work connected with individual non-teaching hospitals or groups of hospitals is carried out by some 330 Hospital Management Committees in England and Wales, responsible to the Regional Hospital Boards for the day-to-day running of their hospitals and for the appointment of all staff except senior medical and dental staff, who are appointed by the Regional Hospital Boards.

(6) The practitioner services consist of:

(a) *Family doctor service*

As the patient's first line of defence, the G.P., or family doctor, is at the very centre of the Service and must be constantly in touch with developments in medicine.

Patients may choose the doctor they wish and they may also change their doctor with a minimum of formality. The doctor has a similar freedom to accept or refuse patients and he may accept paying patients if he wishes. The maximum number a G.P. may accept under the Service is 3500.

The G.P. has complete clinical freedom to treat his patients according to his professional discretion. With a serious illness or a difficulty in diagnosis, the G.P. may call a consultant and secure hospital treatment for his patient.

Only a few doctors work from Health Centres so far; the rest almost always work from their own surgeries, to which people go unless the doctor visits them at home.

About 75 per cent of family doctors practise in partnership, and a common method of entering general practice is to become an assistant to a partnership. *Group practice* is also increasing. In this a group of doctors, including normally between three and six principals, work from a common centre controlled by themselves and jointly employ ancillary help. They cooperate in providing a round-the-clock service for patients and off-duty and holidays for themselves, and they consult with each other about their patients, although each patient remains the responsibility of his own doctor. A recent development in some areas has been the attachment of local health authority staff—nurses, midwives and health visitors—to group practices.

Remuneration was designed to reflect, as closely as possible, the individual doctor's work load and responsibilities and his practice expenses.

97

Under the new system, in addition to the ordinary capitation fee, there is a higher fee for patients aged 65 or over. A basic practice allowance is also paid in recognition of basic practice expenses and commitments, to which there are additions for practising in an area which has been short of doctors for several years, for practising in a group, for seniority, and for vocational training.

There are also additional payments for accepting responsibilities out of normal hours, for visits to patients at night, for treating temporary residents, for maternity services, and for expenses associated with rural practice. In addition, fees are paid for particular items of service, including those which are encouraged as a matter of public health policy, such as vaccination and taking cervical smears. Direct payments are also made for the rent and rates of practice premises and for expenditure on ancillary staff.

General practitioners may also obtain government grants towards improving their practice premises and a finance corporation has been set up to make loans for the purchase, erection and improvement of premises.

(b) The dental service

As in the family doctor service, patients are completely free to choose their dentists and dentists to choose their patients; and dentists may take private as well as National Health Service patients if they wish. Patients are not required to register with dentists, and the normal practice is to visit a dentist's surgery by appointment. Dentists providing treatment in their own surgeries are paid on a prescribed scale of fees; treatment may also be carried out at dental hospitals as part of the hospital service.

(c) The supplementary ophthalmic service

This service, which forms part of the eye services available under the National Health Service, provides for the testing of sight and the supply of spectacles only. Anyone found to be in need of treatment or to require any of the more unusual types of spectacles, or to be suffering from an abnormal condition of the eyes, is referred to his doctor for introduction, if necessary, to an eye hospital or a hospital eye clinic.

(d) The pharmaceutical service

Through this service, everyone receiving treatment under the family doctor service is entitled to drugs, medicines and certain appliances prescribed by his doctor as part of the treatment.

(7) *The hospital and specialist services* provide all forms of hospital care and treatment in general and special hospitals for in-patients, out-patients and day patients.

They also provide specialist opinion and treatment, either in hospitals and clinics, or, where this is advised, at the homes of the patients. The domiciliary consultant service has grown rapidly since its introduction at the start of the service and forms a valuable link between hospitals and general practitioners.

A blood transfusion service, a pathological laboratory service and an X-ray service are at the disposal of every hospital. A screening service for detection of cervical cancer is provided. Venereal disease clinics are held at many hospitals and treatment is given confidentially so that attendance is encouraged and maintained. The hospital service also has a major role to play in the treatment and supervision of drug addiction and provides in-patient and out-patient clinics for addicts.

(8) *The treatment of mental disorder* is provided as part of the National Health Service. Patients can consult their family doctor and receive specialist advice at hospital out-patient clinics as they would for any other illness. They can enter hospital for in-patient treatment without formalities.

(9) *The importance of rehabilitation* as a facet of medical treatment is firmly established, and today hospital treatment does not stop at relief of pain, or alleviation or cure of pathological conditions, but aims at helping people to resume normal living as soon as possible.

Experience has shown that efficient medical rehabilitation reduces the stay in hospital, the incidence of permanent disability and the period of incapacity for full work. Rehabilitation methods have been applied with advantage in the care of the chronic sick, the aged and the handicapped, and have enabled many to become self-sufficient or to be discharged from hospital to resume an independent life in their own homes.

(10) *The local authority health and welfare services* provide a wide variety of health and welfare services which, together with the family practitioner services, complement the provisions made by hospital authorities in order to give a comprehensive service.

Services provided by the local health authority include:

(a) *The maternity and child welfare services*, providing care for expectant and nursing mothers, and advice and general supervision for them and for children under five years of age.

These services are provided to meet the needs of mothers and children in the areas in which they live. Doctors, health visitors and midwives are in attendance at the antenatal and child welfare clinics held in the maternity and child welfare centres. Health visitors and midwives working from these centres visit mothers in their homes to advise and help them and to encourage them to attend antenatal and child welfare sessions. In this way many illnesses and defects are referred for treatment earlier than might otherwise have been the case. An increasing number of antenatal and child welfare sessions are provided by general practitioners for their own patients in their surgeries or in the welfare centres with a midwife or health visitor in attendance. In some areas the welfare centres are staffed by general practitioners in conjunction with local health authority staff.

Mothercraft teaching, often associated with relaxation classes for expectant mothers, is one of the features of the work at antenatal clinics. Such teaching continues for mothers who attend the clinics with their young children, through individual consultation, group discussions, demonstrations, and special classes. In some areas evening clubs for both parents are held.

(b) *Health visitors* to visit people in their homes, to give advice to expectant and nursing mothers on the care of young children, people suffering from illness, including mental illness, and any injury or disability requiring medical or dental treatment, and on measures necessary to prevent the spread of infection.

(c) *Home nurses* to attend people who require nursing in their own homes.

(d) *Domestic help* in households where it is needed owing to illness.

(e) *The prevention of illness—care and after-care.*

(f) *Vaccination and immunization.*

(g) *Mental health services.* Demand for these facilities is increasing with the shift in emphasis from hospital to community care.

(h) *Social workers.*

(i) *Ambulance service.*

(j) *Health centres* at which facilities are available for the provision of general medical, general dental and other services whenever necessary.

(k) *Welfare services for the handicapped.*

(l) *Health education.*

(11) Under the *welfare foods service* expectant and nursing mothers, children under five years and one month and certain handicapped children can obtain a pint of milk a day at a reduced price, or free of charge, from their usual milk supplier by means of tokens. Other welfare foods are distributed by local health authorities. These are dried milk as an alternative to liquid milk, orange juice, cod liver oil and vitamin A and vitamin D tablets.

(12) There is a long tradition in Britain of *voluntary help* for the sick and handicapped. A number of voluntary organizations provide extensive services of various kinds for them in cooperation with, or supplementary to, the provision made by central and local authorities. These are of two main types. There are those which play a valuable part in providing the small personal services and the continued personal interest that are so important to sick or handicapped people. For this work, the

agencies depend largely on the work, part-time or full-time, of unpaid volunteers. There are also several organizations providing highly specialized services largely through paid workers.

A great deal of help is given to hospitals by voluntary bodies and individual helpers, e.g. the operation of canteens for out-patients, trolley shops and library services for in-patients, and the provision of other amenities for patients and staff.

8: The Family Care Team: Philosophy, Problems, Possibilities

LISBETH HOCKEY

BACKGROUND

HEALTH and welfare services in the United Kingdom have developed unevenly and in a piecemeal fashion. When the National Health Service Act was implemented in 1948 it inherited a legacy of a complex and fragmented administrative structure which made its tremendous task even more formidable. The aim of the Health Service was to provide a full range of health and medical care for all members of the population, financed from national revenue and given free at the time of need. Responsibility for care was divided at administrative and field levels, resulting in an artificial tripartite framework, hospital, general practitioner and public health nursing services being controlled by three different authorities. The hospital sector is the most demanding in manpower resources, and in 1968 it absorbed 56 per cent of the total cost of the Health Service. Because it is highly labour- and cost-intensive, its facilities should as far as possible be reserved for those patients who cannot be treated elsewhere.

At present, over 90 per cent of illness is dealt with outside hospital by the general practitioner or, as he is often referred to, the family doctor. In addition to the treatment of his patients' manifest disease conditions, he endeavours to provide a wide range of preventive services, presymptomatic diagnostic tests, and obstetric care. To assist him, he has the help of district nursing staff of various grades for the nursing of his patients, health visitors to give preventive care and midwives for domiciliary midwifery and maternity nursing, all of whom are employed by the local health authorities.

Conventionally, these workers have been deployed on a geographical basis, each being responsible for the delivery of care to persons living in a circumscribed area. Because the general practitioners' areas are not geographically defined, indeed are often rather widely scattered, such a working pattern resulted in the doctor having his patients advised and cared for by many different members of the local authority nursing staff. Similarly, each member of the nursing staff cared for patients on the lists of many different general practitioners. Difficulty of communication between doctor and nurse under such circumstances has been shown to militate against rational division of labour, the doctor undertaking functions which might have been delegated.[12] Moreover, lack of adequate contact and consultation between different workers may cause them to give conflicting advice, thus undermining the confidence of the patients.

MEDICAL TEAMS AND THEIR PATIENTS

The increasing trend for general practitioners to work in groups or partnerships led to the establishment of larger medical practices with more diagnostic and therapeutic facilities. This trend was stimulated by a financial incentive by the government for the improvement of premises and towards the cost of secretarial and other ancillary help employed by the doctors. In the ten-year period 1958 to 1968, single-handed practices decreased from 32 to 23 per cent, whereas partnerships or groups of three or more doctors increased from 32 to 50 per cent.[7, 15]

General medical practice is based on the concept of a personal family doctor service. Although each individual is free to choose the general practitioner under whose personal care he wishes to be, members of one family unit are encouraged to register with the same group or firm of doctors. It is usual for the patient to see his own doctor by appointment, but if attention is needed at a time when he is not available, another member of the group who has easy access to the patient's records and often also some knowledge of the patient is available. This ensures continuity of medical care. Moreover, if the members of a family are registered with the same group of doctors, even though with different members of the group, problems affecting the family as a whole can be more easily dealt with.

The grouping of doctors has had at least two major desirable effects. In the first place, it furthered the combination and integration of different medical skills, with members of the team pursuing their own specialized medical interests and making their expertise available to the practice as a whole. It is now commonplace to find in a group practice a combination of specialities, and vacancies are filled accordingly. For example, there is often one female member, possibly specializing in gynaecology, and perhaps other doctors with special interests in either paediatrics or geriatrics. One member of the group may be an expert anaesthetist, and act in this capacity when his colleagues require general anaesthesia for their patients. Group practice makes it easier for doctors to hold part-time appointments at local hospitals, where they are able to gain further experience in their specialized fields.

Secondly, the grouping of doctors showed and opened up opportunities for the combination and integration of medical with nursing and social work skills, and provided a realistic setting for the operation of full family care teams.

FAMILY CARE TEAMS

Philosophy

Although the Health Service had achieved a great deal, its weaknesses became more obvious as expectations grew. Lack of adequate communication between workers caring for the same family had been one of the most glaring weaknesses and the need for closer cooperation became urgent.

Pioneer experiments sprang up, with local authorities attaching or allocating nursing staff to general medical practices to care for the practice patients rather than for a geographically defined population. The idea was to build up nursing teams consisting of health visitors, district nurses and midwives, to support the medical team. Auxiliary workers with no professional qualifications are sometimes included in the team to help with routine duties in the clinic and the basic hygiene care of elderly patients. In addition to the nursing staff, some local authorities link social workers to one or more general practices to assist with more intensive social case work. Where premises allow, room is made available at the practice for nursing staff and social workers where they can arrange their own sessions with patients, giving treatment or advice or perhaps just listening to the wide range of problems that bring patients to a doctor's surgery.

Frequent consultation with the doctors is possible, case conferences are held and the team's knowledge of patients is increased, thus making their care and advice more effective.

The experimental schemes linking nursing staff with general medical practices produced encouraging results and their numbers increased steadily. They doubled in the two years ending 1st January 1969.[5] Most doctors seem delighted at being able to delegate some of their non-medical tasks to the nursing staff and having nursing and social work expertise readily available; many have written enthusiastic articles about their experience of teamwork.[6, 11, 18]

The nursing staff obtain greater job-satisfaction by working in partnership with doctors. They have access to their patients' medical records and are thus able to follow their treatment and progress with greater professional awareness. Their skills are used to better advantage, because doctors who know them are more inclined to trust them with more sophisticated treatment. This is further facilitated by frequent contact. Similarly, nursing duties can be distributed more rationally among the various grades of workers, fitting responsibility to qualification. Some of the nurses' views have also been published.[17]

The range of services made available to patients is increased, which means either a higher standard of care in absolute terms, or less need for patients to attend hospital for services now provided by the family care team at the doctor's surgery or Health Centre. This saves the patients' time and effort and preserves over-strained and expensive hospital facilities. Examples of services which used to be exclusive to hospitals but now tend to be given by the team are: blood tests of various kinds, electrocardiography and measurements of vital capacity, audiometry and minor surgical procedures.

One of the key concepts underlying family care teamwork is flexibility, and each practice develops its own individual spheres of activity over and above the necessary routine care. Some teams endeavour to strengthen the preventive aspects by arranging classes in various types of health education; some focus particular attention on the elderly and provide additional services such as assessment clinics for them; others offer more to mothers and young children by running parent craft classes and baby or toddler clinics. Much depends on the type of area, the needs of its population and the interests of the team.

The members of the team stimulate and support each other. By discussion and collaboration they pool their resources, dividing but integrating their functions. Together they are able to provide a comprehensive 24-hour service for their patients.

A team has been defined as 'a number of persons doing anything conjointly'. The family care team shares a concern for the family in health and sickness. The conjoint action of the members of the team lies in the giving of care, which embraces a great deal more than the mere administration of treatment. An important function of the team is its constant availability to the patients. The contribution of the patient himself to effective team operation must not be overlooked. Through the pooling of resources the team's contribution greatly exceeds that of the sum of its parts.

Problems

Changes are rarely entirely smooth and painless, and innovations tend to bring new problems. The formation of family care teams is no exception. Although the disadvantages of family care teams seem minimal and the new problems by no means insurmountable, they must be recognized.

The main disadvantages which have been reported are, first, the loss of intimate knowledge of an area by the health visitor,[2, 10] and secondly, increased travelling time for the non-medical members of the team.[1] As indicated in the introduction to this paper, the conventionally deployed health visitor was responsible for the preventive care of people living in a geographically circumscribed area. Through the constant visitation of families in that area, she acquired an intimate knowledge of it and became a well-known figure who could be readily approached for advice. In the new working situation, she is no longer identified with the area and its community and it has been suggested that needs previously discovered may now be missed. There is at present no evidence to support or refute this suggestion.

It is inevitable that the visiting of scattered patients in a practice often entails increased travelling for the members of the team who had previously been working in compact areas. At the same time, it is possible for visiting to be planned in such a way that excessive travelling is avoided.

The problems of family care teams seem to be mainly of three types:

(1) Personal relationships, including leadership and management.
(2) Education.
(3) Legal considerations.

Personal relationships. Teamwork entails not only active collaboration but also mutual understanding, tolerance and empathy. The need for careful preparation of workers for work in family care teams was stressed by Abel.[1] Once doctors and nursing staff with the more progressive and popular personalities have been linked in working partnerships a residue of incompatible individuals is likely to remain. There are, in most areas, people who find it difficult to adapt to new working methods and whose attitudes appear resistant to change; there are also those who are not prepared to meet others half-way; and in all those cases efforts to create a team approach tend to be abortive. As the long-term benefits of this way of working become more apparent it is hoped that a greater number of medical and nursing personnel may be attracted to it. At the same time some individualists will probably always prefer to work alone.

Groups of people working together as teams usually require a coordinator. Some family care teams where members have learned to understand and appreciate each others' roles seem to be working happily without an officially designated leader or coordinator. Others, fortunately the minority, seem to have various degrees of friction in trying to establish leadership positions. Leadership and management demand special skills which need to be acquired like any others. Medical or nursing proficiency does not necessarily include management ability and it is not always clear who should manage whom and who is willing to be managed by whom.

Education. The range of work in a group practice often calls for new skills in nursing personnel. Problems have arisen where demands made by doctors exceed the nurse's professional competence. It is important that all workers, in whatever capacity, should be adequately prepared for their role and that education and training should be constantly one step ahead of new demands.

Legal considerations. Some members of family care teams have been troubled about the legal implications of the new working pattern which gives non-medical personnel added responsibilities. These problems are gradually being resolved as nursing competence for new tasks is established. Whilst the British doctor accepts medical responsibility for his patients he is legally permitted to delegate to nursing staff those tasks in which the nurse's proficiency has been established.

Possibilities

Family care teams seem to have considerable scope and a potential not only for expansion of the work but also for adaptation in times of emergency.

Primary visits. A fairly recent development is the use of a nursing member of the team for first visits to patients. The purpose of the nurse's visit is to assess the patient's condition, not to diagnose. She notes and records the patient's condition, reporting back to the general practitioner immediately. She conveys the type of information on the basis of which the doctor is able to make a decision about the need and urgency of a visit by himself. This enables him to plan his home visits rationally, with the least amount of unnecessary travelling and inconvenience to his other patients and himself. This extension of the nurse's role gives her more scope in the use of her expertise and may relieve the general practitioner of a proportion of domiciliary visits which frequently do not require his professional skills.[16] At present, there is still division of opinion about the advisability of nurses paying advance screening visits for the doctor. Nurses themselves seem to enjoy this added dimension to their work,[9] but there is some apprehension on the part of administrators.

Transport for patients. In some medical practices, transport in the form of a minibus is available to bring groups of patients to the surgery for medical or nursing attention. The idea was pioneered by Floyd,[8] and the Department of Health and Social Security has since made some minibuses available and also sponsored a research project on transport schemes which is now in progress. The advantage of bringing patients to the surgery is twofold: it saves valuable professional time, and it provides an opportunity for elderly and lonely housebound patients to get out and meet other people. A team approach is essential to enable all the patients to be attended to promptly and efficiently.

Community wards. Most general practitioners from time to time have patients whom they are well able to treat medically, but who require more supervision and care than is available in their own homes. Often such patients have to be admitted to scarce and expensive hospital beds. To overcome this, an experiment was launched recently by Hasler and colleagues, whose report on another study is mentioned in the bibliography.[11] A small ward in a local hospital was made available to the medical practice for short-term care of patients. The ward is staffed by the family care team, and the members of the team work either in the ward or in the community, as the need arises. The team is led by a senior nurse member who allocates the staff and coordinates their activities.

The team in an emergency. An example of flexibility of the family care team and its adaptation to sudden need and emergency was demonstrated in an epidemic of influenza A2 1968 Hong Kong in a busy general practice in Scotland. During a six-week period over 3000 additional patient/nurse contacts were made which the medical members of the team could not have absorbed. The conventional pattern of that particular practice was changed during the crisis. Although normally the primary assessment visits were often undertaken by nursing staff, the roles were now reversed: the medical members paid all first calls in order to ensure an early diagnosis and initiation of treatment, and the non-medical members took over responsibility for follow-up visits. The health visitors in the team made a special contribution by visiting vulnerable patients in an effort to prevent infection by giving advice and early help and support. Kuenssberg, reporting this experience, states that "the ship, the rigging and the crew were thoroughly tried and tested and were not found wanting. The team emerged as a co-ordinated and co-operative unit . . .".[14]

CURRENT TRENDS AND THEIR IMPLICATIONS

Medical progress continues to be a major factor in the changing pattern of mortality and morbidity. Even progress contains the seeds of new problems. The prevention and effective treatment of infections and the staggering advances in surgical techniques allow more people to reach old age, with its inherent hazards, and more people are exposed to the possibility of developing chronic disease conditions. Survival after severe accidents, often resulting in brain injuries, means that more people require physical care. There is no sign that mental disabilities are decreasing. It follows that the heavy demands on medical, nursing and social services are likely to continue or even increase. As new treatments become available the costs of care tend to rise and the financing of the Health Service poses increasingly serious problems.

National policy for future developments in the fields of health and welfare is based on an extension of care in the community, and hospital care must be reserved for those who really need the complex diagnostic and therapeutic facilities which can only be provided there. Measures to reduce the length of hospital stay are encouraged so that a quicker throughput of patients may be achieved. Greater collaboration between hospital and community services must be aimed at if unnecessary use of hospital in-patient and out-patient facilities is to be avoided.[13] These trends and developments greatly increase the burden on the domiciliary services, especially those of the general practitioner, but whereas the population is growing steadily, the number of general practitioners has recently dropped.[7, 15]

It is essential, therefore, that medical skills and time are used to the greatest advantage and this has been facilitated by the linkage of nursing staff with general medical practice. Anderson and co-workers,[3, 4] who have studied the development of linkage schemes from their inception, consider it to be the most significant experiment in the National Health Service.

The formation of full family care teams represents a further step towards greater utilization of resources, increased job satisfaction and, most important, an extension of patient care. It seems to be not only a desirable but a necessary development if the increasing demands of the health service are to be met.

SUMMARY

The National Health Service in the United Kingdom has committed itself to the provision of preventive health, medical and nursing care for all members of the population. The demands are increasing and all available resources of finance and manpower must be used to the best advantage.

This paper describes the formation of family care teams. These include general practitioners, health visitors, district nurses, midwives, and sometimes also social workers, secretarial staff and receptionists, all working from a general medical practice. The grouping of doctors to form larger practices has facilitated this development. The pooling of a variety of medical, nursing and social work skills enables the members of the team to give a more comprehensive service to patients, and team operation appears to provide greater job satisfaction for individuals.

The disadvantages and problems of family care teams are discussed, as are their potential scope. Flexibility is an important feature and each team develops its own working methods and interests. Four examples of team operation are described briefly: the use of a nurse member of the team for primary visiting, transport of housebound patients to the doctor's surgery, a community ward staffed by the family care team and team action in an emergency situation.

In conclusion, some implications of current trends for the Health Service are discussed, and it is suggested that the formation of family care teams appears to be a desirable and possibly a necessary development if increasing demands on scarce resources are to be met.

DISCUSSION

Dogramaci: The image of the British nurse has been of a person who set an example in bedside nursing, in extending tender loving care and so on. But do I now understand that the doctor is delegating some of his responsibilities in seeing patients and sometimes in making a diagnosis to the nurse, and that in times of emergency she works as an assistant to the doctors, as part of the team? The image of a bedside nurse has already largely disappeared in some countries such as the United States, where bedside nursing is done by assistant nurses rather than nurses themselves. Does all this mean that this image will be changed?

Hockey: I do not think the image of the British nurse is being changed, but we certainly have a different grade of nurse who will perhaps provide more of the 'tender loving' bedside care. This is the State Enrolled Nurse, who is a professional worker in her own right and not an assistant nurse. She has two years of bedside training, whereas the State Registered Nurse has three years of highly technical training. I think that the two-year trained State Enrolled Nurse is likely to be a much better bedside nurse than the three-year trained highly technical nurse. We also have auxiliary personnel with various amounts of in-service training to help with the simple hygiene care of old people who would normally have a member of their family caring for them.

Hill: Isn't the enrolled nurse stepping into a vacuum created by the fact that many of the fully qualified nurses are going up and up in the so-called status and academic scale and doing more complex technical jobs? In fact, although they are called nurses their roles are perhaps different, and perhaps we should call them by another name. But isn't a vacuum being created by the aspirations of all the professions, whether medicine or nursing or anything else? You are filling it in nursing quite nicely with the State Enrolled Nurses.

Hockey: This is perfectly correct, but surely a ceiling must come at some stage as we cannot keep on rising in our aspirations indefinitely. However, I do not see any danger or harm in this trend for the time being while there is scope for more rational deployment of resources.

Barbero: Caring is an area of investigation that is not often examined in detail. We rated six paediatrician-nurse teams on a scale that in essence showed whether there was caring. Three teams had a much more business-like organization than the others, and a minimal input into 'caring'. The other three showed many features that would be involved in the fundamental relationship of caring for people. With the group that cared there was a very high incidence of individuals returning for care; and if people could not return for an appointment they went to the extra inconvenience or expense of cancelling the appointment. In health education, which to us is the most crucial question, a heightened level of understanding seemed to be occurring in the 'caring' group in contrast to the business-like group. This is an important feature, not commonly described, of some kind of team action, and maybe of individual action as well.

A series of observations indicate that at least with traditional training the physician is not the best person to do health maintenance or health management, although he is very effective in diagnosis and in the identification of therapeutic goals. In one study nurses were contrasted with physicians in their management of some chronic problems such as hypertension, diabetes and other such disturbances. It was clear that in terms of understanding and management the nurse management approach was more effective than that of the physician.

Baker: Did you say that the number of group practices had increased from 30 per cent of all practices to 50 per cent?

Hockey: No, but groups of three doctors or more have increased from 30 per cent to 50 per cent. In other words, two-partner practices or single-handed practices account for the other 50 per cent.

Baker: Is the hospital the proper place for training a nurse who will spend most of her time working in the home?

Hockey: Perhaps the training of all nurses should begin in the patient's home. You are right that a full hospital training as given at the moment is not an adequate preparation for a nurse working in the community. She needs additional training to cope with the complexities of social problems and the initiation of social services. She needs to learn to recognize the hidden, more obscure needs of her families. She needs to be able to work with many other people who have different skills and backgrounds. All this has to be acquired and it is not acquired in the hospital setting. At the moment some short additional preparation for domiciliary nursing is given either after completion of the basic hospital training or, less often, integrated within it. I believe that the future of nurse education may lie in a two-year basic period of training for all nurses and specialization after that. One can reach a reasonable nursing proficiency in two years, provided that selection in the first place is adequate.

Fişek: What is the attitude of a young graduate nurse to community nursing as compared to hospital nursing?

Hockey: The image of the nurse in the community has been changing very rapidly. When I was a district nurse in the community, we went round on bicycles and boiled our equipment in old saucepans. Nurses now have infinitely better working conditions; they go around in cars and the full range of pre-sterilized equipment is available to them. In other words they are able to do very much the same kind of jobs as nurses in hospital. This has greatly enhanced the image and the status of the district nurse. By and large community nursing is more popular because the nurse in the community has more independence and she is better able to combine nursing with her domestic commitments—increasingly now of course the service is being staffed by married nurses. So on the whole the shortages in community nursing are minimal,

112

whereas many hospitals are faced with serious recruitment problems.

Fişek: I once asked a Turkish district nurse whether she wanted to go back to a hospital. She said that she did not, because she has a respected position in the community and is well accepted there, but she did not have the same thing in the hospital.

Hockey: This is absolutely right, and applies equally to the U.K. Especially in a country area in Britain a nurse—who may incidentally also be a qualified health visitor and midwife—is a person to whom the whole community turns. Like your own rural midwife, she has tremendous trust from the population, her work is very rewarding and she has a personal satisfaction which she is not always able to find in hospital work.

King: How are the manpower needs of district nursing likely to be met in the future, when more and more practices switch over to the concept of group practice and require more people? Is there going to be a shortage or will the manpower, or rather womanpower, needs be met?

Hockey: There will probably have to be a channelling of resources from one area to another. Again, I think the unified health service that we are expecting in the future will help towards this development. We shall have area boards and I envisage that the nursing staff will be interchangeable, working in and out of hospital, which will have tremendous advantages. Apart from filling the needs it will enable nurses to maintain their competence and be kept up to date by regular periods of work in hospital. This will help all round. I think we have the manpower there to staff all services reasonably well, but at the moment there is a wrong allocation of manpower to the various sectors of the services.

Hentsch: In fact there is a trend now to start the young student nurse's education by introducing her first to community rather than to hospital care. She is familiar with the community and she can best start her understanding of nursing from there, instead of being thrown into hospital which is a completely unknown world to her.

Kisseih: The training of the nurse in community health care right from the beginning of her professional preparation is very necessary, especially in developing communities where many of the major killers are diseases which could be prevented. In some of the African countries, especially the former British colonies, the basic nurse training programme does not include any public health nursing. Consequently, nurses qualify without the slightest idea of what is expected of them in social and preventive health work.

The difficult conditions under which the few public health nurses work also deter the hospital nurses from specializing in community nursing. In order to attract more nurses into public health nursing, therefore, the salary scale and other conditions of service of the public health nurses, including provision of living accommodation and transport facilities,

113

are being improved in my country. The basic nurse training curriculum is also being revised to include public health nursing, psychiatric and obstetric nursing.

Another grade of nurse having a great impact on rural health work in Ghana is the community health nurse. She is a female with at least ten years' basic education, who trains for two years in community nursing. She is an auxiliary to the public health nurse but, at a health post where the staff consists of a health post attendant, two community health nurses, a midwife and a sanitarian, the community health nurse takes overall decisions and is supervised only about once a week by the public health nurse from the nearest health centre.

Rural health work is carried out by nurses and other health personnel because of the shortage of medical officers in the country. Whenever the nurses are required to carry out certain medical duties, they are expected to acquire the necessary technique through systematic preparation, and under the supervision of the nearest medical officer, whose supervision, however, might be limited to a weekly or even a monthly visit to the station.

Seden: Where the developing countries still have 'granny midwives' how do they handle the situation between them and the trained rural nurse or midwife? What measures do they take? We have this problem and we are trying to bring the reality just as close to the ideal as possible.

Kisseih: In Ghana, we have these 'granny midwives' who are called 'traditional midwives'. The attitude of the Ministry of Health towards these women is that until they can be replaced with trained midwives no action is to be taken to stop them from practising.

Some time ago, a register of some of these traditional midwives was kept to enable the regional medical officers of health to keep them under close observation. However, this has been discontinued, as some members of the health professions felt that the traditional midwives might regard the registration as official recognition of their work.

At present, there is no definite policy with regard to their practice. In some of the regions where the maternal and child health clinics are well established, the medical officers in charge, together with the public health nurses, instruct these traditional midwives in hygiene and care of the baby's cord. It is envisaged that as soon as every area of the country is served by a trained midwife, the traditional midwives would disappear.

Israel: In India, the indigenous *dai* is the traditional midwife and she commands a great deal of respect in her own village. She is one of the opinion leaders and what she advises the women will follow. This was a problem faced by the family planning teams, because with family planning the *dai* is likely to lose her job of delivering the babies. So in the village programmes we have tried to involve the *dai* as much as possible; we make her a depot holder for contraceptives, and the incentive scheme in which people are paid for bringing in patients will help to solve her financial difficulties. There is also a move to train these indigenous *dais* and to provide them with midwifery kits. We cannot escape the fact that the *dais* are there and they will remain for some time, so we hope that we will be able to include them in the programme and make better midwives out of them.

Banks: In countries where midwifery is a mother-to-daughter tradition it is possible to train the young *dais*, who are intelligent and learn easily. There are two tricks to this. One is not to send them back to their own village if the break with tradition is not acceptable, but to post them to another village, and the other is to give them an attractive kit, perhaps in an aluminium box.

Hill: Health is only part of a culture, and just because we have materialistic success in our scientific centres in the West, we should not destroy the cultures of developing countries. Cecily Williams who described kwashiorkor is very forceful about this: we should not discard the old if we cannot replace it by the new.

9: Paediatrics and the Community

GIULIO J. BARBERO

It is most fitting to hold a meeting on teamwork for world health in Turkey, since, in addition to the work of Florence Nightingale, this area has been the scene for a number of other similarly significant contributions. The centre of the cult of Asklepios, the god of medicine, was located at Pergamon. In his honour, the town built the Asklepieion, a temple with a medical library and a theatre holding 3500 spectators. One might fancy, although no evidence exists for this, that this theatre in the god's honour was one of the first means for mass health education, which is certainly an important activity for teamwork in world health.

A second contribution arises from a trading problem Pergamon experienced with Alexandria. Fear that the quality and renown of the library at Pergamon might eclipse that of Alexandria led Egypt to stop the export of papyrus to Pergamon. As a result, Pergamon invented parchment, *charta pergamena*, which remained for centuries a durable basis for the written language. Thus, the art of communication, so important in teamwork, is well rooted here. The words carved over the doorway of the Asklepieion still bear witness to the boundless pride of Asklepios and all subsequent healers: "In the name of the gods, Death may not enter here." Through the following centuries Arab scholars in this part of the world kept alive and developed many important aspects of the art and science of medicine.

Moving from the past to the present, my role in this meeting is to present some aspects of teamwork concerned with child health now being developed in the United States. A major change occurred in the pathway of medicine there some 40 years ago when the medical schools moved towards a more scientific outlook and incorporated large amounts of basic science into the curriculum. Since the values of the scientific method in medicine added many new benefits of great importance to child health, it only gradually became evident that this change was siphoning off considerable activity from the study of the delivery of health care to groups and individuals.

After the Second World War, large programmes of medical research were undertaken, necessitating great activity in the development of manpower and tools for this effort. The realization then slowly emerged that the neglect of, and unplanned approach to, medical care was leading to major problems, such as a markedly fragmented health system, increasing specialization resulting in fewer health professionals for general

117

population needs, and spiralling costs due to ever-increasing techno-logical depth and complexity. During the same period most of the traditional infectious and nutritional diseases of childhood markedly diminished, due to technical developments and general socioeconomic improvements. Activity in child health shifted from problems of mortality to preventive maintenance and to long-term handicaps affecting the quality of life. At the same time, it became clear that large pockets of illness existed, particularly in rural and urban families in the lower income group, with inadequate funding and manpower being deployed for their needs.

In this light, the national priority in medical research was recently levelled off and new programmes were introduced for regional health care. Funding was made available for the health care of the poor, and specialized programmes were set up for high-risk pregnant mothers and for the younger and older members of the population. At the same time, a whole series of experiments were started, such as neighbourhood primary health centres in areas with great health needs. All these activities formed the beginning of a national examination of the ingredients required for a primary health care system, with the back-up services necessary in the complex situations of the present day.

TEAMWORK BETWEEN COMMUNITY AND CHILD HEALTH WORKERS

It is with this background in mind that the question of teamwork in child health arises. Through all the legislation, there has been new emphasis on the need for the consumer (the population desiring the health care) to have a voice in the development of the service by the health providers. Already the government, which is supposed to represent the general population, has set up the first phase of a team by bringing together the consumer and the provider at a local level. This is a complex situation involving a continuing series of evolving states of interaction. This interface becomes particularly crucial in child health, since both the family and the school are significantly involved in the ascertainment, development and remedying of disorders of childhood. Ideally, in a stable and static community the opportunity arises for professional health workers and the local population to work closely together as a team; however, that type of community is not very common, particularly among those with the greater health need.

TEAMWORK FOR PAEDIATRICS AND THE COMMUNITY

The interface between paediatrics and the community is now in a state of dynamic agitation similar to that occurring in the active surface membranes of viable cells. Our experience stems from one form of this culture of social cells, namely a number of comprehensive programmes for children and youth which have been set up in urban and rural areas

118

of the United States, all of which can be considered as individual experiments in health delivery to children.

From this experience I would like to extract certain ideas which seem to me of importance to the subject of teamwork in health. First, in discussing teamwork, it might be of value to extend Miss Hentsch's dictionary definition of a team.[1] A team can be defined as a population of individuals with various skills who have learned to understand each other's language and thinking, and emotionally have developed common goals and the need to trust each other, suppressing some of their individual needs for the common end. The relationship between a community and the child health providers therefore represents a team under ideal circumstances. The various child and youth programmes aim to be actively involved with the communities they serve. Communities are not static but mobile and in constant change, and child health workers must develop an entirely new understanding to work in partnership with a community.

Much can be learnt through experience of the many forms which are developing in the various individual projects. In theory, the health providers should seek out and elicit from the community (or *vice versa*) participation in decisions regarding service needs and quality. The pattern that this takes in practice has been quite variable. For example, which members of the community can truly represent it—the outspoken ones, the quiet ones? And since he often cannot satisfy immediate needs, how can the health professional avoid seeming to oversell his services? How can there be enough time to allow for the gradual evolution vital for the development of quality and depth in teamwork care?

Many programmes have boards with adequate community representation to influence the pattern of care. But at times this sensitive balance of forces has resulted in the total domination of the programme by the community, to the ultimate weakening of the ability of the health workers to play an educational and helpful role. The converse situation appears when a weak community involvement is aggravated by too forceful control by the health workers or by the community being highly unstable. This situation will delay the integration of the community's own health priorities with those of the health professions, which is related to what Miss Kisseih[2] says about the need for built-in measures of self-growth. Such slowing down is sometimes necessary. Clearly, a balance of both sides is vital for the change towards more effective child health maintenance. As a catalyst to such teamwork, it may be quite valuable to have as members of the community individuals who also play a professional role.

The Children and Youth Program at Hahnemann Medical College and Hospital, Philadelphia, deals with an urban low income population. In this geographical area, the incidence of crime, poverty, infant mortality, morbidity, drug addiction, disease and various handicaps is higher than in most higher income groups. The programme has an active community coordinator and staff. A community council in the area has active committees on welfare, housing, health, education and recreation, and ties with the schools in the area as well as with a number of preschool day-care centres. Examples of community involvement in the programme are: in the local school special classes for certain children are subsidized; teachers receive counselling in school about problem children; there are day-care centres for working mothers, a local radio programme several times a week on health and nutrition, listened to by many mothers, a community newspaper, a summer camp programme, a nutrition programme in the local schools for children and their parents, sewing and cooking classes for mothers and pregnant adolescent girls, and special tutorial classes for children with learning disabilities. All these activities are carried out with the help of many volunteers from both inside and outside the community. The programme brings together the various efforts from diverse areas in this common action for the benefit of children. The community coordinating group of the programme must keep itself informed about and ready to develop bridges to various state and private resources that may be of value to members of the community. It has certainly become apparent that efficient utilization of services and therefore their value to a community diminishes as the approach to problems becomes more complex. Assigning responsibility to smaller local communities and doing away with centralized control over large areas may be a key factor ultimately of great importance in community health.

CONCEPT OF CHANGE

It is vital to these programmes that both community members and the professional health workers should be aware that change is continually necessary. This is an exceedingly difficult issue since, on the one hand, it is inherent in man to be restless in response to his recognized needs; while on the other hand he finds great difficulty in repeatedly modifying his positions and behaviour. This process is nevertheless vital for long-term evolution, since institutions, teams or any collection of individuals tend to move from a dynamic stage to a static phase and have increasing difficulty in adapting to new situations. The problem is how to build into any activity a concept of dynamic change without progressively adding to the complexity. Individual issues tend to be focused on, and handled out of relation to, the whole, so that often new dilemmas and obstructions to change are developed in other areas. In any group called a team it seems to me that one needs to foster freedom to examine and test any issue, but at the same time one must relate all steps to the whole in order to prevent a centrifugal spread of disorganization without too forceful restriction to a highly structured pattern. A team should include the conceptualizers as well as the implementers who will interact together to modify the process of change in a useful fashion. Furthermore, the team in the health area should always show movement towards an *ever* distant goal. From some of the earlier reports of this conference, one saw that various types of illnesses decreased through the efforts of the health programme; however, it was apparent that new health problems would arise requiring changing patterns of approach and even different types of manpower for their management.

In this context, it is of considerable interest that many of the Children and Youth Programs in the U.S.A. have been set up in medical schools, so that the student physicians, nurses, and other disciplines can actively experience some of these new ideas during their formative training periods. It should be most interesting to see the effects of this experience on these health personnel in the future.

PRIORITIES OF HEALTH

A major aspect in the concept of change is to be constantly aware of the health needs and priorities. For example, studies by the Children's Bureau of the United States of America have indicated that soon almost half of the population of the United States will be under 25 years of age. Over 300000 children are in diverse institutions away from home. Accidents are the leading mortality and morbidity problem of youth. A large proportion of the children will be in school. One-third of the patients of out-patient psychiatric clinics are under 20. Children have, of course, more acute illnesses than adults, with more than half of these being respiratory in origin. Many millions of children have one or more chronic handicaps. It is also obvious that the more severe the primary diagnosis is, the greater the number of other problems present. These generalizations for a large national population need to be translated by direct examination to a small discrete area of service responsibility. It is also apparent that an area needs recurrent appraisal of its priorities in order to effect any necessary change and improvement in the pattern for its health teams. For our present level of problems our primary health teams consist of a nurse and a paediatrician, backed up by social workers, child psychiatrists and other specialists. Audiology, speech, vision, dentistry, and social, educational and emotional problems are becoming key health needs in the community.

This approach and configuration of the health team may change as our health priorities are redefined. In any health system for children, the problem of providing such care, in the continual battering provided by periodic waves of acute illness, is a real one, requiring sufficiently careful programming to cover such eventualities without destroying the possibility of dealing with other long-term health needs.

121

As a backdrop for the Children and Youth Programs, the Children's Bureau has set up a system for reporting the various areas of activity, and each programme in some way maintains a quarterly report of diagnoses and services. In our programme, each encounter is checked off on a form which is submitted for computer storage of information. We hope this will lead to the development of much information which will be important in setting up change in the programmes.

THE MECHANICS OF HEALTH DELIVERY

Of equal importance to a conceptual attitude to health teamwork and delivery is the development of a harmonious and even flow of the procedures of health delivery. The operational procedures require that all the various members of the programme must be deeply involved, so that true group understanding can arise. The key to the mechanics of health delivery lies in the patient records. In complex or multi-problem situations, the record can become of very little use to the clinical teams. It is often too individualistic, full of uncompleted problems, and too disorganized for the demonstration of a smooth sense of flow in individual patient care for the primary health caretakers. New techniques in record-keeping are therefore vital in health work.

Our own programme has been trying to translate specific condition areas into more global terms, such as: I, Health; II, Brief Episodic Illness; III, Remedial Handicap; and IV, Chronic Handicap. The category number and date are noted in boxes on a form on the front of the record, permitting a rapid review of where the patient stands in the various areas which are to be improved. All new caretakers can quickly appraise what is wrong, what is missing, and what is well and in health.

Another question in the mechanics of health delivery by teams concerns the levels, frequency and types of screening procedures to be used to follow up children already in care. The development of an appointment system is a further illustration of the importance of operational procedures. In our programme the ability to reach the community by efficient handling of the complex traffic problems involved in patient care is vitally important. In other words, there must be as strong a status and support for development of detailed operational mechanisms for health delivery as for new concepts of change.

ATTITUDES OF TEAM HEALTH WORKERS

The effectiveness of teamwork between community and child health workers is influenced by the attitudes of the health workers. Unquestionably, a key issue is the recruitment of individuals who are basically interested in providing helpful service to the people they serve. The manpower shortage does not make this ideal always possible. Therefore, a programme must, at various team levels, have enthusiastic input in order to enhance features of service. Dilemmas occasionally arise about how to handle an individual team caretaker who may be disrupting the service and others on the team. Sometimes this must be handled by removing such individuals from the team, after attempts have first been made to direct their energies into more effective and productive channels. As an example, in the earlier stage of our programme, we were able to observe some teams who were much less focused on service and other teams who had a high sense of service and relationship to their patients and families. The former had a much lower incidence of follow-up, higher referral to other resources, and less movement into health maintenance than the latter teams, who showed a high spirit of relationship and dedication to their patients. This problem of team attitude becomes vital as one moves from an acute episodic health delivery focus towards responsibility for health maintenance and rehabilitation in a broad sense.

EVALUATION OF PROGRAMME

It is becoming clear that part of the programme should be devoted to evaluating the activity and to undertaking research on crucial questions. Much as any large business corporation has found it beneficial to build a research programme into its overall activities, so also should any group active in a dynamic phase of health delivery plan for evaluation and research. Without this, there undoubtedly arise great possibilities for sterility, apathy or ritualization. The necessary curiosity needed to maintain movement is snuffed out by the lack of continuing feedback of learning. The Children and Youth Programs require careful examination of their organization for such programme evaluation; however, this phase of the programme is still too early in its evolution to provide useful discussion material. Specific areas of research need to be encouraged in order to clarify areas of uncertainty in the health delivery process.

In summary, I have presented a number of aspects which strike me as being of the utmost importance in the development of teamwork between paediatrics and the community, as well as in the development of the health team providing care for a community.

Two thousand years ago, a man from this sector of the globe stated it all quite clearly in simple terms. "Life is short, and the Art long; the occasion fleeting; experience fallacious, and judgement difficult. The physician must not only be prepared to do what is right himself, but also to make the patient, the attendants, and externals cooperate." (Hippocrates.)

At a later time, Goya of Spain made an etching of a dressed jackass sitting by the bedside of a dying man, feeling his pulse. Under the picture, Goya wrote, in his pointed fashion, "What diagnosis will he die of?"

One would hope that after our discussions on teams for health we shall not be 'jackasses' in our reach for the ideals of Hippocrates.

DISCUSSION

Hill: What about the cost of this kind of programme?

Barbero: We estimate the cost per child as about $180–$200 per year. This includes the data system and a community coordinating effort in a number of areas. The initial cost started at around $400 per child and has gone down rapidly in subsequent years.

Israel: A very high percentage of children seem to have eye conditions as handicaps. Are these minor handicaps or is there a considerable amount of blindness in this particular community? If so, what is the cause?

Barbero: There is very little actual blindness. They have strabismus and other visual impairments. However, the preferential use of one eye from failure to focus the other effectively even though both are present is a valid handicap for rehabilitation.

Bridger: In what ways does the strategic planning take the process of change into account, and how is this implemented at your own level?

Barbero: Our core team consists of a nurse, a physician who is the team coordinator, a nutritionist, a dentist, a community coordinator, a social worker and others. This group meets frequently to examine their own supervisory activities and to define their areas of interaction. The problem here is that there are frequently different conceptual points of view; but, as a team begins to operate, it can come together itself around the specific circumstances: an individual with very little training but with some innate skill can sometimes become highly adept as a team member around an individual question. The problem is how to develop this kind of functional interaction by developing team coordinators who catalyse the decision-making process but do not necessarily take over by fiat.

King: This kind of programme obviously involves very large numbers of staff of different kinds. At the same time I understand that the community has very large numbers of unemployed persons. How much is being done to incorporate less-qualified personnel into the health team to provide this massive quantity of care? Is the attitude of the existing professional bodies assisting or counteracting this?

Barbero: One of the continual dilemmas has been the interaction between the non-professional and the so-called professional, who finds it exceedingly hard to let go. The programmes, however, have been set up to experiment with having more and more personnel from the community itself. This will be an evolving process of learning. There is going to be a continuing confrontation, but I think it will be a fruitful one. Those who have emerged from the community itself can often teach the professionals many things, as representatives of the community in some ways. They are also beginning to have a stake not only in their specific need orientation but in the wider goals of the general programme. The interaction is wholesome.

Young: Health and nutrition are clearly related; do you see much ill health due to malnutrition, particularly undernutrition, and what can you do about it in the circumstances?

Barbero: There is some malnutrition. One out of five children under three years has anaemia of less than 10 grammes haemoglobin/100 millilitres. A fair number of children fail to grow because of environmental deprivation. We are much concerned now about the impact of this on long-term brain development. The team must then intervene in the home situation, and they must learn to allow the parents to take part in the process. Such parents may either have been battered themselves in their own childhood or they may have great current specific problems in health and social living.

Seden: Do you have special criteria in recruiting the members of this team? Do you also have a special programme for their in-service education or on-the-job training?

Barbero: Most of the activity in these programmes is on-the-job training. The manpower problem is really quite grave and we have to take those who are available. Team interaction allows for evolution over time so that a common goal begins to be seen. There are some ways of evaluating this. In some of these programmes there is a tremendous turnover of personnel and in some virtually none, so somehow a kind of cohesive quality begins to evolve in the programme. In our own programme we have had no turnover of personnel, which has permitted the process of team development to occur in a stable form. We have been able to encompass the no-no man and the yes-yes man[1] in the struggle for some kind of learning.

Hockey: Is any attempt being made to educate parents in their own home situation, and if so, is it accepted?

Barbero: The home visits are done by the community aides, backed by the nurses and the social workers. The nurses sometimes go with the community aides, if it becomes clear that a different frame of reference is necessary. The community aides work rather closely with some of the nurses and social workers. They are very well accepted in the homes because they are neighbours of the people they visit. They are the best individuals to ascertain health problems in the area and to point out some needs. They are also very involved in many of the activities of the community, whether in recreation, welfare, health, or coordinating some other resource useful for an individual. So home visiting occurs rather frequently. Each nurse, for example, spends one day of her week in home visiting, and the community aides are always within the community. Some of the specific community programmes are carried out in the homes of community people.

125

Hill: The members of your team are orthodox medical personnel, doctors, nurses and so on, plus the home visitors. Are you likely to use the physician's assistant (as at Duke University, North Carolina) or the nurse practitioner (of the kind at work in Denver, Colorado)? These intermediary personnel are being trained in the States in large numbers now.

Barbero: These nurses are not the traditional nurse. They do various screening functions or supervise the nurses' aides in testing vision, speech and hearing. They also take down part of the primary family history and may take over the initial contact with the patient so that later the physician can move in and focus on the critical issues arising out of the relationship with the nurse. In essence, these nurses are a sort of nurse practitioner.

Bridger: You mentioned the possibility of conflict between the community with its community objectives and the professionals with their health objectives. There would also be times, however, when everybody could join in shorter-term goals very successfully when they were perceived as good, attainable and desirable. To what extent did progressive learning develop between those specifically concerned with health, on the one hand, and those concerned with community objectives on the other? In other words, how far were the healthy aspects of conflicting as well as common aims made use of?

Barbero: Conflict is always present because what a community needs for its health far transcends the capacity of any programme. The basic needs of a community are jobs, security and housing. These are the health questions. They are far more important than any of the things we do, so frustration in dealing with these areas can shoot right down into a programme. People hope that Nirvana is here as one begins to relate to them at the onset. The dilemma is to get this progressively into a better balance and to utilize slowly but steadily the difficult fact of life that our adolescents are having to learn, namely that you have to get into the "nitty-gritty" of working and digging away together.

Ordoñez-Plaja: The no-no man[1] is very useful because when you argue with him you are not arguing in a very rational way, and that is just the way you will have to argue in Congress or in the State legislature. On the other hand, the no-no man will show you many faults in your planning, which will make you think twice and be ready to have the big fight at the legislative level. I agree entirely with you that it has to be done that way, otherwise you will be stopped before starting.

Barbero: One of our problems in Philadelphia is that we have a fairly large amount of lead poisoning. This is not seen unless the children show major neurological damage. The real problem at the preventive level is the size of the iceberg below the water-line. In trying to understand how we might grapple with this problem we tended to minimize the

126

tremendous assets the community had for dealing with this problem at a political and physical level. The health workers became very frustrated because the City of Philadelphia just could not deal effectively with the de-leading of many of the old houses. But soon we found a ground swell arising out of the continual communication between our community council and other community groups. They could move into the vacuum and create a political pressure that no set of health providers could in any way do. I think within a short time we are going to have legislation and resources to tackle this problem properly. This was a tremendous area of learning for the health team.

Hill: How did you get that message across to the community?

Barbero: In this community council the opportunity occurs to talk about our problems and to become aware that none of us have the sole means to handle them. Out of this some action emerges. A series of these councils in different areas have now been formed and other groups are trying to modify certain kinds of basic needs. These groups then generate their own activity. Our part was to present the dilemma: "Here is a dilemma of housing and there is no legislation that enforces the prevention of such lead paint intoxication of children." Then a planned constructive action seemed to emerge. It went from the emotional to the organized and structured. The community could tell us much more clearly what was important in dealing with many features of it. For example, it was part of their recommendation that all the activity should occur in the community and not in the medical institution, and they took this over with excellent judgment.

10: Paramedical Paradoxes—Challenges and Opportunity

TIMOTHY D. BAKER

ALL nations today have a great opportunity to improve health care without increasing health costs. This opportunity lies in the improvement of the training and utilization of paramedical personnel.

In discussions of paramedical workers, however, controversy is generated by the lack of agreement on definitions. Initially, I shall propose a system of categorization that may be useful as a frame of reference. Despite disagreements on the definition of the term 'paramedical', there is almost universal agreement that the paramedical worker has a vital role on the health services team in the delivery of curative and preventive services. I present here some economic justification for this vital role of the paramedical.

The general agreement on the importance of the paramedical worker makes it difficult to explain the low priority accorded to their recruitment, training and supervision in many countries. Some of these problems of training and utilization form the third section of the paper.

In a concluding section I list some potential solutions to some of the paramedical paradoxes.

DEFINITIONS

Not only are there disagreements on the exact definition of the term 'paramedical', but some authorities reject the term, using 'paraprofessionals', 'allied health professionals', 'subprofessionals', 'ancillary' or 'auxiliary health personnel' as terms to describe various types of health workers other than physicians. Since the term paramedical may include, at least for some people, everyone from the professional midwife to the health centre janitor, it is clear that a system of subclassification is essential for meaningful discussion.

Table I classifies health workers by length of training, income and the type of practice. It does not indicate professional or subprofessional levels, as professionals are in both high- and medium-income groups. Specific work function was specifically omitted, as there are wide overlaps in function among the three groups.

TABLE I

HEALTH WORKERS BY INCOME AND TYPE OF PRACTICE

Type of practice	High income, long education (12 years basic + 6–13 years professional)	Medium income, medium education (10–12 years basic + 2–5 years professional)	Low income, short education (6–12 years basic + 0–2 years professional)
Unsupervised independent general clinical practice	Physician (GP)	Assistant medical officer, licentiate, behdar, health officer (Gondar), feldsher, nurse	Dresser
Hospital or group practice	GP and specialist: e.g. surgeon, pathologist, radiologist, physiatrist, orthopaedist	Nurses—general duty and specialist, surgical technician, laboratory technician, X-ray technician, physical therapist, etc.	Nurses' aide, practical nurse, dresser, laboratory assistant
Antenatal, delivery, and postnatal care	Physician-obstetrician	Midwife	Auxiliary midwife, dai
Drug compounding and dispensing	Pharmacologist	Pharmacist	Dispenser, compounder
Mental health	Psychiatrist	Psychiatric nurse, psychiatric technician	Psychiatric aide
Dental practice	Dentist	Dental hygienist	Dental aide
Public health	Health officer (M.D.)	Health visitor, public health nurse, health educator	Home health aide, etc.
Environmental sanitation	Sanitary engineer	Sanitarian	Malaria assistant, sanitary inspector, etc.
Average cost of training: X		$0 \cdot 3 – 0 \cdot 5 X$	$0 \cdot 1 – 0 \cdot 2 X$
Average earnings per year: Y^*		$0 \cdot 2 – 0 \cdot 5 Y$	$0 \cdot 1 – 0 \cdot 2 Y$

* Including consideration of private practice as well as government salary.

Another parameter that has not been included in Table I is supervision. In most cases, there will be supervision within groups as well as across professional lines. For example, the ward matron or supervisor will assume responsibility for most supervision of staff nurses, while the physician will also give orders for patients under his direct responsibility. Some middle-income health workers have responsibilities within a health system far greater than some high-income professionals in solo practice.

It is one of the paramedical paradoxes that this supervisory responsibility and authority is seldom accompanied by appropriate levels of increased salary.

A point that should be emphasized is the vast difference in scope of responsibility between independent duty, generalist paramedicals and paramedicals who work with the benefit of supervision.

Although the generalizations in Table I may not be completely applicable to every country, the system has overall applicability to most countries.

ECONOMIC IMPORTANCE OF PARAMEDICAL WORKERS

Major economies can be realized as functions are transferred from high-salary to low-salary workers, because the main costs in the health industry are for services rather than goods. This principle is based on the assumption that productivity does not decrease at the same rates as salary.

Examples from dentistry show the magnitude of increases in productivity that may be expected from use of auxiliaries and aides. An American Dental Association survey showed that each additional full-time auxiliary working with a practising dentist increased the dentist's productivity by approximately 30 per cent.[1,2] A U.S. Navy study showed that each middle-level dental technician could boost the productivity of a dentist well over 50 per cent.[3]

There are limits to this principle; otherwise, we would have the janitor performing all health sector functions. Downward delegation of functions is limited by (1) quality of care expressed as end-results of services, (2) acceptability to consumers, and (3) perhaps most important, acceptability to the professionals who set standards for care. Physicians in developing countries often state that nothing but physician care is good enough for their people, when, in point of fact, only a small portion of the people have the benefit of any modern medical services at all.

The high costs of physician services

Based on the premise that a physician earns $5000 per year, the cost of providing only the salaries for one physician for every 1000 people would be from three to ten times the total annual health budget for countries such as the Philippines, Thailand, Sudan or Pakistan. Since the private sector covers an appreciable part of the cost of the health industry in many countries, it might be more appropriate to use the gross national product rather than the government health budget for comparing health expenditures of developed and developing countries. In the United States, Canada and Switzerland (using appropriately higher levels of physician income), the cost of maintaining one physician per 1000 population is less than 1 per cent of the GNP. On the other hand, in less developed countries such as Tanzania, Sudan, Burma and Uganda, the cost of maintaining one physician per 1000 population at $5000 per year would take from 5 to 8 per cent of the GNP, a level which no developing economy could support. (The figure of $5000 per year per physician in the less developed countries is a compromise between the earnings necessary to keep a physician in his native country and the considerably higher earning opportunities in richer countries. Salary levels of residents in the United States, registrars in England or contract doctors in Kuwait help to determine the level of income necessary to keep a Philippino physician in the outlying barrios of Palawan, or a Pakistani physician on the north-west frontier.)

The question may be raised "Why shouldn't other countries follow the example of Russia and provide doctors for everyone at a reasonable cost, by pegging the doctor's income at the same level as the miner, truck driver or other useful members of society?" The answer is simply that countries which have the ability to limit the freedom of migration as effectively as the Soviet Union might well consider this solution. In most countries of the world, however, governments are unwilling to limit freedom to migrate.

These facts show quite clearly that many nations simply cannot afford the luxury of having one physician for every 1000 persons. This really should be self-evident, but it is not. Unfortunately, the proliferation of medical schools has become a status symbol for developing nations. A past Health Minister of Nigeria stated in an address in Edinburgh that he planned to train 1000 medical graduates per year in Nigeria. The country could not conceivably support such numbers of doctors. They would migrate to countries where the doctor shortage is expressed in economic demand rather than biological need. As mentioned earlier, unless countries can afford to pay something close to the world market price for physicians, or adopt restrictive migration policies, they will not keep the physicians that they have trained. Developing nations cannot afford to invest their scarce resources in training doctors for rich nations. An obvious solution to this dilemma lies in increased and more effective use of paramedical personnel.

Physicians, paramedicals and health indices

Improved health standards and greater numbers of physicians do not necessarily go together. Historically, we find that in the United States from 1910 to 1960 the number of physicians per head remained essentially constant. During this same period, infant mortality decreased by at least three-quarters and the age-adjusted death rate dropped by two-thirds.

Internationally, if one compares countries of similar economic development, there is little correlation between the number of doctors per 100000 population and health indices such as infant mortality.

Thus, it appears that more doctors do not necessarily raise health standards. Perhaps investment in training a higher ratio of paramedicals would show greater benefit. Studies by Cunningham[5, 41] and Morley[9] in Nigeria showed that either nurses or grade 2 midwives were effective in lowering the under-five mortality rates.

In summary, great economies could and should be realized by the increased and more effective use of paramedical personnel. It is equally true that there are barriers to the use of paramedical personnel, based primarily on problems of training and prestige. These problems will be discussed in the following section.

PROBLEMS OF UTILIZATION AND TRAINING OF PARAMEDICAL WORKERS

Manpower distribution—pyramid or hour-glass?

A curious phenomenon in many less developed nations is that there are more doctors than nurses. In essentially every country, health manpower broadens widely at the base, with large numbers of orderlies, aides and non-professional health workers. However, the obviously inefficient pattern of a constricted number of middle-level professionals seems to occur most commonly in those countries least able to afford the highly paid physician.

Table II shows the ratio of nurses to doctors in several representative

TABLE II

NURSES PER DOCTOR IN COUNTRIES OF DIFFERENT
LEVELS OF ECONOMIC DEVELOPMENT

Country	Number of nurses per doctor
Finland	3·7
Sweden	3·1
Japan	1·2
Turkey	0·6
Sudan	0·6
India	0·4

countries. Although the table refers to nurses, similar imbalances occur in the ratios of other middle-level professions to doctors.

There are several possible reasons for the development of this imbalance. One might be the relatively low status accorded to paramedical workers in many countries. "Western consultants at collegiate schools of nursing in underdeveloped countries report that nursing shortages exist only because too few women wished to enter a downtrodden and unskilled career."[7] Another reason, perhaps related to the first, is that physicians have probably tended to allocate health training resources to their own profession.

Whatever the reasons for the genesis of this situation, we should be concerned with its correction. The solution lies in increased training, which leads us to our next paradox.

Despite many statements and exhortations on the importance of paramedical training, in practice their training receives low priority in both quantity and quality—particularly in the less developed countries.

Table III shows that the less developed countries of Asia and Africa

TABLE III

PERCENTAGE DISTRIBUTION OF PROFESSIONAL SCHOOLS BY
REGIONS OF THE WORLD

	USA and Canada (N = 1351)	Europe (N = 1291)	Oceania (N = 55)	Other America (N = 383)	Africa (N = 34)	Asia (N = 273)
Medical schools[15]	7	14	14	26	50	63
Dental schools[16]	4	10	13	22	21	22
Nursing schools[12]	89	76	73	52	29	15
Totals	100	100	100	100	100	100

N = number

seem to give far less priority to nursing schools than to medical and dental schools, while Europe, Canada and the U.S.A. at least give a quantitative priority to nurse training. It is hard to explain the low priority given to nursing education in areas which can least afford the luxury of a disproportionate number of doctors.

International agencies have shown interest in the problems of paramedical training and utilization, but their accomplishments have been small in relation to the size of the problem. Table IV shows the relative numbers of physicians and paramedicals trained by three agencies.

TABLE IV

PERCENTAGE DISTRIBUTION OF TRAINEES BY PROFESSION

	Rockefeller* (N = 3850)	AID† (N = 1734)	WHO‡ (N = 17396)
Physicians, including public health physicians	65	40	56
Other health personnel	17	42	28
Nurses, including public health nurses	18	18	16
Totals	100	100	100

* 1917–1950.[10]
† 1955–1959.[8]
‡ 1957–1966.[17]

134

In addition to the quantitative imbalance there is almost invariably a qualitative difference between the education of physicians, who receive the greatest investment per student per year; nurses, who receive a moderate investment per student per year; and ancillary personnel, who receive a very low investment. (In Ibadan training a medical student costs $5000 per year. In Dar es Salaam the middle-level 'rural medical practitioner' costs $1600 per year. Medical auxiliaries trained in Bumbuli, Tanzania, and Omdurman, Sudan, cost less than $500 per year.[4]) The faculty-to-student ratios are almost invariably less favourable in the training institutions for lower-level personnel. In many cases, instructors in lower-level training institutions have no particular training or skills in education and teaching.

As Fendall says, "Recruitment to the ranks of teachers of auxiliaries suffers primarily because such teachers have neither status nor remuneration comparable to the importance of their task. Such teachers, unlike their colleagues at schools or universities, are teaching to a minimal rather than a maximal core of knowledge. They must be thoroughly conversant with field conditions, theoretical knowledge, and vocational skills. It is more difficult to teach to a minimal core of knowledge and limited vocational skills than it is to teach to a maximal . . ."[6]

Training in paramedical schools, like the training in many medical schools, is frequently more traditional than relevant. Examples may be found in programmes that attempt to take a four-month medical school course in anatomy and boil it down to four weeks for training dressers, without finding what elements of anatomy are essential for the dressers' work. Another example is the reliance on hospital bedside training for those nurses who will spend much of their career working in clinics or health centres.

In addition to the problems of curriculum and faculty, health training institutions seem to be equipped in inverse proportion to the numbers to be trained. As Fendall says, "Not only is there a dearth of teachers trained to the needs of auxiliary training, but there is an equally appalling lack of teaching aids."[6] I shall return to this point in the next section.

Another problem in current systems of paramedical training is the lack of any formal, easy route which would encourage progress from one level of occupation to a higher level. Even in the Soviet Union the *feldsher* is not automatically given credit for previous training when he or she enters medical school. In many cases, upward mobility of capable people is blocked by the need to return to the beginning of another programme of study.

In areas where populations are too dispersed to support highly paid professionals, an all-purpose health worker with low wage aspirations is probably necessary. Unfortunately, it is virtually impossible to train a health worker to "know everything about everything" and to serve in remote rural areas. Perhaps the solution to this paradox lies more in the field of communication and transportation than in the field of health training.

There is an overwhelming need for better training of more paramedical workers. There are multifarious problems in expanding training and improving utilization. What are some of the solutions to this dilemma?

POTENTIAL SOLUTIONS

(1) A first step towards solving the paramedical problem is for one or more foundations to take responsibility and interest in the problem. An example of the effect of such interest is this Ciba Foundation symposium on *Teamwork for World Health*. Hopefully, this conference is the first of other conferences that will involve more participants who are directly responsible for the training and supervision of paramedical workers. In the future, foundations may provide training fellowships for paramedical school instructors and facilitate the exchange of information on new developments in paramedical training between countries. The Ciba Foundation's interest will focus attention on this problem and make it a respectable area for investigation and experimentation.

(2) A second important solution to the paramedical utilization problem is increased governmental interest in the economy of efficient ratios of high cost:medium cost:low cost personnel. In virtually every country in the world, provision of health care is under scrutiny as "costing more than the country can afford". Finance Ministries may be as important as Health Ministries in encouraging paramedical development.

(3) Third, application of new teaching techniques in paramedical schools would provide a more efficient and more effective method of education. There is a dearth of good textbooks for training ancillary health workers. Since many of the training needs of ancillary health workers are the same in different countries, economies could be achieved by having 'universal' textbooks. These textbooks could be translated with necessary local adaptations and changes. There are problems inherent in translation programmes, but they can be overcome if the programme is given proper priority.

There is not much hope that advanced techniques such as teaching machines and computers will be used in schools where getting chalk for the blackboard is still a major obstacle. However, well-constructed programmed-learning texts would have great value in training auxiliaries and could serve as reference books for their future work.[11]

(4) Better utilization of paramedical personnel can be achieved through training supervisors in the art of supervision. Where nurses or physicians must serve in positions of overall supervision, they should

certainly be given special training, rather than being 'experts by assignment'. Furthermore, when ancillary personnel are promoted to supervisory positions over other ancillary personnel, they need refresher training as well as training in the elements of supervision and management. This leads to our next point.

(5) The difficulty in advancement from one job category to another in the health sector can be partly overcome by choosing supervisors from within the profession. Just as nurses seem to make the best supervisors for other nurses, so might well-qualified and capable auxiliaries make the best supervisors for other auxiliaries (providing, of course, that technical supervision is always given by appropriate professionals).

(6) Paramedical and medical educators should devise practical tests for advanced placement, or exemption from certain subjects in order to recognize the experience of other health workers restarting on the educational ladder.

(7) The very thorny problem of supervision of paramedicals on independent duty in remote areas might be partly solved by recourse to radio systems for consultation, supervision and instruction. Such systems have worked well in Micronesia with its far-flung, sparsely populated islands. In Alaska, school teachers or health aides in remote Eskimo villages have been given some health training and they consult with physicians in base hospitals regularly or on an emergency basis as medical problems arise.[13] This radio technique has also been used with success in some areas of Africa and in the Australian outback. Radio communication is not inordinately expensive, even for developing nations, and should be tried in many more countries.

CONCLUSION

Improvement of the training and utilization of all members of the health team offers the greatest opportunities and challenges in the health field today. In most countries the greatest return will come from increased investment in lower-level health workers.

SUMMARY

Relevant training and effective use of paramedical health workers are fundamental in improving health services and controlling costs of medical care throughout the world.

In discussing training and use of paramedical workers, we must consider the great diversity of job titles and work functions covered by the term 'paramedical'. This article classifies health workers by type of practice: independent duty/close supervision; hospital/outpatient/preventive services; generalized/specialized; and by level of income and practice.

The following paradoxes are discussed:

(1) The general acceptance, in principle, of the importance of para-medical workers in contrast to the low priority, in practice, given to their training and career development.

(2) The ill-defined career ladder by which a paramedical worker may be promoted from low through middle to high level positions.

(3) The great responsibilities thrust on some independent duty paramedical workers, contrasted with their brief, often inappropriate, training and minimal or inadequate supervision.

(4) The unfortunate imbalance found in many developing countries between expensively trained, highly paid professionals and the more economically trained and maintained paramedicals.

Some potential solutions and new approaches to paramedical training are presented.

DISCUSSION

Hockey: How is the quality of care measured by the end-results?

Baker: This is probably the most difficult problem in medical care research. Measurement of morbidity on an age-adjusted basis can be used to evaluate the quality of a *complete* system. In a partial system, such as that in the United States, where the private physician, the hospital and the health department are separate, it is difficult to assign responsibility for failures. In hospitals, case fatality rates can be used for end-result evaluation. Even here one gets into difficulties comparing one hospital with another. Some profit-making hospitals would come out very well in a case fatality evaluation system, because healthy patients with unnecessary surgery have fewer fatalities than sick patients with necessary surgery. Measurement of quality of care by end-results is a most important problem, but it is still a problem, not an established technique.

Russell: How far has the training of what I would call 'auxiliaries' been investigated in detail? Syllabuses that were set 10 or 12 years earlier for boys and girls who had just left primary school or who had had a few more years of education were still being taught last year to people in south-east Asia who had senior school leaving certificates, intermediate and even pre-university levels of education. The authorities concerned seemed rather baffled when asked why they were not reviewing the situation, yet this sort of training must be kept under constant review. In most developing countries one has auxiliaries because one cannot have anything more, but there comes a time when a total change in policy is needed.

Baker: Certainly as the educational level rises one must be able to adjust the system. The best way to do this is to relate the system to what a country thinks it can support in a given period of time. If it can pay a salary that will attract a person with only eight years of education, then one should design a system to train eighth grade graduates until the country's educational levels are sufficient for 12-year graduates to be hired.

Long-range plans should be used for health manpower—20-year plans rather than the conventional five years. Education should be geared to the number of physicians, nurses and ancillary personnel needed to meet the various service needs. One should aim for as high a level of prerequisite education as is reasonable in relation to the needs of other sectors of the economy.

Young: What is to happen to the people trained for eight years when the 12-year trained people take over? Sir Arthur Lewis[2] raised this type of point in 1962: in the early stages of the evolution of an educational system in a developing country, the person who has an education of eight years is valuable for primary school education and will command a salary which is a relatively high proportion of the gross national product. But later, when the man or woman with 12 years' training becomes available, the eight-year person will be displaced. Likewise, the 12-year person will be displaced later by the graduate or somebody of higher educational attainments. At each stage you have the danger that people educated up to a particular level will command a salary which is a higher proportion of the gross national product than that which they will receive when education has developed further. These people can then become frustrated, since there is no occupation available to them which commands the salary they have been used to. Have you any solution for this problem in relation to paramedical or other auxiliary training? I am concerned about the training of both the health workers, and those who are teaching them.

Baker: Older physicians have had less training than young physicians, yet both continue to practise medicine. Older nurse supervisors often have less training than the younger nurses whom they supervise. The discrepancy in years of prerequisite training points up the need for continuing education and re-training to keep older, less well-trained but more experienced workers effectively employed.

Young: It is tremendously important that in all this training, there should be instilled into the people who are being taught the need and the desire to re-educate themselves. What they learn at any particular stage is to be regarded as intermediary, and they must be imbued with the idea of self-education for the rest of their lives.

Baker: I agree completely.

Hill: You said that in the long-term we could work out the numbers of physicians, nurses and paramedical personnel needed, but has anyone assessed yet what the job of a physician is? We use 'physician' as a blanket term. The story of this conference to me is that the role of medical personnel, whether doctors or anyone else, is determined by the job rather than the blueprint of the health service or, indeed, medical education. Some years ago the Robbins report,[1] dealing with higher education, including medicine, in England, said: "We have not made the national need the main basis of our estimate." In other words, the educational system has nothing to do with the national need. So just what do you mean by the long-term when we haven't assessed what it is? The Todd Report[4] gives a study of medical education in England with which to some extent I disagree, but it did not give an assessment of what job the doctor is to do. Sir Arthur Lewis[3] says that in developing countries educated personnel are few, they are an *élite* and they are holding developing countries, to some extent, to ransom. One answer to this economically, he says, is to over-produce dozens and dozens of graduates, so that they must seek jobs lower and lower in the hierarchy and therefore be paid salaries which the country can really afford.

This question about the eight-year training compared to the 12-year training will tend to settle itself in the long term, if we look at what is economically feasible. Would you still hold to your opinion about the long-term projection, Dr Baker?

Baker: You can over-produce in one country only when you are producing something which is not exportable. Today you cannot over-produce physicians in the Philippines because they will go to other countries. Medical educators, directors of health services and ministers of health are reluctant to limit the migration of personnel. This is not a popular technique for keeping down the salary levels. Personnel without a degree that is recognized throughout the world *can* be 'over-produced' to saturate the medical care market and to provide effective care for all the people at a price the country can afford.

The relevance of the type of training is tremendously important. Interest is developing in relating sub-tasks to be done to the type of health worker best suited to do the tasks, and the curriculum needed to prepare the various types of health workers.

Russell: Probably the greatest need is for job descriptions to be worked out for the various types of post, especially in the developing countries, and then to fit the training to this. Once you know what you are training for, you can develop a training programme for it, but this is only really beginning to be done. For example, Indonesia was recently doing this exercise in the nursing field and it has been done in some parts of India. It seems to me perhaps the most important issue in the training of auxiliaries.

Banks: We may be at cross-purposes over the grading question. If one excludes nurses, aren't the paramedical workers that we are discussing the sanitarians, laboratory technicians, dental technicians, assistant pharmacists, and so on?

Baker: I am discussing the system of health workers from the most expensive to the least expensive. Each of us has a different idea of what a paramedical worker is. I think one should look at each description of each category of person being discussed, which will be different for different countries. The sanitarian is generally a man with a college education, at least in the United States, so I would not put him with the others you listed. I would put the sanitary inspector along with the auxiliary nurse midwife, nurse's aides and dispensers, compounders, dressers, and so on.

King: In Zambia the missionary doctors, after a period of mission service, have played a very useful role in teaching auxiliaries. This is working extremely well, and their level of commitment and experience of the country have conditioned them excellently for this type of work. In auxiliary training one of the things very much required is an institute of medical education specifically concerned with the whole range of medical education, particularly at the auxiliary level. Ideally there should be one for each WHO area and they might well be attached to the institutes of tropical medicine in the industrial countries. A development of this kind is required for all the different aspects of auxiliary training.

Baker: I certainly agree. As much importance should be given to the training of auxiliaries or middle-level health workers as to the training of professionals. The training of health workers other than physicians has received inadequate priority; giving adequate priority to this training is one of the best ways to secure better medical care without increasing costs.

11: New Concepts in Medical Education

E. BRAGA

THE rapid development of the health sciences and the increasing potential of medical attention, as well as the growing importance of social and preventive medicine, are forcing institutions responsible for the education of medical and allied health professions to change their objectives. In the developing countries these schools and institutions are often very strongly tied to ideas, programmes and structures taken over from countries with which they have had, or still have, political and/or cultural links. In a few instances such an association has worked satisfactorily. In most cases, however, these cultural or educational links have prevented the countries from creating their own teaching institutions for the adequate training of such personnel. As a result they need to develop new approaches and ideas relevant to their health problems and needs. In the developed countries the panorama is also changing, for even the most advanced ones are at present revising their programmes for the preparation of health personnel in a true fight against traditional patterns. Dissatisfaction is thus universal.

Any attempt to define new concepts in medical education will have to be based upon the principle that such an important field cannot be considered separately from the wide area of university education. It would be useless to try to analyse eventual changes or innovations being adopted here and there, for what really matters is the interplay of the educational structures and schemes and also their interrelationship *vis-à-vis* the actual health needs of society.

It is particularly difficult to forecast future trends for, as recently stated by Kerr[3] in discussing the crisis of the 'multiversity'—that is, the university which grew step by step in response to social needs and pressures:

"One major controversy involves two conflicting views about the role of the university—its past traditions, and present and future directions. There are many persons, particularly among the faculties, who still hold the aristocratic view of the university. They wish the university to be small, to be élitist, to be high-prestiged, to be remote from society, to concentrate on the historical and the theoretical. Others hold what might be called the more practical view, in which the university must be larger, more egalitarian, and more closely involved in the life of society. This conflict takes place not only between individuals and groups, but sometimes in the minds of most of us who are active in the modern university. As professors, we look back nostalgically toward the earlier university, the more aristocratic view. But in our concern as citizens, we may take a quite different position: that

143

the university must serve society. These differing views move the university in quite different directions and cause some of the strains both within the institution and within the people who participate in leadership."

Similar views were recently expressed in the following statement of an eminent European educational authority[1] in a meeting of Ministers of Education of French-speaking countries:

"Very often two essential functions of the university, e.g., the production of cadres demanded by society and the satisfaction of cultural needs of countries, are placed in opposition to each other. This derives from the concept that, although necessary, the first function lacks purity, whereas the second, supposedly disinterested, should be regarded as more noble. The present crisis, however, demonstrates what common sense has already been showing for quite a time, that is, instead of being in opposition these two functions are actually inseparable and thus complementary."

It is apparent that this conflict results intrinsically from the timidity with which educational planning, in its ample context and connotations, is being undertaken. Despite the true world-wide explosion of education during recent years, the lack of comprehensiveness of educational planning, particularly in the developing countries, and above all the poor adjustment of such planning to local characteristics and needs, have resulted in serious imbalances and distortions. According to a recent UNESCO study[5] a number of constraints have been playing against a more rapid adaptation of educational programmes to the present and future needs of countries. The following negative factors deserve to be mentioned: (a) fundamental inertia and social conservatism of the educational systems, resulting in an alarming increase in the gap between the pace of renewal of such systems as compared to the speed of evolution of society; (b) attitude of reservation with respect not only to the idea that education is an investment of capital importance, but also to the notion of educational planning; (c) lack of continuity in the administration of education; (d) sociopsychological resistance, even amongst administrators, with respect to planning; (e) absence of integration of educational planning into other fields related to national development, etc. etc.

The list is long and highly relevant, and the more one looks at it the more one sees that it applies, almost in its entirety, to the question of medical education. In fact, similar constraints lead into systematic isolation and this negative factor emerges as the main characteristic of educational programmes in the health sciences. This isolation can be exemplified not only by the typical sub-division of teaching of these sciences by a number of schools, faculties and institutes, but also by the lack of relationship between such institutions and the various agencies and organizations which should absorb and utilize the manpower produced by them. Besides a consistent lack of identification of needs there is also an absence of analysis of educational objectives and possible approaches to meet them. Most of the medical schools of the world thus appear as institutions modelled by a scholastic tradition based on a strong hierarchical system, and dominated by a very rigid administrative structure.

Great efforts are, no doubt, being made everywhere towards re-examining the educational systems for medical and allied health personnel, and towards formulating adequate plans in regard to this. Although there is still a long way to go, the old walls seem to be bending, if not cracking, and the prospects for significant changes can be well illustrated by the Technical Discussions held in Geneva in May 1970 on the occasion of the 23rd World Health Assembly.[6] In fact, during these Discussions 225 participants from 90 countries and 11 inter-governmental and non-governmental organizations attending the Assembly discussed the various aspects of the education and training of health workers; the need for quantitative and qualitative improvements in their education and training; the adaptation of curricula and teaching methods to national or local conditions; and, of course, the need to innovate and adapt.

The Discussions actually endeavoured to clarify how countries could orient their programmes for the preparation of health personnel in order to solve the problem of expanding health services in the face of financial and manpower limitations. The debates brought out several important points, namely: (a) that health planning, including health manpower, must take into consideration local and regional characteristics; (b) that coordination at all levels should be closely maintained between health agencies and educational institutions; (c) that the functions of each member of the health team, both at professional and auxiliary levels, should be defined on the basis of the society's health needs and the requirements of teamwork; (d) that the content and methods of training should be adapted to local circumstances; (e) that continuing education of all members of the health team is essential for the good quality of health work; (f) that the training of teachers of medical and allied health sciences, both from the quantitative and qualitative angle, deserve high priority; and (g) that evaluation and research are important factors in orienting the adaptation of educational programmes to the conditions and needs of a given area.

Although the education and training of health personnel has already been considered in a variety of national and international meetings, the World Health Assembly Technical Discussions of 1970 served to bring together those responsible for the planning and administration of the health services of practically every country of the world in order to discuss a problem common to all. As a preparatory measure for the meeting, the World Health Organization asked its Member Countries in 1969 to comment on their views and experience on the following points, including the basic issues to be debated:

(1) *Factors to be considered in developing education programmes for health personnel*, such as (*a*) coordination plans for public health and for education for the health professions; (*b*) education programmes for health personnel as an integral part of the national health plans; (*c*) pilot studies on the planning of health manpower according to the local socioeconomic and health conditions; (*d*) methods of evaluating the programmes of education for health personnel; and

(2) *Adapting education programmes for health personnel to the local, national or regional health needs*, such as (*a*) attempts to redefine responsibilities within the health team, including the development of new types of health personnel and of pluri-professional health teams; (*b*) adoption of schemes for the joint education of health personnel through the community health approach; (*c*) establishment of relationships between health services (Ministries of Health, social security agencies, etc.) on the one hand, and universities and medical schools on the other; (*d*) teachers' training and continuing education programmes.

The comments received—an impressive collection of homogeneous answers—formed the basis of the 'background document'[6] which served as a guideline for the Technical Discussions. The document clearly indicates that the dearth of health personnel is universal and that certain approaches to its solution are also becoming universally acceptable. It also states that ". . . if any single word could express the main concern, the word would be *adaptation*". In fact, the process of adaptation is inherent in planning, and, as the Director-General of WHO[2] stated in his address to the Fourth Rehovoth Conference:

"The success of all plans depends, in the last analysis, on the availability of people competent to carry them out. There is a shortage of trained persons everywhere and at all levels. But no educational system can be effective unless its purposes are defined. The members of the health team must be trained specifically for the tasks which they are destined to perform, taking into account the circumstances under which they will work. These tasks can only be defined in accordance with a plan in which the nature of the services to be provided is defined, priorities are allotted, and the staff needed to provide these services determined both in numbers and in terms of the training required for the duties envisaged. The training provided must then be tailored to meet these needs."

Five elements emerged from the Technical Discussions of 1970 as fundamental to the efforts of national health administrations for securing health personnel best suited to local needs and resources. In fact, the participants agreed that to provide the best possible services to

146

all segments of the population, urban or rural, in a developing or developed country, one cannot depend only on the highly trained physicians. Well-trained doctors should be ready to assume leadership of a team of health workers, including auxiliaries, in order to ensure both quality and efficiency of service. Adaptation of education for the health professions, including medicine, to the local health needs and resources, and a judicious distribution of functions between physicians, other health professions and auxiliary level personnel, seem to constitute the most promising solution to the problem of expanding health services in the face of manpower and financial limitations. National health administrations should thus be willing to provide for:

(a) close cooperation between those responsible for the provision of health services to the public and those responsible for the education of the required health personnel;

(b) reasonable distribution of functions between various members of the health professions and their auxiliaries, with attention to teamwork;

(c) effecting changes in the education programme, both as to the types of personnel to be trained and as to the content of their training;

(d) continuous education of all health personnel, both to refresh and to advance their basic knowledge, including pedagogic sciences for teaching staff;

(e) continuous study of the interrelationships between education and services and also of the performance of each of these two constituents—through systematic evaluation and operational research—with a view to introducing such changes whenever indicated.

The above points should be taken into account in the overall process of developing health manpower. Yet there can be no blueprint for the education of medical and allied health personnel: an approach which may be suitable in one situation may fail and cause stresses in another. A few basic principles may, however, serve as guidelines in this respect.

The first is that the education of health personnel should be regarded as a means towards the development of health services, rather than a final goal in itself. The second is that the types of health personnel who may be needed and the kinds of education programmes to be designed to prepare them must be determined by the nature of the local health problems and the corresponding health plans. The third is that education in the medical and allied health sciences—a very expensive undertaking especially for developing countries—should avoid fragmentation and subdivision, at least for the sake of economy, bringing together analogous programmes, faculties and facilities, through multiprofessional schemes for health workers of different kinds and levels. Multidisciplinary teaching also seems indicated both from the educational and financial angle. Finally, such schemes should be closely integrated with the local health services covering the whole range of institutions providing health attention and not solely with a teaching hospital. This means that teaching should be 'community health' or 'total health' oriented, rather than based only on the traditional individual care of hospitalized individuals.

As stated by Perkins[4] ". . . traditional education offers little nourishment for the most crucial needs of new countries, or for the needs of some older countries now in the process of modernization". In fact, there is at this time a considerable disturbance in medical schools of ancient foundation in countries where even recent educational reforms are being attacked by the student body itself. It is not enough to dismiss this spirit of protest and revolt as being altogether without foundation. It should rather make us search our own hearts, look back into our memories and ask ourselves if what we received in our time, and how it was given to us, was really the best for the great changes in scope and methods embodied in health practices today. And where we find indications for change we should not let tradition hamper us in our approach.

SUMMARY

"There can be no international blueprint for the development of health services. There are many alternatives, some of which may be suitable in one situation, whereas in others a different policy may be preferable."

This statement by Dr M. G. Candau, Director-General of the World Health Organization in his address to the Fourth Rehovoth Conference,[2] is perfectly applicable, *mutatis mutandis*, to the development of educational programmes in the medical and allied health sciences. Everyone agrees nowadays that countries should adopt an ecological approach towards their health services, and that the education and training of the manpower required should be adapted to local circumstances, as part of each national health plan. As a rule, however, such educational programmes do not aim to meet the requirements of societies undergoing rapid socioeconomic changes. Except in countries whose political patterns have led to centralized forms of public administration, the predominant structure for the education and training of health personnel is mostly in isolation from the institutions and agencies which absorb and utilize them. It is difficult to predict for how long this situation will last, even in countries which can afford the maintenance of structures which are, to say the least, rather uneconomical. In situations where teaching personnel and financial resources are limited, pluriprofessional schemes comprising the integration of the biological and health sciences during an introductory period, followed by horizontal integration between the

148

educational institutions and the existing health services throughout a 'community health' phase, seem to be the present trend. Such an approach, including also multidisciplinary teaching, cannot easily be implanted other than in new undertakings; yet the traditional orthodox schools of medicine and allied health sciences are gradually trying to associate with each other, especially for the preparation of their students under the total health, teamwork concept.

DISCUSSION

Bridger: International bodies tend to reach 'diplomatic' conclusions and to leave out the action which should be taken to achieve the desired objectives. How far did the Twenty-Third World Health Assembly go in defining the kind of help and instructions that could be given to WHO in developing new educational programmes in the health sciences?

Braga: An organization such as WHO has to be discreet, naturally. It is an instrument of its member countries and not a supranational organization. We are not supposed to judge what countries are doing or to force a country to do something differently. What we can do is to expose countries to the exchange of ideas, to expert committees, or to some novel approach. For example, some time ago WHO was invited by the Camerouns to see whether it would be possible to help them develop a medical school. A mission of highly qualified experts went there and recommended that a more or less traditional medical school should be organized, but the country simply could not afford this. Later, another mission tried to explore this situation from a different angle. Their suggestion was to organize a faculty of health sciences for the joint education of the basic members of the health team, and to establish models for the training of middle level and auxiliary personnel. This received the blessing and financial support of the United Nations Development Programme (UNDP). Work has already started and the Camerounians are very proud that this is being developed. Dr King, of course, is doing a beautiful job in his medical school in Zambia, and healthy rivalry between national institutions is also important.

The international body has to be able, or courageous enough, to say whether what a country wants is a good thing. Yet it has to be a sort of discreet salesman of new approaches.

Rebhun: I am glad Dr Braga emphasized the problem of adaptation, which I also made earlier in connexion with environmental health engineering practices in some of the developing countries. The main reason why academic personnel leave developing countries is not a financial one, I think. If this were the main reason there would be no academic personnel left in my country, because the salaries are only a fraction of those in the United States. Difficulties of adaptation may be one of the reasons why they leave. In environmental health engineering, many people from developing countries find that their education or training in the developed countries was not adapted to conditions at home. An extreme example: a person whose thesis was on environmental health problems in space ships and then goes back to a developing country where of course he cannot work on that subject, becomes frustrated and goes back to work for the American space programme. The problem of adaptation is one of the crucial problems in training health personnel. One possibility would be to use special programmes in graduate or undergraduate schools, as is being done in a few places.

Braga: This is precisely one of the points we are trying to stimulate. An expert committee meeting in Geneva about three years ago made very specific recommendations about the need to adjust training in environmental health, particularly in some areas of the world.[1] There is also the reverse picture which Dr Baker mentioned. Brazil, for example, is well supplied with environmental health engineers but the auxiliary personnel are scarce. But there are areas of the world which have neither category and WHO is now trying to stress local training in those areas. In Morocco, in cooperation with the local university, WHO has started a programme not only for advanced training in environmental health but also for the teaching of this subject at undergraduate level in the normal civil engineering course. Sanitarians and others are also included. WHO is trying to stimulate more training under local conditions for people who are going to work there.

Kisseih: Professor Young asked earlier what happened to people with lower professional preparation who supervised others with higher professional qualifications. This is very common in my profession, where many nurses find that the younger ones enter nursing with a higher education standard and are trained at a higher level. The only way out for these senior nurses who intend keeping their leadership posts in the nursing team is 'continuing nursing education'. Some are quite prepared for this and are willing to go back to school to acquire the necessary qualifications. Some, on the other hand, are inclined to think that it is only experience that matters. Fortunately for the nursing profession in Ghana, a majority of the senior nurses are prepared to improve on both their general and professional qualifications by returning to school periodically.

With regard to the term 'paramedical', I think this idea might have originated in the Soviet Union, where every non-medical member of the health professions is expected to progress to the level of the medical officer. This was made very clear to us during a tour of the Soviet Union organized by the World Health Organization in October 1966. All the nurses from the non-Communist countries at this seminar tried to impress on the Russians that nursing was a profession in its own right and that a nurse should not be made to feel that in order to satisfy her professional needs she must qualify as a doctor; but they did not take us seriously. They only laughed at us and stated that if we were to be honest with ourselves we would admit that in the health team the medical officer was always the team leader. In that country, apart from the medical officers, all other members of the health team were paramedicals.

I am glad that this word is now going out of fashion. All the members of the various health professions should be colleagues, since they each have a different role to play in the team. When we advocate higher nursing education in the universities for our nurses in Ghana, this is simply to make them more efficient in a team where many of the other members, including the pharmacists, the nutrition officers and the social workers, are also highly educated. Higher nursing education is never meant to drive the nurse from her own duties, as I understand is the problem in certain countries.

Christie: During the early planning of the University of Ibadan in Nigeria, the question was discussed very keenly of whether the right policy was to give students a full training according to Western standards or to give them a training like that of a *feldsher*, or of a peasant/doctor. Is that problem still an active one, or has it been solved?

Braga: This is still a serious question, possibly because those of us involved in the education of health personnel have not had sufficient training in what we call educational planning. In an educational programme you must first define the objectives precisely. Then you can establish the curriculum for the sort of personnel that you have to train. After that you have to evaluate whether you are reaching the objectives. This is the difficulty we have, because planning in the field of manpower for health is a recent development. We are learning more and more but we are still self-educators in this area. We have not been well prepared for the task and we may have not been doing the right thing. Medical and technological sciences have developed a long way, but the educational approach itself still has some way to go.

Christie: Aren't the problems in Africa really quite different from those in China? If a lower type of medical education was offered in Africa, people would get their medical education elsewhere so that they could do postgraduate studies elsewhere, which the *feldshers* cannot do. The argument at Ibadan was that there would be two forms of life, the higher forms educated abroad, and the lower forms educated in Nigeria. They would not agree to that.

Braga: It seems there are points common to all countries and certainly we have to have a universal consensus on some requirements for the education of all sorts of health personnel. But the type of training to be provided should be designed and provided locally, for people who will be working locally. The recognition of titles and diplomas is something else which involves many legal, political and cultural aspects, and although there are many examples of such recognition by countries through bilateral and even multilateral agreements, I do not really feel that we shall ever have a universal convention on this matter. But to be different does not mean to be inferior. Sometimes a person trained for a specific situation in a less developed country is as good as the man trained to deal with other health problems in a more sophisticated environment. If they are exchanged both of them will be in trouble, but in time they will overcome the difficulties and adjust themselves, provided of course that they have acquired that scientific knowledge which should be common to the two educational programmes. When we speak about medical education and medical schools we agree that we have to have some minimal requirements. We still debate whether medical training can be shortened. We still do not know, but we have already reached some consensus about the average length, the course content and the disciplines which are common to the education of a number of health workers in many areas. I fail to understand why education in the veterinary sciences is not combined, at least in the pre-clinical years, with medical education. If the demands or needs in the years to come are mainly in the developing world, where very little exists, ingenious solutions will have to be found and all possibilities, financial and otherwise, considered.

Hill: The difficulties in developing countries are those of timing and of the backdrop of general education throughout society. Two examples might explain this. Three years ago, I had to report on a medical laboratory school which was set up by the British Government in Pakistan, where we gave people with rather low secondary school education one and a half years' training. These boys were in great demand throughout Pakistan and we could not get them out fast enough. I was very impressed with this and subsequently I talked to the Minister of Education, who was also very impressed, and he said "You know, we have a thousand BSc's in Pakistan whom we cannot employ". I asked why they were not put in the hospital laboratories, and he was horrified at this. These BSc's are unemployable because they were intellectually too arrogant to do technician jobs, which in England our BSc's do.

The other example is about timing. When the university first started in Dar es Salaam they had an old medical auxiliary school and they decided to have a course lasting about four years for local graduates for which they got a diploma. The entrance was 'O' level, the lower secondary level, and then they found that no students with 'A' level went into medicine but chose the other faculties instead. The boys who had got in with 'O' level found that their diplomas had no international recognition.

After a lot of discussion they now do five years with an 'A' level entry requirement, which is going back to square one, 'keeping up with the Western Jones's'. So it is a very difficult question of timing, within this backdrop of education in general throughout the country.

King: In spite of all that we have heard of the importance of innovation, WHO is sometimes rather too conservative. When a team is called upon to advise on the setting up of a medical school and the doctors of a country want the conservative pattern, it is difficult for WHO to advise anything else. It is thus difficult for WHO to be radical. In Zambia, the original WHO blueprint that we were given for a medical school was much too conservative, particularly in regard to the type of teaching hospital that was advised. One of the most urgent needs would seem to be to teach medical students more under the conditions in which they will subsequently work in the district hospitals, rather than in a vast concrete colossus costing £12 million, of the type that we are now building in Zambia. I did my best to press these controversial views somewhat too late, and the only support that I had was from my colleagues in public health. The rest of the profession was completely against so radical an approach.

Russell: The medical school in Zaria, Nigeria, is now using training facilities in district hospitals and health centres. This medical school will be developed largely in the rural areas, not in a large centre at all. It should be a very interesting experiment.

In medical colleges in various tropical countries I find that very often 'tropical medicine' is being taught as such. Not only that, but one comes across various courses in tropical medicine. While I feel reasonably sure that Pakistanis or Thais are not, for example, doing research on Chagas' disease, it seems there is something wrong with the thinking that regards 'tropical medicine' as something special in a tropical country. I would like to see tropical medicine go out of the syllabus and out of the thinking in tropical countries, where medical students should be simply trained to practise medicine in the context of their own country's needs.

Many of the doctoral theses in paediatrics and preventive and social medicine would really equate with a dissertation for a Diploma in Public Health. There was often little original work or thinking, and this was disturbing; the difficulty seems to be to get deans of medical colleges and staff who have perhaps been trained in Western countries to see that the time is ripe for a complete change in outlook.

Dogramaci: A great deal of blame must be laid on the developed countries that sponsor medical schools in Africa. Ibadan was sponsored by London University, and the ambition of every French-speaking African country is to adopt the syllabus of Paris. The professors in Paris or London University are not even able to improve their own curricula, yet the developing countries are trying to do something even

153

more dangerous and adapt these already out-dated curricula to their own conditions. Professor Christie asked earlier whether the medical education was of middle level or of a high Western standard. I do not agree with this. The standard could be very high, but not in Western terms. We could accept medical teaching which is adapted to the local conditions, with standards much better than in Paris, New York or London, but best suited to the needs of a particular country. This could be done by two means. One is to tell Paris, London, New York, to accept these experimental curricula for postgraduate work, and the second is to thank WHO for telling Camerounians to go not to Paris but to Sherbrooke in Canada.

Wolstenholme: When the new medical faculty started in Ethiopia it had a combined pre-clinical division, with no separate departments of anatomy, physiology, pharmacology and so on. I doubt if any of the medical schools in London would not benefit by something of the kind, but this was deeply resented by the Ethiopian students and it took a great deal of argument to persuade them otherwise. They regarded it as a deliberate experiment on an underdeveloped country.

Braga: WHO has been attempting to overcome this sort of feeling by taking local people, particularly the ones being prepared for teaching positions, to places where these new approaches had been adopted, such as Latin America, the United States, Canada, and Hacettepe University in Turkey. This method seems to be rather successful.

Young [*Comment added in proof*]: I have been a member of the Inter-University Council for Higher Education Overseas for some time. It was this Council that advised the British Government to make available funds for the foundation of university institutions such as that at Ibadan, while the University of London, by virtue of the fact that its Statutes permit the granting of degrees to external students, agreed to institute a 'Special Relationship' with these new institutions so that their graduates could receive the internationally recognized degrees of the University of London. This arrangement was in no way imposed on the newly established University Colleges in Africa and elsewhere. Indeed, those institutions were most anxious to have such an arrangement as a protection against any possible criticism that their courses and degrees were of second-class quality. The 'Special Relationship' between the University of London and University Colleges abroad has now almost completely come to an end, and the newly fledged universities are arranging their own courses and examinations.

I am myself one of those who believe that developing universities in African and other territories under British influence would have done better to have based their courses on a less highly specialized pattern than that for degrees of the University of London. But the fact is that in the early days they would have regarded any degree specially designed for them as being an inferior product, and a poor substitute for the 'real thing', which is what they demanded.

Dickson: Dr Baker made a plea that the Ciba Foundation should concern itself further with paramedical education. Interest in their role derives principally from the lack of health services in remoter parts of the world. But it could also be viewed as one way of creating employment for people seeking work of this kind. Recently someone pointed out that the famous Oxfam poster with the pot-bellied child should be taken down, because except for isolated pockets of starvation it no longer related to the major social problems of Africa: it should be replaced with a picture of school-leavers outside a labour exchange showing a notice 'no vacancies'.

What we need to export from the West to the developing countries is job creativity. At present very little thought is being given to this. There are the Intermediate Technology people* with E. F. Schumacher in London, and in the United States there is the group† inspired by Frank Riessman, co-author of *New Careers for the Poor*.[2] A great many young people have the heart to care for others but lack the required educational qualifications. It becomes particularly poignant in my work in Britain, when I see young offenders specially released to care for handicapped children, giving themselves with such devotion that at the end of their temporary attachment they say "This is the job I would like to do." If only we could get that lad accepted professionally we would be killing two birds with one stone: we would be giving help where help is needed, and we would be enabling him to achieve fulfilment.

Here is a marriage of two needs: the need for staff in the caring professions and the need of young people to have such work. Hardly anybody is interesting themselves in this. If this is a too delicate problem for WHO, could not a smaller Foundation like the Ciba Foundation give a cutting edge to research in this field?

---

* Intermediate Technology Development Group, 9 King Street, London, W.C.2.
† New Careers Development Center, New York University, N.Y. 10003.

12: Philosophy of Management: The Place of the Professional Administrator

B. L. SALMON

I HAVE a plaque in my office with the following inscription:

> "Nothing will ever be attempted if all possible objections
> must be first overcome."

I do not think I have attempted to overcome all or any of the objections that might be raised as a result of this paper and, indeed, I view this session as a challenge to explain my concept of management, in order to have a better understanding of management problems. The objections (and I am sure there will be many) have to be discussed and overcome after the event, in accordance with my plaque.

Let me start by stating categorically that I do not claim to know all about the subject of management, nor am I an academic or theorist on the subject. Indeed, my thinking and my attitudes are the result of practical experience of management and of trying to understand, and indeed change, management attitudes in a business situation and also in a hospital situation. I must dispel the illusion that business and industry, any more than the Hospital Service, have a complete understanding of management.

At best we are all in a learning situation, and our understanding is only in the emergent stage. Management is not a science, nor is it something that is static: it is changing all the time, with the result that it is ever more difficult to keep up with its principles and concepts. Much of what was accepted practice 15 years ago is today out of date: we are all developing at such a pace that one of the problems managers are faced with is continuing and continuous change, and therefore they need to be able to change to meet the new situation.

But there are principles and concepts of management that have developed as a result of experience, of thinking and of experiments, and today it can be claimed that the manager's job can be both studied and understood. Thus managers can learn about the skills of management in order to improve their effectiveness as managers.

Let me therefore try and define management in the simplest way possible: it is the process involved in the function of managing. Managing is the function of ordering and coordinating other functions and the persons fulfilling them to achieve an end product or to give a service. More

157

recently, a further dimension has become increasingly important, i.e. creating the climate within which subordinates and colleagues can share in setting objectives and effectively fulfilling their independent roles.

Associated with this definition there is a requirement to appreciate certain important principles involved in the modern concept of management:

Principle No. 1 is that managers should be in a position to make decisions fitting to their jobs, and, furthermore, that any decision should be taken, wherever possible, at the level or position where the responsibility for it is the relevant one for the job. A manager has got to know his authority and the powers, discretion and constraints associated with it. Equally, he must still earn the right to exercise it through his own performance, attitudes and behaviour, but this does not mean that the senior manager is absolved from responsibility for his subordinates. Delegation of authority is possible without abrogating responsibility.

Principle No. 2 is that only a limited number of managers can report directly to a senior manager. This can be any number depending on circumstances, the nature of the situation and the characteristics of the tasks involved. If a manager has too many managers accountable to him he is unable to devote the time necessary to the individual managers for whom he is responsible. If he has too few he will find himself doing the jobs of his junior managers and he will be unable to delegate satisfactorily. This second principle of mine is a pragmatic approach based on my experience. Theoretically one can argue that the key principle concerns the tasks and objectives of the manager and that in practice these tasks and objectives fail to be achieved if the manager has too few or too many staff reporting to him.

Principle No. 3 concerns the selection and development of managers. All managers have appraising and training functions to perform, and these are closely interrelated. They also need to have a good deal of awareness, matching people to jobs and circumstances, for a subordinate manager must be helped, counselled, trained and developed to carry out his job by a senior manager. This doesn't mean that the junior manager takes no decisions but it does mean that the senior manager has a responsibility to ensure that his junior manager is helped to make the right decision. It also means that the senior manager advises and helps in the career development of his subordinates. And this is one of the senior manager's prime responsibilities. Likewise, junior managers are required to act in the same way with their supervisors and supervisors with their staff.

Principle No. 4: managing involves coordination. In complex management situations today, a manager may have structural authority over other managers, and obviously on occasions he gives orders and makes decisions, but inevitably he must also communicate with colleagues and with experts and specialists, whose advice must be sought if he is to make the right decision. Coordinating the advice of interdependent and different viewpoints is a major task in itself. It requires not only the capacity for balancing and optimizing on the part of the manager himself but an awareness of the nature of the different specialities. Equally, a manager must have an understanding of groups and the factors and forces which can operate in them to affect the decision being made. Whether a manager takes advice or not is *his* decision but managers usually have the opportunity of being helped and being influenced. These aids are often known as the 'tools of management' and it is basic that a manager must understand what the tools are and how to use them.

Principle No. 5 concerns communication and the responsibility of a senior manager to keep his own staff and managers informed. If a manager is to do his job successfully he must understand the policy and changes of policy which are agreed. Information must pass not only up and down the different lines but across them, otherwise the subordinate managers will be working in a vacuum.

Principle No. 6: a manager is responsible for the function or part of a function, which may or may not be technical, and for the people carrying out that function. The people are vital. This means that every manager has personnel responsibilities, none of which are diminished because there is a personnel manager to advise. The personnel manager is required to manage his own staff—that is his executive role—and the rest of his job is advisory.

Management thinking today is still based on principles of hierarchy and accountability of the individual. Although I realize this has been challenged at this symposium, my comment is that if the hierarchical system is to be replaced, it will be accomplished by evolutionary means and therefore it is necessary at least in the short term to work from within the hierarchical framework towards the future. Broadly speaking, in any management situation we are concerned with three levels of management, namely first-line managers, middle managers, and top managers. Furthermore, within each level there are grades as well. Usually there are two, or perhaps three, grades to each level of management. These grades may be different and not congruent throughout an organization, depending on the tasks to be performed and the degree of responsibility associated with the job.

At the lowest level of management, or 'first-line management', it is the manager's function to carry out, i.e. execute, the policy decisions that have been programmed by the middle managers. The title 'first-line manager' implies that he has no managers under him. He may have technicians, foremen, charge-hands or staff. Senior supervision is often included within this level of management. The first-line manager's job is to see that the policy as programmed is correctly executed by all his staff; he must be encouraged to bring his own people into that decision-making and he must be given scope to make his own decisions and plans within his terms of reference.

Over the first-line managers are managers at middle management level who are responsible for the programming of policy decisions, that is, setting the purpose, direction and the limits within which those who execute the policy may decide to act. Middle managers manage other managers.

At the top level, top management are responsible for setting the policy, and top managers manage middle managers.

Perhaps I could clarify the three levels of management by saying that *first-line managers* are primarily concerned with the execution of day-to-day decisions, *middle managers* are primarily concerned with programming decisions and are therefore the short-term planners, and *top managers* are primarily concerned with policy decisions and are therefore the long-term planners.

Today a manager cannot carry out his function, however good he may be, unless he has services or tools of management available to him, for one cannot expect him to be expert in all fields. He must therefore seek the expert's advice. But, whatever the services or tools are, those responsible for them are only advisers and it is the manager at all levels who must take the decision. If he does not heed the expert's advice, it is his decision, and it is at his own peril for he is accountable for his performance.

One of the most difficult tasks of the manager is to understand what the tools of management can provide and how best the experts can be briefed. A manager has therefore to understand fundamentally the techniques involved, but it does not mean that he has to be expert in that science or service. Among the services—tools of management—available to managers are work study and ergonomics, computers, management accounting and budgetary controls, operations research and personnel services. And there are a host of others!

I want now to dwell for a short time on management philosophy, for it seems to me that unless managers can understand what the objectives of an organization, and their own personal objectives, are, they cannot manage successfully. However many levels of management there are we must not forget that managers are human beings and not machines, that they must be used to the best advantage of the organization, and that this cannot be done unless there is a desire amongst all managers to understand themselves and each other and to work together for an agreed goal. Above all else, management thinking must be flexible and fit in with the requirements of the organization. Furthermore, it is important to remember that the needs of the organization and the individual manager must be reconciled. This entails, for the manager as well as the organization, assessing those areas where there are congruent, complementary and diverse objectives.

Good management essentially requires good communications— upwards, downwards and across the board. It also requires a philosophy such as management by objectives, which inevitably means that managers must have detailed specified job descriptions so that they can agree their management objectives with their senior managers at regular intervals, say quarterly, and the manager must be appraised of his attainment of these agreed objectives.

Since the material with which we manage is managers, we need to understand ourselves. The individual has needs as well as the organization and both needs ought to be met, although in practice this rarely happens. Managers must become committed to the principles of 'management by objectives', not as a technique, but as a personal conviction and a management philosophy.

I have given considerable thought to the subjects of business management and hospital management in the United Kingdom, and, although there are differences, the essential requirements of management are the same. The fact that business is profit-orientated and a hospital is not does not alter the manager's role—he has different objectives. I am convinced that good management is a philosophy that is applicable in any situation—in business, in the Hospital Service, in international organizations, or in any work where managers are required.

I have spoken at length on management structure and management philosophy, but I have left to this time my own thinking on structural authority. This is certainly a necessity today in the context of any large organization, but one must not think that once having laid down the structure everything will automatically work smoothly; in any event, structural authority is limited. It is the mechanistic approach to an organization; it may look sensible in diagrammatic form on paper but that is about all. What is required for the 1970s is that managers understand their jobs and their authorities and understand how to work together. Commitment by the individual manager is of prime importance. Structural authority gives one the right to control, command and instruct, but in addition to this there is the requirement that those with authority should understand their managers, work with them, and help them to commit themselves to the agreed objectives. A manager today cannot wear blinkers and remain an efficient manager. He will have to consult colleagues, senior and junior managers, outside experts and inside ones. He must be able to take part in group discussions and contribute to the group. This is abundantly true in the Hospital Service, for not only is there the involvement of managers with managers within the medical or hospital or nursing administrations, but these arms of the Hospital Service must be considered totally and in relation to each other.

161

Throughout a hospital group, doctors and nurses and hospital admini-strators at different levels are working together with technicians, para-medical personnel, domestic staff, porters, cooks and a multitude of others. For a hospital group to be managed efficiently all the services and resources of the hospital must be coordinated—and not just at the top level.

It therefore seems to me that there are two spheres of authority, one structural and one influential or sapiential. In addition to structural authority, every manager must know how to use his sapiential authority and to make use of the sapiential authority of other managers. As I see it, there are spheres of authority and spheres of influence, and every manager is concerned with both. Managers can only succeed if they understand their sphere of influence and know the sphere of influence of other managers. This sphere of influence, of course, involves the use of specialists and this is one of the most difficult aspects of management to understand, for specialists and experts, whether they be doctors, accoun-tants, lawyers, computer programmers or engineers, cannot be taken as a homogeneous group—we need to differentiate the specialists concerned according to their capacity to relate to the individual, to the team and to the organization or institution, in terms of understanding the situation, the problems and the character of management. One can have a top-flight surgeon, brilliant at his job, but quite irrelevant in the top management category—where regretfully men like this sometimes abound. On the other hand, another top-flight surgeon could give the kind of medical/organizational advice which resulted in a better long-term decision than the contribution of the Senior Hospital Administrator or the Chairman of the Board.

Thus there are certain specialities which may be studied and practised academically, professionally or organizationally. But the capacity of the specialist adviser to earn the right to share in the management and deci-sion-making at any one of the three levels of management depends on his ability to fit in with the organization and understand its requirements and problems.

To sum up, may I say that the real job of a manager is to understand his people and their jobs and to take the decisions that are appropriate. He can only function successfully if his role is defined and if he knows what is required of him. Good management depends on good communica-tions and on having the right man in the right job. There is no such thing as an ideal structure; there is, however, an appropriate structure for every situation, but please remember that, however appropriate it may be today, it will inevitably change tomorrow.

Perhaps at this late stage it is appropriate for me to admit that I have no knowledge or experience of international organizations, but I would like to suggest that the basic principles that I have enunciated apply to the international situation. I realize, of course, that the complexity is intensified; that one is concerned with cross-cultural environment, and therefore that the interdependence factor in management will be even more difficult to achieve. I realize, too, that the location of the enterprise, team or institution, becomes additionally important when the organism is outside a national setting. What I have attempted to do in this paper is to emphasize the essentials of management; and it is the management of an institution or organization that is the means by which teams or groups can be developed. Without this context a team or group has no purpose and no meaning today.

DISCUSSION

Hockey: Before I ask my question I would like to say that Mr Salmon was chairman of a very important committee which produced a most far-sighted report on senior nursing staff structure[2]. In applying management principles to the hospital structure, this report, where its recommendations are accepted, has completely revolutionized nursing in hospitals. It has given order and good sense to a very unwieldy structure that has existed for many years, and has at last given nurses in management positions and roles their 'proper status'.

My question is: is the philosophy of management dependent on the size of the establishment? It seems to me that it should not be, but at the same time there are organizations which seem too small to allow the three levels of management to exist.

Salmon: I cannot quantify it, but I think the philosophy of management is applicable even in the smallest organizations. In these the three levels of management are combined under an entrepreneur who makes all the decisions because there is no other manager to function. Therefore, unless the organization is almost a one-man business it is still possible to have the three levels.

Hill: Could you develop the argument about top management being concerned with policy and that it is unnecessary to be an expert in every subject? Is it necessary, in the international sphere, for the Director-General of WHO to be a doctor? In the national sphere, do you think the Minister of Health in England should be a doctor? At the hospital level what do you think of the medical superintendent as distinct from the lay-manager?

Salmon: I think it is more important to choose the Director-General, or the Minister of Health, or whatever he is, for his qualities as a manager and his ability to take part in policy discussions than to promote him purely because of his technical brilliance in the subject. Medical superintendents did a job in the hospital service up to a few years ago, but I would not recommend that they should be reintroduced. The cogwheel system[3] which organizes medical administration into divisions responsible to a medical executive committee, which in turn is responsible to the hospital authority—a committee system of administration—is functioning reasonably well in those areas where it has been introduced, and is a far better way for professional medical people to operate than in a completely hierarchical situation of their own. Doctors do not like a hierarchy above them, though I do not think they mind it below them. They are individuals and one has to bear this in mind in any organization.

Dickson: When working in dependent territories I frequently found that the Governor was a man of enlightenment, genuinely anxious to introduce more liberal policies. Younger members of the Service only recently arrived in the country were sometimes equally anxious to identify themselves with such policies, but between them and the Governor came an intervening layer of provincial commissioners, who were adamantly opposed to such innovations. So nothing happened.

More recently I have become interested in a scheme whereby troops and officers in the armed services are released for military aid to the community. I find that generals see the political implications of this and are in favour of it. The troops find it makes sense and enjoy doing something more useful than normal peace-time soldiering. But between the two lie majors and colonels who are determined that this shall not be: such work does not belong to what they call 'the profession of arms'. So nothing happens. I believe this is a syndrome which is to be found in a great many organizations. What is the solution to this middle-level manpower problem?

Salmon: If the Governor-General or whoever it is really believes in a new situation or organization, he must first train and develop his own staff to think about and carry out what he believes in. He has to get their commitment. If he does not, the troops cannot be expected to do what the commanding officer thinks is required. It may be difficult to do but the solution itself is simple: it is to pass the thinking down the line and to get the group commitment of the brigadiers, the colonels and the majors.

Banks: It is perhaps implicit in what you said that to carry out these principles anywhere there must be highly trained professional managers at all three levels. Their essential duty in every sphere of life is to make the wheels go round, to organize and supply equipment and the like. But I do not yet see how to fit this into the work of health teams, which have to deal with the elimination, prevention, treatment and rehabilitation of disease. I am thinking in terms of the pattern of disease on a major scale, in the developing countries especially. The pattern of disease itself is changing. Disease does not always depend on known factors, let alone controllable factors. You have the environment, you have the host, you have the other living things and above all you have the most difficult material in the world to deal with, the plastic unknown, the human material when it is sick. How can we fit in these highly trained professionals, whom we certainly must have, with the equally essential teams?

Salmon: The institution or organization responsible for these teams should have the management thinking and philosophy which eventually one would want to be created throughout. If you can develop it first at the centre of the organization you can gradually get the seed to flourish. One cannot just build a team in some part of the world and think it is going to flourish without the background and the support that is required from an organization or an institution. I do not know enough about the building of world health teams to be able to comment on difficulties like this.

Banks: This is what I was hoping you would say, that it has to grow. The danger is that people will try to change things too quickly.

King: I agree very much with what has been said about the importance of management in medicine, and I am very concerned with how we can best give our students some glimmerings of the management role. In developing countries very soon after qualification they go out and manage their own district hospitals, so this would seem to be a useful subject to be considered within the context of medical sociology. I am searching around for ways of teaching it.

Salmon: It is urgent and necessary to give information, even to students, on what management is all about. I do not know how this can be incorporated into the medical education curriculum, but I am sure that it will have to be, and that it is possible to use sociologists to teach this in an academic area. The sooner it is understood by all future doctors that management is of vital importance to their profession, the better.

Dogramaci: Last year at Hacettepe University we formed a committee of students to study and criticize the management of our teaching hospitals. They became very much interested in this, they made up questionnaires, and they went and investigated the problems. In this way they not only helped us but they learnt a great deal.

Salmon: That is an excellent idea, well worth pursuing in other places.

Dogramaci: If the first-line managers are in some way dissatisfied with the middle-level managers should they be allowed to report directly to the top manager? Wouldn't it be desirable at times not to have the middle-range manager at all but just to stick to the first-line manager and the top manager?

Salmon: I do not think it is normally possible to work with two levels of management instead of three, because the responsibilities of either top managers or the first-line managers become too diverse. They become responsible for different types of decisions and whereas one can make a decision if one is a first-line manager, if one has to be a first-line manager and a middle manager it becomes extremely difficult to take the two decisions. I do not think the first-line man can report directly to the top manager, but of course it is not just his middle-level manager who is interested in him. Normally both father and grandfather take an interest in the child. What the manager is doing with his junior manager, how the junior manager is being rewarded, how he is working and whether he is achieving his objectives or not, are all problems that are discussed between the middle manager and his senior. The senior manager is often involved directly with his subordinate's managers. I attend many meetings where my managers are present and I see their managers working as well. Therefore the senior manager can see what is going wrong, if it is going wrong, and can take action with his manager.

Christie: Most hospital managers or superintendents have absolute security of tenure. Many of them become more and more ineffective and a few of them, particularly the medical superintendents, become inefficient despots. What do you think of security of tenure among the higher echelons of management?

Salmon: I think very little of it. A manager should stay in his job only if he has the competence and the ability to carry out and to go on carrying out the job, and if he meets the objectives that have been set for him. If he does not meet the objectives and if he is incompetent he should be removed from the job. I do not agree with life appointments on principle. They are anti-management.

Russell: Do you see any special difference between management and administration in government service? In developing countries, particularly in south-east Asia, one comes across the most appalling examples of what one can only describe as gross mismanagement. They usually arise because management is fixed in a bureaucratic pattern with fixed procedures for everything and, regardless of the urgency of any given situation, administrators say these are the procedures that have to be followed.

Salmon: Administration *is* management, when you analyse it. Civil services have a different view of what an administrator should do from a professional manager's view, but they both encompass the same skills. The difficulty in civil services throughout the world may be that they laid down a clear-cut system where merit and reward have little meaning, whereas in business and in some of the institutional worlds you have to be competitive; you have to show merit if you want to get on. This is one of the vital differences. In England, as a result of the Fulton Report[1], the Civil Service is now examining the whole of its own administrative structure. Many changes will probably take place in management within the Civil Service as a result, certainly in England and maybe even outside.

166

13: Teamwork at Ministry level

ANTONIO ORDOÑEZ-PLAJA

NEED FOR TEAMWORK

'DISEASE' and 'health' are two words frequently used in private conversations, in national and international political speeches, in sociological, anthropological and demographical meetings where health themes are discussed; and all the people who use the terms disease and health take as a starting point the idea that their definitions—if such definitions exist or have any meaning at all—or the images evoked by these two words are the same for the listener as well as the speaker. Yet possibly not even a meeting of experts who have memorized the WHO definition* would be able to bridge the communication gap. And when a discussion is held between persons of different cultural backgrounds, the conceptual discrepancies can have incalculable dimensions.

On an island of oyster fishermen, an individual who can stay under water for several minutes would be considered 'healthy' even if he had goitre, intestinal parasites and a cutaneous melanoma. In a large city an individual who can fulfil his office work and resist three hours on the subway is considered healthy even if he cannot swim. But his boss will allow him to miss work and see a doctor if he has a benign skin lesion or an allergic rhinitis.

In the early days of public health we can say that the basic responsibility, or almost the only one, of the health administrator was reduced to the control of epidemics, a term which, by the way, was used at that time solely to refer to contagious diseases. Little by little, preventive medicine has evolved from a magical, and sometimes empirical, phase to a rational and progressively scientific phase. At any rate, the scanty knowledge of an earlier period could easily be assimilated by one person who could assume total responsibility.

At present, when epidemiology has enlarged its field of study to all the diseases which affect important population groups (paradoxically returning to the original meaning of the word), it has become indispensable to utilize sister disciplines—biostatistics and ecology, to name only two—

* "Health is a state of complete physical, mental and social well-being and not merely the absence of disease or infirmity." [From the Preamble to the Constitution of the World Health Organization.]

to carry out acceptable epidemiological research or simply to be able to evaluate and interpret adequately any pathological phenomenon affecting the community as a whole or in part. In the same sense, the measures to correct most of the situations conditioning disease must take into account and must show intelligent use of modern communication science, sociology, anthropology and political science in order to elicit the collaboration of citizens and to obtain the administrative measures that almost always imply decisions at the political level—as in air and water pollution, in the fight to control noise or in the prevention of abuses of therapeutic procedures which are in vogue. From the administrative point of view, the delegation of duties and the knowledge of modern management techniques which concentrate more on human resources than on formulas are essential for coping with complex contemporary problems.

Undoubtedly there are other reasons, but I believe that with those mentioned above, one scientific and the other administrative, we have more than sufficient reasons to reach the conclusion that not even that all-rounder, the humanist Pico della Mirandola, if he were alive and concentrating all his efforts on public health, could handle those problems single-handed. In today's world this vacuum can only be filled by the coordinated work of a multidisciplinary team. The illusion that the computer would be able to replace man is simply the persistence of belief in magic; and it appears that, underneath it all, man still clings to this belief.

DEFINING AND RECRUITING THE TEAM

A team is a group of persons with different levels of knowledge, abilities and personalities who must complement each other and who share a common, unifying goal. The team must have a leader. The leader should be able to evaluate the team adequately and should know the motivations of each member in order to stimulate and to enhance its potentialities.

It is not easy to accept the fact that a team is necessary, possibly because of the persistence in the adult of infantile fantasies of omnipotence. It is even more difficult, however, to create and maintain a team.

Some basic requisites are indispensable for the successful integration of a health team. The members, whatever their profession, must have a common goal: health improvement as an end in itself and as a means of increasing the general welfare. It is absolutely imperative that the members of a health team, besides understanding their objectives, should come to a consensus as to the means of achieving them. They must simultaneously be in agreement in regard to such fundamental points as the definitions of health and disease and about the priorities for establishing goals. Priorities should be established by taking into account research findings and community needs, and they should be established by the team itself. These points of strategy of action could cause conflicts which a good team should make use of to gain a better integration of proposals and the mechanisms to fulfil them.

Since universal definitions of the terms health, disease and welfare are meaningless, we have to accept that only a working definition, and therefore a transitory one, will be useful. It can be reached only if we adjust what we think about health and welfare to what the people think about it and to what they perceive as their most urgent needs in that respect.

Obviously it is not easy to find lawyers, architects, economists, administrators and auxiliary personnel disposed to dedicate themselves to these objectives, since their professional training has prepared them in other directions. However, our experiences in Colombia in the last four years have shown us that this is possible and also useful and convenient.

Under these conditions, the forming of a team requires time. It implies, of course, a knowledge of the human resources in the country, which are generally found in the universities or research centres. Because of this, a good measure of political stability is imperative, since, besides the time required for the selection of personnel, it is obvious that the candidates chosen will not want to leave their own jobs only to suffer the consequences of a public administration where there is little guarantee of being able to carry out emotionally satisfying work. The fact that working conditions offered by the government are generally inferior to those provided by the university is a positive factor in that it guarantees the true and profound motivation of those who make this sacrifice. They do so in order to reach objectives to which they must be completely loyal. Personal loyalty on the part of the team members towards the leader will be developed afterwards.

The leader must work as much or more than any one of the members of the team. He must accept the fact that each member of the team knows more in his speciality area than himself, and he must select the members on this basis. But he must also demonstrate to the group that he has an overall vision of the whole which permits him to make the decisions in the final analysis.

We must clearly distinguish between 'making decisions' after consultation with the group and 'giving orders' to the group or to individuals or to subgroups. The latter is not compatible with group dynamics—it would be a return to the old system of 'bossism', because it means no shared participation or responsibility, the highest elements of teamwork. The leader who becomes a 'chief', or who is feared and obeyed, but not respected, is not part of the team; he is the owner, the master. As for the *time* dedicated to the job, if the chief rests on his laurels while the others work, it will be impossible to conserve morale.

169

SOME PROBLEMS OF TEAM RELATIONSHIPS

In a world in which the generation gap widens daily, it is important that the team should contain representatives of various age groups. Without ignoring the fact that youth contributes great impulse, it seems to me more significant that the young members understand better the behaviour of their contemporaries—and let us remember that they are more than half the world population.

The egotistic person or the *prima donna* is obviously incompatible with teamwork; and this also applies to the leader. The leader can occasionally use a discreet dose of 'display' if it leads to furthering the prestige of the team or aids basic objectives—those to which the group's prestige is committed. Of course, when one member of the group stands out because of the recognition given him by his own team, this is excellent. But if the leader raises one member of the team above the others, then we enter upon dangerous ground because, unless his praise is very realistic and precise, he will awaken envy in someone.

When a show-off insists on his own glory, the situation becomes serious. The team will not tolerate such a situation and, I think, the reaction is reasonable. The group develops a sense of power which makes them feel that *only* they, and *as a group*, can decide when one of their members can, should, and has a right to stand out as noteworthy. If the prestige of one member stands out excessively, the image of the leader and of the group deteriorates. The concrete fact is that in a well-structured team the deviant is automatically sanctioned by the other members, and this is one of the reasons for the force of the team and for its cohesiveness.

In the final analysis, the team members are defending the working philosophy and the integrity of the group—often intuitively or unconsciously—and giving a proof of their loyalty to the leader and to the objectives he represents. Its counterpart is most stimulating. Any attack or external aggression against one member of the team is perceived as aggression against the group as such. All group members will react in the face of external forces with all their vigour and internally comfort and support the man under fire. The person under attack feels totally supported and, at the same time, functions always in accordance with the philosophy and behavioural patterns of the group through loyalty and/or convenience, if we want to examine this in the most pragmatic and realistic manner.

Teamwork requires, among other things, that the members have an image of their team-mates which coincides as precisely as possible with reality. In addition, each member must have a self-image which adjusts to reality as much as possible and thus coincides with the image the other members have of him.

When the leader selects a friend to join the team, he is taking a serious risk. On the one hand, he imagines that the friend's behaviour at work will be an extrapolation of previous behaviour on the socio-affective level. This presumption is probably much more false than true. The conditions are completely different. His attitudes and behaviour at work will not be determined by the same values as those he uses in social relations. On the other hand, neither the friend nor the team members will be able to ignore the fact, in terms of image, that he is a friend of the leader.

Discordances between image, reality, behaviour and motivation can create situations of intolerable tension. Friendship alone is a bad basis for selection. Obviously, a new member of the team can be a friend of the leader or of any member of the team, but the selection should not be made *on* that basis, but *in spite of it*, if we want to avoid the fallacy of 'affective extrapolation'.

To conclude, the following observations are intended to lead us to a discussion of ideas:

(a) A problem in Latin American countries, and perhaps in other developing countries too, is that, historically, we have not been able to make the citizens, or even the political leaders, rely on or have faith in teams. Leadership has generally been based on the concept of the 'strong man', who is responsible for all and who is the only one who can get things done.

(b) Thus, a *team instead of a strong man* is a new idea. It is a concept which has had to be sold to our society and which has had to convince it that group dynamics is valid. No one has wanted to rely on a team or feel that group participation could be a fulfilling or a rewarding activity. We must therefore not only convince political leaders and representatives and people in general of the efficiency of teamwork, but also show them its advantages. In this way, a team will be beneficial because it will be *used* and team members can be trained for group activity which will be much more productive than individualistic competition.

(c) We must try to institutionalize our concepts of teamwork and also avoid the rigidity which often occurs in highly developed systems, where individual contributions are ignored and creativity stifled.

This paper should be viewed as a first draft or a preliminary report, resulting from four years of biased observation because of my personal participation in the health team in Colombia.

Because of a forthcoming change in government in Colombia (in August 1970), at least the three top members of the health team will disappear from the scene. A big open question remains: what will happen afterwards? Will the objectives be strong enough to keep the group together under different leading personalities? Will the new

171

members adjust or tolerate the established behaviour and ways of action of the team?

A discussion of these and related questions will be most helpful for me so that I can start writing the second draft on this subject—which I intend to do in the months after August with the perspective that only the past tense can give.

A participant-observer is a biased observer, and I am fully aware that when we have done something with love we tend to fall in love with what we have done.

SUMMARY

(1) *Need for teamwork*

    (*a*) Health and disease are complex concepts influenced by the cultural and physical environment.

    (*b*) In earlier days public health was limited to controlling and/or preventing communicable diseases, and a capable person could by himself handle public health matters.

    (*c*) Today no single person can have enough of the knowledge about technical, cultural and political variables necessary to make sound decisions.

(2) *Defining and recruiting the team*

A team is the only means to replace the impossible 'know-all-boss'. The team should be interdisciplinary and at the same time share similar goals and ideas.

Loyalty to the leader could develop later, but should not be considered as a prerequisite for selection; in fact, it is desirable that loyalty does not exist at the time of recruitment.

The team should not be selected on the basis of the leader's personal friendship or on what could be labelled 'affective extrapolation'.

At the early stage of team building we should look for persons who fit in with the leader without implying by this that they should be 'yes' men. As the team grows we should look for persons who fit the team. Emotional stability is an important trait, but what we should try to achieve is a team in which personalities compensate and complement mutually; that is, there should be what could be called 'compensatory neurosis in the group'.

(3) *Functions of the team*

The ultimate goal of the team is health improvement as an end in itself and as a means of increasing general welfare.

Misuse of the team by the leader for selfish motives, for political reasons or for other purposes destroys the concept of the team.

Unpredictable behaviour will seldom occur if the self-image of the team members coincides with the group image.

DISCUSSION

Salmon: Is the leader of such a team project chosen by the other members, or is he selected for his knowledge of management and of what is required?

Ordoñez-Plaja: No democracy yet goes so far as to have a Secretary of State elected by a team! He is always appointed by a head of state or by parliament, directly or indirectly.

Salmon: Can the members of this team have their own career development and proceed from the team to further responsibilities? Or once in the team do they stay there until the team dissolves?

Ordoñez-Plaja: All the members of my team were chosen from universities and research centres. I insisted that they spend at least two hours a day in teaching and/or research so that they would never become bureaucratized and would always have one foot in their home base. When a new government comes they can either work with it if the objectives are maintained, or go back to their previous work. This is a good measure for avoiding insecurity.

Hill: Had the members of your team any preliminary training directed towards the fact that they might go into teams later on?

Ordoñez-Plaja: They had no preliminary training in working as a team, but they had in-service training. They were picked from different specialities in a span of almost a year. We had very long interviews with them and ensured first that they had the right motivation to help. The second thing was to be sure that they would like to be part of the team and that they were not yes-men. One of the great risks in building a team is to think that the yes-man is a wonderful man, but he is the worst person you can get in a team.

Bridger: Just as different cultural backgrounds can lead to conceptual discrepancies about 'disease' and 'health', may they not also produce different ideas about what we each refer to as 'the team'? I found myself agreeing with some things you said about teams and disagreeing violently with others. Such potential cultural sources of misunderstanding should receive special attention.

Ordoñez-Plaja: I agree.

Bridger: Have you ever used group methods of selection not only to improve the criteria and methods by which you choose people, but also to develop understanding of groups and teamwork?

Ordoñez-Plaja: In studies we did with Roderick O'Connor from Atlanta we realized that those methods were made to measure people in other cultures and that we had no parameters for measuring our own people in Colombia. We then developed our own methodology for selecting people. For instance, we asked what they thought about the WHO definition of health. We rejected people who said it was wonderful. The WHO definition is not a definition; it tries to get so much in that it does not say anything—it is more a definition of death, according to many religions, which you can get in the other world, or Nirvana, or certain moments of a honeymoon. You cannot expect to have perfect physical, mental, and social well-being otherwise. On the other hand, if someone who was sceptical about this definition gave another definition of health and disease we usually rejected him too. We wanted people who had interesting questions and interesting doubts. There are so many people who have answers to all the questions but they do not know how to make good questions and think about them. We have been thinking about health and disease intensively for four years now and we do not have any definitions at all, but in the process we have discovered many interesting things. For instance, health might mean something to you and something absolutely different to your neighbour. When you reach that point, you have done something much more interesting than attempting a new definition of health and disease.

Dickson: When I was a schoolboy and played football it was the captain who was in charge and it was the captain in the field who claimed our loyalty. Today in national sport one often is not even aware of the name of the captain: it is the manager who commands. Now the manager is essentially a non-player, operating from the sidelines. Does this mean, in the context of our discussions, that leadership is no longer invested in one of the participants, but is exercised from outside the group?

Ordoñez-Plaja: In our culture, particularly among the new generation, there is a growing feeling against show-off people. If we have succeeded as a team it is because no one is taking any public advantage in being either the leader or a member of the team.

Horn: Did the members of the team really do two hours a day teaching or research, in fact and not just in theory?

Ordoñez-Plaja: Most of them are doing at least two hours of teaching and research, or learning. I think that they are not bureaucratized. On the other hand, in this way they are always in contact with young people, and that is crucial. We are unfair to the new generation. We criticize them for their hippy behaviour, their marijuana smoking, and so on, but we forget that we raised them. After the Second World War we told them that war is very bad and that peace is wonderful, yet when they burn their conscription cards we send them to jail. We have raised a generation in such an ambivalent way that they should be schizophrenic and when they behave like schizophrenics, we blame them.

We should be in permanent contact with youth and make them participate in decisions, or at least make them produce intelligent questions instead of burning automobiles and throwing stones. Now,

174

would that work? I do not know, but at least we have to make the effort. In our team group I lowered the average age from about 46–48 to 35 years. I have young people in charge of divisions with a big budget who are only 26 years old. They have performed wonderfully and have been a great help to me.

Dogramaci: The good leader does not give orders but makes decisions. How much are your leaders tied down by the opinions of the members of the team? And if a straight yes-yes man is useless or dangerous, how about a no-no member of the team?

Ordoñez-Plaja: I still have one no-no who is against anything, especially if it is new. Some members of the team said that we should eliminate him but I think it is useful to have him. A yes-yes man is always dangerous. A scapegoat is very useful because everybody will hate him, and that is a unifying factor.

As regards the first point, the leader has to maintain the combination and the balance between the technical decision and the political decision. At the beginning this is very hard. Four years ago I thought that politicians were all 'bad' people. But I have learned to respect them. The leader, because of his position, has knowledge of many political and other factors that have to influence a technical decision, and that is in part what gives him his power. On the whole, when it comes to a critical decision, I think the most important thing in group dynamics is to take all the blame when something goes wrong and give the credit to the team when things go well.

Hockey: First, why do you confine your sources of team selection to universities and research stations? Why not use experienced field workers who have left university some time ago? Secondly, surely no selection can be so good that no incompatibility is noticed later on. How do you deal with genuine incompatibility of temperament?

Ordoñez-Plaja: I recruit most people from universities or research centres because that is where you get most of the good people, but not all of them. Regarding incompatibilities, I am very sceptical about the so-called emotionally stable person. We all have a degree of neurosis and the important thing is to have a balance between those neuroses. One member of the team gets very easily depressed, and his counterpart, a sort of Sancho Panza, never gets depressed and always has his feet on the ground. When the first one is depressed I put them to work together and they balance each other. I have two or three who balance me when I get depressed or too happy. I have an excellent man who acts as the buffer when everybody gets excited or nervous. Everyone turns to him; he is always calm and objective, and he is probably the only emotionally stable person in the team.

Israel: Your situation is ideal to some extent, in that you can select the leader and you can be rather selective of the team. But in most cases, and certainly in India, the formation of teams depends very much on seniority. Certain people have to be the leaders of the team and certain others members of the team. This calls for more thought with regard to the orientation of these teams so that they can be utilized in the best way possible. Many of the workers who come for training tell us that when they go back, they will be working in a situation where they will have to follow the orders of the leaders of their teams, who in this case are medical people. We therefore decided to get the leaders of the teams together with the other members in small workshops or seminars, in which questions of the team concept, leadership and group work were discussed. However, the administrative level that you have been talking of is a much more difficult level to deal with. At a recent meeting it was decided that the National Institute of Health Administration and Education would hold workshops for the administrators, to orientate them by special methods to the importance of the team approach. Did you have this sort of experience in your country before the present phase, and did that lead you to take up this way of selecting the team?

Ordoñez-Plaja: I was in a most fortunate position because I was in office for four years, whereas previous Ministers of Health had been in office for an average of 11 months, in which time one can hardly do anything at all. That gives power to bureaucracy and none to the leader. I have no magic formula, and every country has its own laws, but when a man is very bad I have found it very useful to give him a free hand and he will make a great mistake before too long. Then you can get rid of him. The other thing is to transfer such people to other institutions where they can do no harm. Another thing I did was to give all of them a chance to start a new life with some additional training. The most difficult part of the problem is when you cannot do that and have to do the best possible with what you have. In that case I would probably commit suicide, because when a group of people get bureaucratized there is very little chance to change them. If it is a disease more than 20 years old you cannot do anything with them, except that you *can* transfer them to other jobs with the same salaries. If you give them less work and the same salary, they are very happy and they do not interfere with important things.

14: Mental Health Care: A Growing Concern to Communities

J. A. C. DE KOCK VAN LEEUWEN

PREVIOUS speakers and discussants have already brought into the open many aspects relating to the problems of working with teams. Again and again we have been confronted with the fact that teams are composed of human beings and that we have to reckon with all the aspects that characterize such beings. Dr Ordoñez-Plaja, for example, specifically mentioned the risks of jealousy in teams and of taking into consideration the motivational states of all the team members.

I shall direct my presentation towards the human side of our work, intending thereby to offer you some concepts that may help us to understand better how teams operate and why certain things sometimes happen.

I am well aware of the fact that in conditions in which our biological existence is at stake, it is almost a luxury to talk about mental health. But as soon as our circumstances change, we do well to take care of this most human side of human beings.

If we include in mental health care the concept of *emotional hygiene*, serious problems arise, because the application of hygienic principles to the field of emotional health implies the acknowledgement that the behavioural sciences have developed themselves to a state of adulthood. We are all familiar with the principles of personal and environmental hygiene. We know, for instance, that morbidity and mortality figures have been influenced, and are being influenced, much more by supplying clean water and adequate sewage disposal than by any medical measure as such, including the discovery of antibiotics. Now, if we are prepared to accept that we not only possess the necessary knowledge of bacteriological and chemical threats in our environment but also know which behaviour in the emotional sense improves health and which behaviour leads toward illness, we can envisage a tremendous new area in which we have to work.

Reasoning by analogy of course can be a very fascinating game, leading to unexpected views. It has to be proved, however, that the analogy holds true and that it does not just serve the purpose of fantasy.

To prove the validity of the points that have been raised, it is necessary to turn to the psychoanalytical concepts of personality, whose essence leads to the conclusion that our behaviour characteristics are deeply influenced by the way our parents and other emotionally relevant people treated us as a newborn and as a child. The conclusion is amply based on daily repeated experience and definitely not simply on the outcome of personal analysis. Even if we look at experiments with animals of different kinds, we find more and more that our concepts of instinct have to be revised quite thoroughly, because much of animal behaviour also seems to be more the result of 'environmental actions' than of genetic patterns. This does not of course imply that in trying to explain human behaviour one could dispose of the concepts about the fulfilment of inner drives. All that has been said is that the form in which the inner drives manifest themselves is at least co-determined by interaction with the environment.

One of the most fundamental findings concerns the concept of security. It seems that if we do not provide enough security in early developmental periods the result is that the grown-up person shows signs of not being able to relate to his fellow men in such a way that he himself and the other people derive any emotional gratification. In other words, the problem of loneliness that is spreading in our industrialized countries may be due to the fact that the development of our technologically dominated culture prohibits the creation of emotionally secure climates.

Much of what has been said has been formulated earlier and more concisely by others, but in this presentation I want to draw your attention to some practical implications of these facts.

We cannot imagine human existence without *interaction*, be it between mother and child, between spouses, between teacher and pupil, between police and justice and offenders, between bosses and subordinates, between government officials and the public, and last, but not least, between doctors, nurses, auxiliary personnel and patients. All these interactions carry emotional loads, and these loads can either be used in a proper way or they can be used to cause damage. This implies that every human being must be made aware that his behaviour affects the emotional health of the people with whom he interacts.

If we set ourselves to achieve this goal, there are certain techniques that can be used. All of them are based on the same principle, that is on improving the 'feedback' mechanisms between the people who interact with each other. By education in the traditional way we have learned to be polite, respectful, careful of the feelings of others, and so on. The effect of this type of education is that we tend to hide quite a bit of our thoughts and feelings. By doing so we falsify the feedback to our partner, who in his or her turn does the same to us. If under certain conditions we break down these culturally established barriers we can describe the result on the basis of the following diagram:

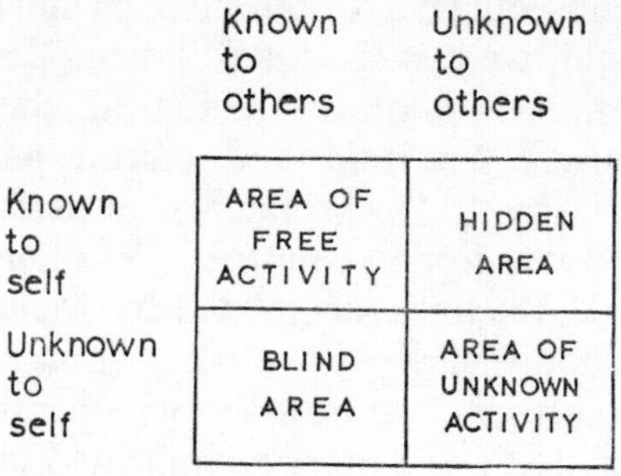

	Known to others	Unknown to others
Known to self	AREA OF FREE ACTIVITY	HIDDEN AREA
Unknown to self	BLIND AREA	AREA OF UNKNOWN ACTIVITY

FIG. 1. Interaction between individuals (after Luft[1])

Knowledge is spread over ourselves and over others. We know certain things about ourselves that we do not tell others under normal conditions. Others, however, know certain things about us that they do not tell us if there are no special reasons to do so. If both parties cross the habitual barriers the result can be an enlargement of the area of shared knowledge. This enlargement can facilitate to a tremendous degree the way we can cooperate with each other.

We know from experience that health education in the classical field of food and environment already requires a tremendous effort to be successful. If we have to add the above-mentioned message about emotional hygiene the effort required is almost too much. Still, we cannot dispose of this challenge by denying that it exists or saying that we have already so much to do that we cannot add to our burden. Whether we want it or not, our behaviour towards the other person with whom we communicate influences their health. Of course, the analogy with bacteriological or chemical harm does not go as far as the acute toxic effects of an overdose, but it can definitely be compared with the effects of chronic exposure to low doses.

Our industrialized countries are in the middle of finding out how their cultures have developed in such a way that great numbers of their populations are to be considered in a suboptimal state of emotional health. They are paying a tremendous price for making the wrong choices as far as care for emotional health is concerned. They use their technological power to provide everybody with every conceivable contraption that can be mass-fabricated. The result is a steady growth of material income, but we are also familiar with the threatening situation of over-pollution of air, water and soil. We have been violating—perhaps because we were ignorant of their existence—all the basic rules of ecological systems, and we are still violating the rules of our emotional ecological system, because their effects are less clear and much more difficult to measure than environmental pollution.

If we turn to the consequences for our medical and nursing professions of what has been said, we can see the following development. In our systems the main emphasis is on the biological, chemical and physical side of our existence. We train and recruit people in this field. We gladly give priority to these factors, especially in the aid we give to our friends in developing countries. We split up our work load and create tasks along the lines formulated by Taylor[2] and many of his successors. Our prime concern is whether something is being done efficiently. By using this criterion we assess whether the lowest paid, least trained individual is doing the most complicated task that can be entrusted to him. We stick to our policy that it must be possible to create auxiliaries of auxiliaries, and so increase the force of people working on behalf of our health and welfare.

By this I am implying that the consequent division of labour along the lines I have described leads to a situation in which the last link in the chain runs the risk of doing a highly monotonous and almost inhuman task. We are therefore neglecting the principles of mental hygiene which lead us towards creating more complicated tasks in which people can put whatever creativity they have; but this calls for a radically different type of thinking.

Of course the picture I am drawing is lopsided. I am fully aware of the many factors that have been brought to bear to counteract the over-emphasis on materialistic policies. However, as one who is experienced in group dynamics, I am deeply concerned about the way we people in general are dealing with each other. Each new group that constitutes itself immediately starts to find out what the pecking order is, who can boss whom. And it is only after considerable effort that this habit can be overcome and replaced by more considerate behaviour directed towards cooperation. Even the teams in our health care system more often than not suffer from this peculiar and very often destructive characteristic. The problem of course is that the members of the team are suffering without knowing how to stop it and how to change it. The abuse of tobacco, of alcohol, of drugs and of many other health-damaging habits in our industrialized societies is explained—at least partially—by the tranquillizing effect they have, that is they lessen the subject's awareness of the pain he is suffering.

It has been said that Holland has a well-developed and elaborate system of mental health care. If we take the number of psychiatrists per head of the total population this statement seems to be valid, because we have by far the greatest density of psychiatrists. However, this crude measure can easily be misleading, because it may well be that we charge our psychiatrists with work that in other countries is done by other disciplines. If we look for figures about psychoses and neuroses there seems to be a strikingly similar pattern in different countries, although again comparisons are very dangerous, because the definitions and the systems by which the casualties are counted are almost impossible to compare.

In following my presentation so far, you may wonder where this will lead you. The answer is that it is my sincere conviction that unless we are able to free ourselves from the dominance of economic and financial principles, we are heading for a disastrous future. We have the means to improve the state of our mental health, but this requires our own personal effort. It is not something that can be done by inventing a machine. It is not something that can be taken over by a computer. It is something that asks for personal sacrifices. Our efforts in the field of health education have taught us that as long as we manipulate our environment we are successful, but as soon as we touch the area of changing personal habits it seems that we have almost no success unless our lives are literally at stake.

If we fail to develop skills in relating to each other in non-competitive ways, we shall fail to survive. Our medical teams should be, and could be, examples of a better way of functioning. The conditions for this are, however, that they should not be concerned only with cost-benefit analysis in terms of money and material but also with 'what do we do together and with each other'.

The ultimate goal of our actions must be that all members of the communities we work in and for should be aware of the fact that they are emotionally responsible for each other.

DISCUSSION

Hill: I am accountable in the end to my superiors, the Board of Governors and my university. Where does accountability come in in the psychological make-up of the team?

de Kock van Leeuwen: In real team cooperation the accountability ought to be the accountability of a team, and it is a fundamental problem that this whole concept of accountability has focused—until now—upon one man. This leads to very peculiar management consequences. It is a long-standing idea that where teams operate well the team leader says he is responsible when things have gone wrong, while it is the team that succeeds when things go well. In fact, if the team really operates as a team, people operating on an equal basis with each other know very well where a failure comes from and they do not accept this kind of ultimate responsibility of one person. On the other hand each appointed superior is well aware of the fact that if something goes wrong officially he is accountable, but if he is able to indicate where the mistake has been made without him failing in control it is the man who is sitting there who gets the full blame.

The whole psychology of operating together needs a thorough revision. The hierarchical pyramids which are the essence of the military apparatus are in my opinion only useful under certain specific conditions. If there is an emergency and immediate action has to be taken, then one man has to decide that action. If there is ample time to discuss whether policy *A* will be better than policy *B*, and for preferences to be manifested, then the decision about the policy is shared by all the group members. This sharing should be acknowledged, not only in terms of success but also in terms of failure if a team has failed. This should not be done in terms of accusations towards one or more members, because it is the team that fails. On the other hand if I am the chosen or appointed team leader and formally accountable, yet follow a certain policy—determined by majority feelings—that I think is wrong, then I am not a good team member. I then should not have joined in agreeing to that decision unless I myself was convinced that I could follow this policy and be responsible for it. So what you often see is that weak team leaders follow suggestions of subordinates and when something goes wrong they blame the others. That is definitely a wrong policy. Our whole system of accountability tends to counteract good team operation. We as doctors always speak in terms of ultimate responsibility, with the nurses operating under our responsibility. But nothing is less true, because the nurse has her own work, much of it completely out of the physician's control, so he cannot feel himself responsible for what she is doing and he cannot bear the ultimate responsibility. It is a joint responsibility.

Salmon: Is it possible to work on a basis where one man can be accountable but where a team can advise the leader, who ultimately is responsible for taking the decision? In a capitalist world this seems to me the only practical way to operate so far, but this does not necessarily mean that one cannot work with teams; it depends on the management of the team, how the leader reacts on its members and the trust that is established between his advisers and himself.

de Kock van Leeuwen: You have hit the nail on the head. One of the problems is of course that the final accountability system gives the team leader an outlet which is highly undesirable. If a team leader thinks he runs the risk of being overruled by the team in which he cooperates, he often tells them that he cannot sell the solution to his Board or somebody else higher in the hierachy. In such circumstances he is bringing in a force that cannot be influenced by the others, and this can be very destructive in a team operation. The advisory team can operate, and it is the only way we can operate under our present circumstances, but it has some innate very destructive tendencies. In particular the team leader must be well aware of the fact that if he uses this kind of mechanism he really destroys the team operation.

182

Horn: Did you say that unless we are able to free ourselves from the influence of economic and industrial factors we are heading for disaster? If so, what does that mean?

de Kock van Leeuwen: No, I mean that if we make ourselves completely dependent on economic and financial factors and cannot free ourselves on behalf of the emotional side of living, we are heading for disaster.

Christie: Are you suggesting that the incidence of emotional disorders in the highly technical advanced countries is higher than in those that are relatively undeveloped?

de Kock van Leeuwen: No. Comparative research shows that the figures are about the same. But emotional disorders in Western countries manifest themselves differently from the way they manifest themselves in developing countries. Loneliness is a phenomenon that as far as I know is not so obvious in developing countries, where the communities are smaller and where the people know each other much better than they usually do in metropolitan conditions.

Horn: In the context in which you said that urban loneliness was spreading, your implication, to me at any rate, was that it was due to child/parent relationships.

de Kock van Leeuwen: That is the final consequence of what I said. If a person cannot create a climate of inner warmth in his early days, he becomes unable to relate himself adequately to others. In later life this manifests itself as a feeling of loneliness.

Banks: Recently I had to prepare a report for the World Health Organization on the possibility of integrating mental health care in the basic health services. Theoretically this is not so difficult. It is a matter of organization, getting the lines of communication from the centre to the intermediate centre, and to the periphery, with appropriate psychiatric advice. The main difficulty is that for the basic health services in the rural areas one cannot always talk in terms of teams. At the periphery there may be only one person, an auxiliary nurse midwife. If there is a team she is the basic unit in it, and it is she who has to carry out the orders. Auxiliary nurse midwives are the salt of the earth, but they are locally recruited girls, sometimes barely literate, recruited at anything from 15 years of age and even earlier, given a few months training, or if they are lucky up to two years, and then posted to the villages. It is that girl who will have to carry the responsibility if we introduce the concept of mental health care prematurely into the rural areas. One can visualize a situation where she is given a supply of sedative pills to hand out at her own discretion. I have deliberately stated the extreme, but it is an extreme that applies to millions of people and we had better face up to it.

de Kock van Leeuwen: Where sheer survival is at stake mental health care has almost no place. If I am dead no mental health or mental

183

hygiene is needed. In circumstances where a lone girl has to do all the jobs it is almost impossible to do anything more than help her to maintain her own psychological health—which is a task in itself and is very often forgotten. Miss Hentsch said that very often we delegate difficult tasks to nurses and auxiliaries without taking into consideration all the complications that go with it in terms of emotional stress. More often than not, I think, we tend to train these girls without thinking about how we can help them to carry the emotional load that they must bear. I would focus primarily, not on spreading mental health principles under such conditions, but on how to help such a girl to perform her task and remain emotionally as healthy as she was before she started her work.

Rebhun: You made a distinction between the effects of the physical or chemical environmental factors on man's physical health, and the interactions of men with each other on their mental health. Workers in environmental health are told that the physical environment influences mental health as well: air pollution, noise and smells even when not directly related to physical health may have a strong effect on mental health. Would you comment on that?

de Kock van Leeuwen: The physical environment certainly affects the emotional side. Noise abatement is a very urgent matter, because our existence is really threatened by the overdose of noise that we are producing. On the other hand the way we deal with each other has effects of its own which can be discerned and discriminated from the other effects. Here I focused on these ill-effects not because the other ones do not exist or are not important, but because we tend to forget that interaction in itself can also be harmful.

Kisseih: Would you attribute the increase in mental illness to lack of practice of Christianity? You stressed the need to regard our neighbours as ourselves. This is one of the basic principles of Christianity.

As an experienced psychiatrist, would you say that these principles could be replaced by other advancements in modern science? Personally, I feel that if we all lived up to the teachings of Christ, many of our tension problems would be solved.

de Kock van Leeuwen: A fundamental principle is at stake. I do not know if it is confined to Christianity, but I will enlarge it to religious beliefs in general. I think that the pursuit of scientific facts has brought as a kind of side-effect a fundamental disbelief in religion for many people. Now we are finding that the old truths that all religions preach in different forms are being confirmed by work in the behavioural sciences. The message that springs from the Christian religion is not as easy to apply as you imply; that is, the rule is easy, but to conform to it is rather difficult.

Bridger: Quite apart from the religious aspect there would appear to be a further implication in Miss Kisseih's point, a suggestion that possibly

184

one could prevent conflicting and disruptive forces from occurring in groups and between groups. These processes, as for example the struggle for leadership or the way in which we keep our agenda hidden from one another, are factors that operate in all groups. We need to recognize the existence of these forces, whether loving or destructive ones, both in ourselves and in others. In the course of achieving our objectives we can also learn to cope with such forces and conflicts in the groups to which we belong. Indeed, could we not regard this as part of our accountability?

Horn: There are two kinds of accountability: the legal and the moral. If the surgeon makes a mistake and the patient dies or loses a limb, then legally the surgeon may be liable and he can get into trouble. But the moral accountability is much more relevant to what we are talking about. It seems to me that it is not impossible to be objective about allocating moral responsibility. When a dangerous operation was being planned in my hospital in China, we invariably had a number of meetings beforehand to which everybody who was involved was invited, including the patient's relatives, the nurses, the junior doctors and the senior doctors. In the final analysis, the surgeon who was going to do the operation had to make the decision as to what to do, but having listened to the opinions of other people and considered points of view that previously he may not have been aware of he had a good basis on which to make a decision. If he then made a wrong decision, it was quite possible to go back and say: why did you not consider this or that? What was there in yourself, or in somebody else, or in the environment or what-have-you which led you to take this decision and not that one? In other words this kind of moral accountability can be tracked down to its source and does not necessarily have to be automatically allocated to the leader of a team.

Dickson: As one who has acquired his doctorate in a non-medical capacity, I hope to return home with new insights into how one achieves teamwork. Three problems concern me. I have recently taken part in conferences of the volunteer service organizations, who are very conscious that they operate as separate national entities: some of them want, if only to avoid being discarded by the more radical students in their own countries, to present an image of teamwork and become genuinely more international in their approach. When we discussed how one achieved teamwork—was it something that existed as an aim in itself, separate from the particular goal one has to pursue, the actual task to be performed?—it seemed that in fact there were rather limited forms of teamwork to be engaged in. We could think of an operating theatre, of an orchestra, of a sports event, all of which required a team effort. Beyond that, the kind of requests for the services of the volunteers called generally for individual tasks, not for teams. Have we thought

185

sufficiently, then, of what functional factors have to be considered in order to justify a team approach?

Secondly, if we consider a team as something more profound, more far-reaching than the conventional tribute that we all pay to the virtues of consultation, committee work, joint planning, etc., how do we bring this about? I worked in Africa at a time when the phrase 'the district team' suddenly became the 'in' phrase. It meant only that we met once a week under the permanent chairmanship of an Administration Officer, returning afterwards to our own offices to get on with our own jobs. We did not think inwardly as a team nor did we act visibly as a team. Later, in another part of the world, I was in charge of a United Nations Mission comprising members of different nationalities whose excellent morale was due in fact to a common dislike of the host government. Because we all felt unwelcomed by the government concerned, we coalesced into a team. If our relationships with the general community and the host government had been more friendly, would that team spirit have evaporated?

There is often a very real conflict between involvement in the community and the retention of a team spirit, whether among a group of professionals or others.

This problem is very real to me, because part of my job is to send young volunteers, sometimes in groups, to serve various organizations. Which is to be considered as the team—the group of young volunteers, or the institution or community to which we have sent them?

Then, how do you train to achieve this team effectiveness? Another part of my work is dealing with young men in the last few months of their training to be policemen, to deepen their social awareness. We invariably place them in a situation that is different from what they know in the Force. In caring for young offenders, for example, they discover that it is harder to change the attitude of delinquents than to arrest them. Or, as a result of having worked in a psychiatric unit, they may recognize—if called to some incident at a bus stop at night—that they have to deal with a mentally disturbed individual rather than a hooligan or vicious person. Through this cross-fertilization of experience they learn that they are part of a wider approach to the social problems of the country—but this is made possible only because other Departments believe that such a sharing of experience contributes to a team concept. Could the medical student, without lengthening the duration of training, acquire understanding of how others view the doctor? Can the health authorities modify their attitudes on professionalism and specialization to permit those working in other disciplines to see things for a while through their eyes?

Bridger: These questions cannot be answered in a few words. It is really only in the last 40 years that the systematic study of groups has been developed and, indeed, that any fundamental work has been done to relate that experience to organizational behaviour and change. Furthermore, as Dr Barbero pointed out, at the very time when we begin to look at groups as entities, as organisms—organisms that are born and die differently from ourselves as individuals, that have to be cared for differently, and so on—we also find that the changes in the environment, the technological, social and other 'explosions', have created a different set of problems and conditions. The groups and organizations, whether industries, hospitals or schools, have had to change from existing as relatively 'closed' systems to becoming increasingly 'open' and adapting to a more turbulent environment. As an interesting comparison, the features and problems of the teams we are discussing are not like those of our own group here at this meeting, because, in spite of the theme for which we have met, we have not, as a group, the equivalent objectives and tasks we would have if we were a team working in the field. For example, here we can be polite and considerate to one another because we are not involved in tasks providing us with the kind of potential conflict and difficulty encountered by health teams in action—and perhaps crisis.

To answer Alec Dickson, we can begin to understand what happens in groups by distilling the results of our own experience through life and arriving at certain assumptions. On this basis alone, however, we may develop ideas of handling groups more akin to manipulation than towards achieving team objectives. Attempting a more serious study of group processes and behaviour, we may have to feel very 'deskilled' when we try to learn what is happening in the groups to which we belong. Having had so much experience of groups—in the family, the school, in social and work settings—we each develop skills, behaviour and defences in our various group roles which are not easily reflected upon or questioned. As adults, managers or professionals, we feel we *ought* to know and would rather observe others than share in learning about groups by being in them, by confronting others and sharing our observations and inferences, and by testing out different ways of behaving or managing in privileged group settings where we can build the trust required. More particularly we should be prepared to learn something about leadership in teams and the way the *appointed* leader can promote or hinder the efforts of others to demonstrate their leadership capacities through the different functions and opportunities offered by group activity in all its forms.

In the model shown in Fig. 1, the large elliptical area represents the group's situation in its environment and the smaller ones straddling the boundary represent the persons in the group. A number of different dimensions affect the individual as a member of this group. He is part of the environment as well as of the group. He has values and standards

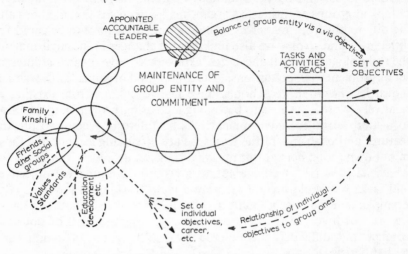

ENVIRONMENTS
FOR GROUP AND MEMBERS

APPOINTED
ACCOUNTABLE
LEADER →

Balance of group entity vis a vis objectives

MAINTENANCE OF
GROUP ENTITY AND
COMMITMENT

TASKS AND
ACTIVITIES
TO REACH →

SET OF
OBJECTIVES

Family +
Kinship

Friends + other social groups

Values + Standards

Education development etc.

Set of
individual
objectives,
career,
etc.

Relationship of individual objectives to group ones

Fig. 1 (Bridger). Model for team development and management.

deriving from his development and experience, as well as belonging to other groups such as family and friendship allegiances.

A team only exists as a group, rather than as an aggregate of people meeting, say, at a bar, if it has a set of objectives. Very few groups ever have a single objective, unless it is such as that of a platoon attacking a machine-gun post. Conflicting objectives, diverse objectives, complementary objectives and congruent ones are often inherent in any situation. Let us assume that somebody has to have the ultimate responsibility and is formally accountable for the achievement of objectives and the performance of the group. One of the requirements of leadership, whether located in one person or in a number, is that of maintaining the balance, which is often a very delicate one, between membership needs and individual purposes and the objectives the group is trying to achieve. At any one time, this problem of balancing might be said to be the essence of leadership. For the individual member the problem is that of reconciling his hopes, fears, aspirations and personal objectives (which are many) with the demands which any one group makes on him for its success. The personal identity and private needs— derived from family, education, background, career, standards, values, religion, and all the other things that go to make that person partly 'inside' and partly 'outside' any one group—emphasize the elements in the balancing process in which a person engages when committing himself to a group task. The individual's personal reconciling process, and the leader's balancing and optimizing in *group* terms, have an important common basis represented by the arrows in the model in Fig. 1. To complete the aspects shown by our model we must at least note the potential forces and factors for cooperation and conflict between members of the group.

Over the years many methods and techniques of training people to appreciate the relevance of group dynamics and leadership for social, professional and management realities have been developed. In practice, the concepts of which I have spoken would be derived from practical experience in group tasks and taking time out to study the processes happening in the group. Such an operation would include facing the problem of resistance to change, and many other features.

Let us now consider the wider picture and the world or society in which our team exists. Let us approach it by examining what has happened over the last 30 years (Fig. 2). Then, most organizations and institutions were managed in a form in which people minded their own

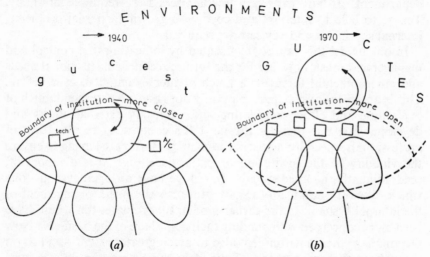

FIG. 2 (Bridger). Model to illustrate organizational change and authority/management implications and patterns of teamwork. Examples of environmental change.

Representing smaller and greater impingement and influence of:

g	G	government
u	U	unions
c	C	consumer
e	E	education
s	S	suppliers and special skills
t	T	technological development

------, etc., such as mobility of specialists and managers.
□, Specialists and advisers, e.g. tech.—technical; A/C—accounts.

business, and where the pattern of authority was the clear-cut hierarchical one within the institution itself—whether authoritarian or benevolent in nature. In those days too the environment played much less part as an influence or force on the organization; government intervened to a much smaller degree; unions had less impact; people applied competitively to the institution for employment, and, in general, change was recognizable but not so turbulent as it has become today. Schools, by and large, still maintained their monastic walls; hospitals were powers unto themselves, and so were the professions and universities.

But today, the government makes an increasing intervention, and the unions, the consumer, the competitor, the supplier, the 'technological explosion' and other forces of social, international and economic change impinge on all institutions. Previously the institution might need the help of an accountant or a combined secretariat and accounting department. In any case very few advisers were required internally. Today, to help to interpret and cope with growing external problems, internal specialists and advisers are required.

In our model this can be represented by indicating that control and management must, now and for the future, reconcile institutional needs and environmental forces to a much greater extent than ever before. This is a tremendous change. Not only does one have to spend much of one's time and effort considering and operating external affairs and developments, but there is the need for continuous re-education of professionals, specialist advisers and managers who are having to ensure the viability of the institution or enterprise. Fig. 2a is a model of, predominantly, a closed system. In (b) we have an open system—one which requires one's team to share more closely in the management of the internal system. In the earlier model, subordinates too would have been more concerned with minding their own share of the business. Now they manage their environment also to much greater extent—and so on throughout the organization. Thus from the classic 'family tree'-type organizational structure and authority pattern we have to learn to change to a form of team leadership—the management of external uncertainty and internal interdependence. Continuing this process entails erstwhile 'subordinates' becoming the 'colleagues' whose commitment is required to share with the accountable leader and other team members in achieving *group* objectives; this can be regarded as an operational definition of participation as against an older pattern of delegating tasks by hiving off defined areas of work with more limited scope for direction to different individuals within the team. Thus, the management of complexity and the management of interdependence are much more important for today and tomorrow than some of the simpler prescriptions on leadership and management with which we have all been brought up.

15: Volunteers—Their Use and Misuse

ALEC G. DICKSON

IN a town in England's North Midlands boys have been leaving home for school 15 minutes earlier than is necessary, stopping off *en route* at an institution for geriatrics. Removing from his pocket what is probably his father's razor, each has shaved one old man—and then on to school. But in this gesture each boy has brought relief to hard-pressed nursing staff and companionship to one old man.

When Hurricane Carla struck the coast of Texas some years ago, mental patients at Galveston left their wards to join in the relief operations, working alongside everyone else. Once the disaster was over, they returned to their wards and sank back into apathy.

A man suffering from a peculiar blood deficiency was recently in danger of losing his job in a small town on the east coast of England: his fingers would become so cold that he could not use them. Teenage apprentices—young 'blue-collar' workers—undergoing industrial training at a nearby firm heard of his plight. To meet his need they developed transistorized, battery-operated gloves, putting to social purpose the skills they were acquiring during training. Today the man is still at work.

When news of the Koina earthquake reached the Indian College of Technology at Powai, on the outskirts of Bombay, the students began to collect money for relief. But Dr Bose, the principal, urged that there was something still more vital that they, and they alone, could produce—a design for a 'quake-proof school: pooling their ideas, they had their design ready in under 24 hours—and then the local apprentices were mobilized to weld a prototype framework. "Do you want me to 'phone the Public Works Department to take delivery of the structure—or would you prefer to go yourselves to the stricken area and put the thing up, making any last-minute adjustments that may be needed?" Dr Bose asked the students—and got the expected answer, "We'll go ourselves." Then the principal strode across to the staff quarters and addressed the faculty: "Are you prepared to sit here whilst our boys blister their hands at Koina?" So the whole college went to the earthquake area, experiencing for the first time a sense of common purpose.

The staff of the closed block at Harperbury Hospital, north of London, was recently reinforced by the temporary attachment of David Smith, aged 19, during the final phase of his training as a police cadet, before becoming a Liverpool constable. His role was that of 'recreational

191

therapist' amongst adolescent psychopaths, all of whom shared one experience: they had 'failed to respond', as the saying goes, to corrective training in one or other of Her Majesty's delinquency institutions. On the last weekend of his attachment, during a bitterly cold March, David Smith—alone and at his own suggestion—took a group of these highly unpredictable young men out camping, to the astonishment of the senior psychologist and his colleagues. "A good time was had by all", reported the police cadet laconically. His most difficult moment? "When the hospital staff didn't want to let any blankets off the premises."

A group of high school students have been going to a somewhat dreary institution for the very old in the East End of London—on Christmas Day, Easter Day and intervening Sundays—offering to give the patients their meals and clean up afterwards, thereby releasing the lower echelons of staff so that they can enjoy the public holiday. Not very dramatic, you might say. Not unless the significance of doing this on Christmas Day, Easter Day and intervening Sundays is recognized. For they are all Jewish boys and girls, for whom these occasions have not the same meaning—and suddenly, by an act of insight, they redeem what would otherwise be a menial chore and transform it into an imaginative gesture of reconciliation.

*   *   *

From these examples, and those shown in Figs. 1–5, it may be evident how infinite is the variety of forms that voluntary action can take: it can be an instinctive reaction to crisis, an escape from routine, a response to leadership, an extra dimension to one's work, a challenge to accepted conventions. Many of our young people today are suffering from what I call the S.O.S. syndrome—a Surfeit Of Schweitzer. Some will hearken still to calls for sacrifice and duty. But curiosity, indignation, companionship—these too are powerful emotive forces: and even the ageing, as Lady Reading of the Women's Royal Voluntary Service has recently reminded us, are never too old for adventure. We are guilty of misuse if we regard this human resource as a lowly category of labour, fit only for those tasks that professionals find wearisome—digging gardens for the elderly, collecting library books for old-age pensioners, or—in a hospital setting—emptying slops. "What did you find most disturbing?" I asked a young Scottish engineering apprentice, specially released by his Glasgow company for a period of service at a London hospital, where he had alternated between the casualty department and the occupational therapy wing. "It's not blood we fear, but boredom", he replied—and spoke possibly for his whole generation.

Who are the volunteers? Until a dozen or so years ago they came still predominantly from Florence Nightingale's social background: it is perhaps only when they are absent that we realize how much we owe to the

efforts of such devoted women. Then suddenly a new image appeared—
that of idealistic young people going straight from school or college to
spend a year or more combating illiteracy and disease in the remoter
parts of Africa and Asia. For several reasons I propose not to speak
about them here. First, because they have become increasingly an élite
body. Second, because the trend has been towards their fulfilling the role
of junior experts, which is not quite the same thing. Third, because it is
the social jungle on our own doorstep which now claims the attention of
students in the West—whilst elsewhere governments are more concerned
that it should be their own young people, rather than foreign volunteers,
who tackle the nation-building tasks of development. And lastly, because in my experience it is far harder to help people in one's own neighbourhood. "We are discovering", said a friend, "that what is called
'community development' in other people's countries, why, that is known
as politics in one's own."

The accusation is often made that volunteering is a middle-class
phenomenon. This arises partly because it has been seen as a spare-time
activity—something you did after 4.0 p.m. if you were at school, between
college and career if you were a university graduate, or when your children no longer made claims on you if you were a married woman. Many
feel today that helping is more than a hobby: it is vital both for the
community's needs and for the individual's own development. So we
have in Britain the police cadet, the industrial apprentice, and—just
beginning—even the soldier being released to tackle social problems as an
essential part of their own training. Half of the young people participating in the work of Community Service Volunteers are, in fact, girls
but in this paper stress has been laid on the males. As caring has been
considered from time immemorial to be the lot of women, it is important
today that young men should learn to care too. Also, it is important not
to contrast courage (a masculine attribute) with compassion (which is
often given a feminine image): the two should blend—and be seen to
blend.

I want to see this process go still further. The experience of giving
must no longer be limited to the fortunate few. Somehow it must be
extended to the disadvantaged, to those very ones who have hitherto been
viewed only as recipients of other people's benevolence, so that they, too,
feel wanted. If we fail to do this, then large numbers of our young will
suffer from what Richard Hauser calls 'social constipation'—a constant
process of taking in without an opportunity to give out.

So we have had blind volunteers working in delinquency institutions,
and young offenders working with the handicapped. And this summer,
building on the experience of a project last August in Southall, near
London, we shall be making special efforts to enable coloured immigrant
teenagers to act as tutors to help younger or more recently arrived

Asian and West Indian children. In Washington recently I asked the staff of VISTA—Volunteers In Service To America—how they would react to a candidate of negligible educational background, reared in an orphanage, and so short-sighted as to require special glasses. Negatively, they replied. Yet this was the actual background of Annie Sullivan, who brought Helen Keller out of an animalistic existence of darkness and silence, the Miracle Worker, perhaps the teacher of the century. In my organization we never reject a volunteer. The great question is not Yes or No—but Where? The answer lies in allocation, not selection.

"Ah, but that is because you are more concerned for the volunteer than the client or patient, who is our major responsibility", some may say. To which I would reply, we are all clients today. A marriage guidance service which has had difficulty in finding an appointments secretary prepared to take calls in the evenings and weekends has now solved the problem: a bedridden woman takes calls at any hour and phones them into the office the following morning. Delighted to feel at last that she is needed, can she be said to be giving or receiving?

"Can anyone tell me what is this thing called 'voluntary work'?" wrote an 18-year-old boy serving for a year in a school for maladjusted children: "All I know is that in this place there are jobs that have to be done—and we do them." The distinction—which he clearly thought so irrelevant—will become, or certainly ought to become, still less valid. Postmen in London S.E.1 have offered to acquaint the welfare authorities at the town hall, responsible for the old, with those instances of human need that come to their notice in the course of their rounds: they have been followed by the milkmen—who also feel that they know when there is trouble in a household served by them. The welfare authorities in the two London Boroughs of Lewisham and Southwark have grasped the offer of cooperation from these unexpected allies. Several consequences ensue. The outreach of the professionals is enormously enlarged, enabling them to extend their services to many more in need of their help. And men in relatively humble forms of public utility feel suddenly that they are potentially in the front rank of social workers. But note that their contribution has not been agreeably peripheral to the welfare departments' functions: it has been within their main stream of work. And it has not derived from the postmen's leisure hours: it has stemmed from a more liberal and humane interpretation of their duties.

Four roles for full-time volunteers suggest themselves. They are:

(a) Front-line relief. 'Gap-filling' is how cynics would describe this. But when social services essential to the nation's well-being are in jeopardy, why should it be more derogatory to hope that young people may step into the breach than it would be in a wartime situation? We shall return to this later.

FIG. 1. We help them. A girl volunteer attached to a school in Southall, near London, with a high proportion of immigrant pupils, helps a group of Asian children with their English.

(*To face p. 194*)

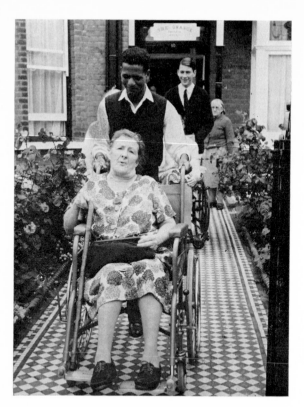

FIG. 2. They help us. A young man from the West Indian community in Britain serves as a volunteer in an institution for disabled people in Essex.

FIG. 3. The handicapped as helpers. An 18-year-old blind volunteer works with spastic children: his major contribution was not in the field of carpentry but in taking each one daily for a period in the heated swimming pool. He himself was moved to offer his help through friendship made with an apprentice - volunteer who had previously been sent to work at his own school for the blind.

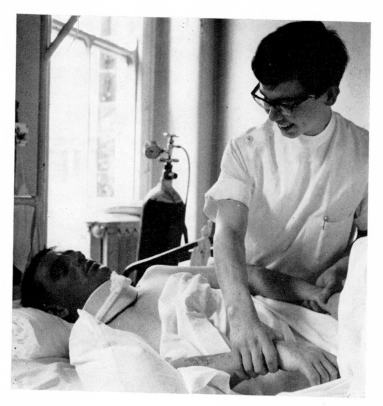

Fig. 4. Spending the months between school and university as a male auxiliary nurse at a Sheffield hospital, this volunteer became aware that some of the paraplegics had participated in the Olympic Games for the Handicapped. This led him to join in the wheelchair games of basket-ball that the patients played weekly in the hospital gymnasium, well aware of the pleasure he gave the disabled men in their ability to outmanoeuvre him.

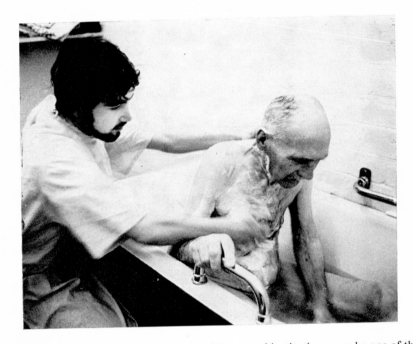

FIG. 5. Bringing relief to hard-pressed staff in mental institutions may be one of the most valuable contributions that volunteers can render. Reacting against the peripheral role of flower-arrangement and taking books around to wards, young people would prefer today to be working in a face-to-face relationship with those in need. This particular volunteer came on duty one morning whistling a popular song of the early 1900s—and had the experience of hearing an elderly patient, believed to be speechless for many years, break into the actual words.

(*b*) The intermediary. I have in mind young volunteers serving in delinquency institutions. Belonging neither to the established staff nor yet to a deviant background, they can serve as models to the boy offenders precisely because they are not identified as professionals.

(*c*) Catalysts. Full-time volunteers can help to involve local young people in part-time opportunities of service. Hospital matrons who would be appalled at the idea of their wards being invaded by hordes of local adolescent enthusiasts may agree to the full-time service of a high-calibre volunteer sponsored by a reputable organization—having won acceptance for himself, it is up to him to secure acceptance for local part-time volunteers and to identify the tasks they can undertake. Sometimes we call this the 'Trojan Horse' role.

(*d*) Agents of social change. Law school graduates in the United States, 'Nader's Raiders', who have helped to compel automobile manufacturers to introduce safer designs and who now hope to enforce anti-pollution measures, come to mind no less than students who have joined in literacy and health campaigns in many parts of Asia. (It is, of course, 'the system' that so many students today feel must be changed: we have to convince them, surely, that participation means a readiness to share pain as well as power.)

How about training? In my organization—which plays in essence a middleman's part, for we administer no projects of our own—we leave the responsibility for the imparting of technical competence to the authorities asking for our young people: our volunteers learn on the job.

But we do brief them, both about the background of the particular project to which they are going and about the nature of the volunteer's role. That can be summarized in two paragraphs. First, you have little to fear from a 'perpendicular' relationship. The director/superintendent/matron has asked for your service and can therefore be regarded as sympathetic to your coming: as for the patients/inmates/clients, we who are sending you to this project would not be doing so unless we had confidence in your ability to help them. It is the 'horizontal' relationship you must beware—that lateral look you will receive as you enter the staff-room from those who may regard the advent of volunteers as a professional threat.

Second, more is required of you than just to do the job allocated to you. Enable those whom you are helping to help others in turn—for the desire to feel needed is not confined to yourself as a volunteer, it is common to everyone. A volunteer, assigned to a school to help Asian immigrant children, knocked on doors in the neighbourhood asking elderly people

195

whether they would allow some of his pupils to talk with them in the evening, so that they could practise their English. Very cautiously, some agreed—whereupon our volunteer rushed back to his class to say "Boys! There are old people living here who are never visited—we will help them, won't we?" So, when Punjabi youngsters spent time with elderly English ladies, each party was convinced they were needed by the other—as, indeed, each was. This element of reciprocity is vital: only thus can we eliminate the 'do-gooder' concept that has been so damaging. In another part of Britain young people have arranged that a multiple store should open specially one evening before Christmas—and have then transported the bedridden and handicapped in stretchers and wheel-chairs so that they can buy presents: to feel that they are no longer perpetually at the receiving end of benevolence, that at last they can give to others, this is to regain self-respect. We have to aim at a chain-reaction in human relationships no less than in nuclear fission, if 'the biological urge to help'—of which Dr Peter Scott, of the Maudsley Hospital, has written[3]—is to be fulfilled.

We have touched on training and briefing. At a more profound level we have also to consider how education can enable us to discern situations of need and to know how best to respond. Many schools in Britain make provision for pupils to have some experience of service to the community. Hitherto this has generally been extra-curricular. Only slowly is it beginning to be realized that, if this is to have genuine educational meaning, it should be related to the actual syllabus.[2] But even now this kind of activity is seen as being something suitable for the timetable only of the least academically inclined, the children leaving at 15 to earn their living—whilst the more intellectual and ambitious are regarded as exempt, on account of examination pressures: for them it is an optional 'extra'.

Of special interest, then, are those schools and colleges which believe that the curriculum can and should bring insight into social problems and their human implications.[1] Students at the Faculty of Medicine, Hacettepe University, Ankara, are allocated a family in a poor area during their first week of study, and they watch over the health of that family throughout the years of their course: in other words responsibility for others is assumed at the very outset of training and not when it is finished. At Walkden County Secondary School, near Manchester, science is taught to 14- to 15-year-olds in such a way that they see its relevance to the relief of suffering. Over three years they have developed an alarm clock for the deaf, linking old out-dated hairdryers with alarm clocks and installing the resulting mechanisms beside the beds of those who are deaf—so that at the required hour they are woken by a blast of warm air on their face. The children have evolved a device that sounds an alarm if a baby is snatched from a pram. And now, most recently, they have, after weeks of experimentation, perfected a contrivance that will

196

alert neighbours when someone living alone collapses in their house and may be unconscious.* For young people of limited academic ability to discover that they have it within them to help others is a wonderful experience. Mrs Barrett, their science mistress, denies that she teaches community service. "I teach science", she insists—but adds in an undertone, "feminine science!"

But it is the *consumers* of volunteers who require training no less urgently. If thousands of our young people are to have a really meaningful experience of service, then professional social workers must rapidly acquire insight into how to make effective use of them. "Don't give me that stuff about 'Service'—just give me a job to do", a 14-year-old boy was heard to exclaim as he cheerfully mended an old lady's iron: how many of us feel confident of being able to offer them opportunities, sufficiently numerous, sufficiently challenging? The question was asked at a conference of Heads of Children's Departments: "Just what can these volunteers do—unqualified, untrained, adolescent and temporary—better than our highly experienced housemothers?" To which the answer came: "They can climb trees with your kids." For it is not expected of housemothers that they should sit in the upper branches of trees, waving aloft their social science diplomas—yet, at a particular moment in the development of most children, to have the elder brother or sister who can initiate them in acts of positive adventure is important to their growth, not least when they are being brought up in the care of local authorities.

Of course many adult professionals do possess this insight. There was the matron who, when asked by a sceptical hospital administrator about her reaction to the suggestion that young people might assist in her wards, replied: "The sound of a dropped tray, followed by a boy's laughter, would do our old people far more good than the swish of rubber-tyred wheels on linoleum floors—I'll be happy to have them." And the Medical Officer of Health for Birmingham remarked recently: "No child is so young but that he can help a mentally handicapped child of his own age or a little younger." We have somehow to enable such professionals to share their insight with others. 'Sharing' is the word. For training, as we all know, is for junior personnel: we who are in positions of responsibility certainly do not stand in need of (re-)training. But if we are invited to a conference to 'share our experience', then none of us feels at the receiving end of other people's superior wisdom. Yet if we return to our work with new insights, then we have in effect undergone a training process.

* We have also been experimenting with a number of approaches, e.g., Operation Wheelchair, where participants discover the day-to-day problems facing the handicapped in a city—gaining access to a public toilet, cinema, library, telephone kiosk, etc.—and then endeavour, on the basis of their findings, to persuade the relevant public authority to make the required adjustments to help the disadvantaged.

Can we let the matter rest there, conscious that we have to integrate some experience of giving into the educational curriculum of all young people, and aware of the need of adults for greater insight into how to use their service? No—for the *structure* of our organizations may also require to be changed. The locomotive-driver cannot be expected, in mid-journey, to change over from coal- to oil-burning: the original design cannot instantly be adapted. In the same way, a hospital superintendent, however willing, cannot suddenly transfer professional functions to volunteers; only marginal responsibilities can be given them without a basic re-assessment of what is required in the nursing process. Nevertheless some new development may help to open the way. The emergence of 'K.A.s'—Kidney Assistants—could be one such example. "I never thought to see Sisters advancing down a ward with screwdrivers dangling where normally their watch would be suspended", said the matron of a London hospital where the introduction of the kidney machine has meant that staff must be trained to combine medical and engineering skills. Since nurses with a knowledge of nuts may take some time to evolve, why should not engineering apprentices or students of technology in the meanwhile join with nurses in helping to run these machines?

The relay race may be an approach that could be applied to the social services. The sprinter, by definition, is good only for short distances: the marathon runner gets there eventually, but at a plodding pace. The technique for getting the furthest, fastest, is that of the relay race. Let us consider how it might be applied to those situations where human need is not being adequately met—in many mental hospitals, for example. "Offer a better wage and better staff will be forthcoming", is the conventional comment: but there may be some fields where the commercial laws of supply and demand do not always prevail. Few, very few, can give care and affection to, say, the incontinent and defective, for weeks and months and years on end: in order to ensure their own emotional survival, many armour themselves with an outer skin of professional detachment. But if this were for a limited period, and if they knew that this was not to be their permanent destiny, then young people might well be found who would devote themselves to the task with an intensity of commitment, being relieved in time by others.

For this to come about—and we are hoping to attempt just this in a number of mental hospitals, with the cooperation of the Department of Health and Social Security—the professionals have to be reassured that they are not in some way threatened. We have to convince them that the use of volunteers will not diminish their role: on the contrary, it will enhance their status, for it implies their becoming in effect leaders of teams, responsible for these young people's induction and supervision.

Volunteering may seem something of a luxury in developing countries, where concern centres naturally on self-help. But the concept of service covers both the members of one's own group and others besides. Involvement may well mean switching from a capital-intensive to a labour-intensive approach. And here the developed and the developing countries have common interests. The social problems facing us both require that there should be a spread of concern as well as depth of concern. And we share together an abundance of young people. Not to use them, not to give them the feeling of being needed, is to misuse them.

DISCUSSION

Seden: There are various age groups of possible volunteers and ways of arousing their interest would naturally also vary in various countries, depending upon their culture, beliefs and acceptance of voluntary work. Have you any general recommendations on how to arouse interest in youth groups and in adult groups? Interest has to be aroused both in the institution and among the voluntary workers, so a more important question is: how does one maintain the interest in the volunteer groups and in the institutions which would be receiving the voluntary services?

Dickson: An enormous harvest is awaiting somebody who can involve those nearing the age of retirement who feel they still have something to give. At the moment there is dissatisfaction among both the young and the old. The young are increasingly having to postpone the advent of adult responsibility through the extension of the educational process, and they are impatient for full independence. On the other hand a new phenomenon is that those nearing retirement are in many cases dreading it, for they do not want to drop out of an active life into insignificance. We in the middle are becoming harassed with the amount of work we have to do and the taxation we have to pay to support both the young in their studies and the old in their retirement. Therefore a new re-apportionment of responsibilities is needed.

Obviously one seeks to maximize the potential of the category of people one is working with. If they are adolescent one takes advantage of the fact that they are young, that they bring a fresh view of things—and professional social workers feel increasingly that this can indeed be an asset. With the retiring, one would capitalize on their accumulated experience and on the fact that they are no longer personally ambitious.

In dealing with institutions I have learnt not so much to offer them assistance, as to ask whether they would aid our volunteers. On the whole people respond more to requests for their help than to having help pressed on them.

As I said, I believe it is the concept of a relay race that we should be applying to many of our social problems, because this is the technique whereby one can get the furthest fastest. We are now planning to adapt this approach by placing teams of young volunteers in some of the most hard-pressed and understaffed mental hospitals in England and Wales. Young people serving in these rather depressing institutions will work with an intensity of commitment because they will know that this is not for a lifetime.

Hill: When Alec Dickson started Voluntary Service Overseas he took a few people to a foreign country. Now the fire which he started at the grass-roots has spread and spread and at the moment Britain sends more than 1500 volunteers overseas every year. As the medical member of the council for the British Volunteer Programme I am now on the horns of a dilemma. Alec Dickson with a few people could perhaps take statistical risks, whereas out of 1500 people I can guarantee 25 are going to have accidents, 25 are going to have mental breakdowns, and until recently many were going to get infectious hepatitis, and so on. I have to look at this from an organizational and managerial point of view, so my difficulty, and the difficulty of the council of the volunteer programme is: is our administrative system going to kill the fires at the grass-roots?

Dickson: I was interested in remarks recently attributed to the British inventor of the Hovercraft, on his resignation from one of our national scientific corporations designed to enable inventors to develop their projects. In a moment of obvious personal bitterness he said that the general aim of management was to isolate the inventor from the factory floor and from the boardroom. The stereotype of the inventor was of a wild Einstein-looking figure with hair all over the place.

You gave him his laboratory, but you did not let him cause confusion in the administration or production line with his crazy ideas. The traditional approach was to anchor the inventor to a down-to-earth man of the world with sound, practical experience of management and finance. This was a certain recipe for friction and futility, this fettering of the imaginative to the conventional and established. The success of Rolls-Royce at the beginning of the century derived from the fact that the engineering genius met up with an entrepreneur equally prepared to take risks, as inventive and creative in the sphere of management as the other was in engineering. Organizations that expect young people in the field to be enormously innovative, bold and imaginative should themselves practise these same virtues back at headquarters, or inspiration will eventually dry up at the source.

Kisseih: In many developing communities where professional health personnel are very difficult to come by, either through lack of funds or unavailability of these personnel, it is amazing how much can be achieved by volunteers.

Twenty-two years ago I was invited by a local authority to establish a Maternal and Child Health Service in a very remote area of Ghana. It was in this area that I became first acquainted with the terrible effects of the disease called yaws. My first reaction was to recommend to the local authority the sending of a delegation to the Ministry of Health in Accra to request the services of a Medical Field Unit in the eradication of yaws. But knowing the limited financial resources of the Ministry of Health, I decided to use another means. I was aware of the existence of a Red Cross Mobile Clinic in the nearest district. This could call at my station once a week to treat the patients suffering from yaws. Volunteers could also be used in collecting the patients and sending them from the various villages to my centre for the weekly treatment. I therefore visited all the neighbouring villages and appointed the more enlightened villagers as team leaders of this operation. With their help, parents were persuaded to send their children who were suffering from yaws to my station every Thursday. Some of the volunteers provided transport. Within a short time the volunteers, the Red Cross Mobile Clinic and I were able to eradicate yaws in that area without any extra cost to either the government or the local authority.

As the head of the country's nursing service, I am sometimes amused at the requests from some of my officers in the field for money for simple work that could be easily performed by volunteers. As I said earlier, our main shortage of health workers in the nursing service in Ghana is in the area of public health nursing. I was therefore very interested when a benevolent society asked if I could assist them in making their society more useful to the community. I immediately visualized a group of volunteers assisting in health education and health work at various levels. With the help of some of my nurses, therefore, a programme (see below) was drawn up for the training of some of these women who could read and write. It is our hope that they, too, would eventually train others.

PROGRAMME FOR THE TRAINING OF MEMBERS OF A BENEVOLENT SOCIETY IN HOME NURSING

Target students: Literate and mainly illiterate women and men.

Objectives: (1) To increase participants' awareness of the health problems in Ghana and those in their localities in particular.
(2) To develop understanding of the role of the benevolent society in the promotion of health in the community.
(3) To give participants knowledge of the minor ailments that can be managed by them (participants).
(4) To develop understanding of the aims and principles of home nursing.
(5) To develop skills in therapeutic procedures and techniques.
(6) To develop skills in health teaching.

Duration of course: 3–4 weeks.

DISCUSSION

Method: (1) Lectures (one day per week).
 (2) Discussion.
 (3) Practical work.

Place: Hospital and selected homes.

Evaluation: Oral and practical examination, 20–30 minutes' duration.

COURSE CONTENT

Unit I: Factors which influence health.
 Health problems in Ghana including common ailments and diseases.

Unit II: Role of the benevolent society in promotion of health.
 Principles and aims of home nursing.

Unit III: *Nursing care*
 (*i*) The plan of care for the patient.
 (*ii*) Organization of home and environment.
 (*iii*) Significance of fever and respiration.
 (*iv*) Bed-making.
 (*v*) Personal cleanliness of the sick.
 (*vi*) Prevention of pressure sores.
 (*vii*) Prevention of spread of infection—hygiene, disinfection and sterilization.
 (*viii*) Serving of meals and fluids.
 (*ix*) Care in relation to common diseases.

NOTE: Due to the varied educational background of the students, the course would be mainly practical.

Unit IV: *Therapeutic procedures*
 (*i*) Application of heat and cold.
 (*ii*) Administration of drugs and fluids.
 (*iii*) Surgical dressing.
 (*iv*) Care of patient suffering from diarrhoea.
 (*v*) Principles in the use of the nursing bag.
 (*vi*) Care of the umbilical cord.

Unit V: *Health teaching*
 To patients, relatives and groups.

CONTENTS OF NURSING BAG

Two thermometers (one rectal, one oral)
Bandages
Plaster
Wool swabs
Gauze swabs
Lint
Scissors
Blade (razor)
Two bowls (small)
Newspaper
Nail brush
Towel
Soap

Tincture of iodine
Cord powder
Shea butter
Eusol
Flavine
Vaseline
Dettol
Methylated spirit
Boric lotion
Nivaquine (tablets)
Aspirin (tablets)
Junior aspirin (tablets)

Hentsch: The League of Red Cross Societies has prepared a guide[1] for the training of volunteers in the field of social welfare. This is now being experimented with in various countries and the results have yet to come. We hope that we can make some contribution to the participation of volunteers in social welfare through this guide.

Dogramaci: In some developing countries volunteers such as Peace Corps volunteers coming from other countries are looked upon with suspicion. Some people think they have another purpose, such as spreading information about their own country. Dr Wolstenholme has already reminded us of a recommendation he made at an earlier Ciba Foundation symposium on the *Health of Mankind*[2]. This was the establishment of an international health service, not duplicating but in parallel with WHO. So I wonder whether an international corps of volunteers could be established where people from every country could work and be sent anywhere by an international agency rather than under the flag of their own country.

Dickson: At the ECOSOC meeting in Geneva next month a proposal for a United Nations organization of volunteers will be considered. [This has now been accepted.] But I feel that only to internationalize the flag under which volunteers serve is not sufficient. We should also be reconsidering the role of the volunteer: is he an expert-in-the-making, is he an 'animateur', is his function to fill a staff vacancy or to bring about change? My concern at the moment is to see young people undertaking service in their own country, for I sense that throughout the developing countries there is no longer quite the same fascination at the news that another plane is bringing more young people from the German Development Corps, the British Volunteer Programme, or the American Peace Corps. Every government is tormented by the problem of how to involve thousands of its own young people. This is a more complicated task than the despatch of a *corps d'élite* to other countries. We should perhaps think in terms of how volunteers coming from abroad might work alongside the students, and even workless youngsters, in developing countries; we should try to dovetail the two and not see them as two separate entities.

King: In many ways nutrition is a particularly suitable field for voluntary activity, in that one of the greatest needs is teaching and the knowledge required is limited. Some schools in Zambia are starting nutrition clubs and these are beginning to do voluntary nutrition work. In future years I hope that we shall see the growth of just this type of voluntary activity, with the developing countries helping themselves in the way that has been suggested. The training mechanisms needed to make these volunteers useful are one of my present interests.

Dickson: Volunteering has hitherto had a faintly middle-class image in the West, though I do not believe that this is sociologically basic to it. It is a matter of availability. Because the middle-class can take time off, it is from this background that volunteers have principally come. That is why it ought to be a positive act of policy to make time available for others—young industrial workers, for example—to have this experience.

Yet paradoxically it is closely related to what might seem to be the complete opposite, namely the tens of thousands of young people in the United States who cannot, or do not, volunteer because they are unemployed. Finding new roles for them in paramedical work, devising new careers for the poor, has great significance even for volunteers because it obliges the professionals to re-think what the institutional or job structure should be, and what responsibilities can be given to the relatively unskilled. I see the role of volunteers as impinging on and overlapping with the problem of the young unemployed. Something much more profound than young people happening to have a period free at the end of the week or at the end of their university studies is involved.

Braga: Local volunteer work on a national basis is certainly much easier than on the international level. WHO itself is an international organization created and maintained by its member countries, yet whenever WHO is asked to provide an expert the member country making the request always has to say whether it is willing to accept the person we suggest. So whenever you consider volunteer contributions you have eventually to connect this with some political angle. A person from a particular country may be accepted but not persons from other countries. This is the kind of difficulty there would be, even with volunteer activity.

Dickson: Another difficulty that U.N. Agencies must face in this respect is the time factor. The trouble is you cannot preserve a volunteer and put him in the refrigerator until such time as he is needed, perhaps two years or so later. He wants to help *now*, and unless you are prepared to accept his offer immediately, he dismisses your organization as an unfeeling bureaucracy and 'does his thing' elsewhere. You cannot even 'can' a project. It may have seemed very live and real when the request was originally made, but when twelve months have gone by and there has been a change of government, a change of Minister, a change of policy, the project may have lost validity. An adult expert may (perhaps) be prepared to accept this situation: professionally he has 'arrived', he is being remunerated according to his status, and he may feel that, given time, he can make himself useful. But the volunteer has only a limited period available: if the project has gone stale even before his arrival, he may find himself condemned to a very frustrating experience. It is the telegram that came yesterday, requesting the urgent despatch of someone to help, that will give the volunteer most satisfaction.

International bureaucracies are still bureaucracies. A great many young people do not want to serve abroad waving the Union Jack or the Stars and Stripes: they would prefer to go as human beings helping other human beings. But neither do they want to go under a heavily structured organization, even if it is the United Nations. This may force the U.N. Agencies to review their own administrative procedures. This could be to the benefit of all parties. Other organizations in accepting the young have had to take a new look at themselves, and this is not the least service that volunteers can give. They may force those at headquarters to be more alert and sensitive, which could be as important as the contribution they make to villagers 10000 miles away.

GENERAL DISCUSSION

Dogramaci: Our symposium title is Teamwork for World Health. In order to ensure that teamwork works successfully for our common aim of better health, when we reorganize our various curricula we should perhaps see to it that teamwork starts from the early days of education. At Hacettepe University we tried to do something about this by establishing for the first time in Turkey a faculty of health sciences for training medical technicians. We had to stop training medical technicians temporarily, but now we are continuing with nurses at two levels, each trained for four years but one course being for students with university entrance qualifications. We now have two schools of nursing, one school of physical medicine and rehabilitation, and one school for dieticians, all under the roof of the university. All the students work together in the same wards, and to some extent in the rural health centres, although not yet as much as we would like. Thus they know each other, make friends and try to understand each other during their training. Would such an approach contribute to teamwork in their future careers?

Christie: There are similar faculties of health science in North America. Yours is one of the earliest and is something that the rest of the world is probably following.

Israel: All through this symposium the need has been shown for the reorganization of thinking on the international as well as the national level on the training of all categories of health personnel. A broad framework of needs in health work seems to be required, and within this framework there must be scope for flexibility according to each country's own special needs and special cultural differences. Such training, whether for a doctor, social worker, nurse, sanitary engineer or sanitary inspector, must concern itself much more with practical exercises in community health, and with more field practice in team spirit and leadership. I think above all it must develop in each of the workers a deep concern for other people, whether it is for their own colleagues in the team or for the patients.

Bridger: Much of the discussion at this symposium has dealt with the extent to which teamwork can be developed among the doctors, nurses and so-called paramedicals in the total health field. This goes beyond the development of professionals and hoping that 'good sense' and purpose will enable teams composed of those various professions to work well together. We could learn much from the matrix-type organization used in space technology. In this, members from different professions and disciplines are matched against the demands of various

207

projects and allocated after consultation and agreement. A project may be temporary or 'permanent' but in any case everyone has two affiliations: generally these are functional responsibility to his professional grouping and operational accountability to his project management. For any individual, therefore, management and membership of a professional team may have to exist alongside and together with management and membership of a multidisciplinary project team.

Hentsch: The emergence of Red Cross Societies in developing countries has meant that members of the LORCS secretariat have had to work more closely together. To meet the needs of these developing countries, who were seeking from us something different to what the long-established countries want, we have come together as a team in a way that we had never done before. The different professionals on the staff are discussing together how best to plan guidance and assistance to the new societies about what will be their specific responsibilities as auxiliaries to the health authorities.

Hill: Mr Salmon talked about the top, middle and lower levels of management. I would go below that and talk about the storekeeper and the maintenance man. Ghana and Nigeria, for example, have very few of these men. You cannot get balls of string, you cannot get exercise books within the hospital campus although they are available in the town. This is not because of a shortage of exchange but because no one is thinking about this. The doctors are up in the clouds and the job of storekeeper is not taken account of. In Bombay on the other hand they have such a surfeit of 'storekeepers' that nothing gets through.

This brings me to the question of aid. Instead of quantity, I would like to see some quality in this aid. Instead of injecting into the froth at the top, which we do by sending out professors, I would like to inject into the body some ex-corporals or sergeants who could show people how to deal with stores and communications. Ghana in fact is tackling this in its Institute of Public Administration. Though this institute is for the top management, they are very concerned with this other problem. In teamwork we must not forget the non-medicals—the maintenance man, the storekeeper—because medicine cannot get on without them, and many places are not running well because of the lack of them.

Banks: I have been mildly depressed by the gap that our discussions have revealed between theory in the most advanced areas in the world and what is practicable at the grass-roots. Is it possible to span this gap by some sort of practical experiment? The Ciba Foundation does not just produce books, and I am sure that the Director would like to have suggestions for practical developments. The men who came nearest to suggesting answers about teamwork in health were Mr Salmon and Mr Bridger. In their vast experience in other fields I wonder if they have had any comparable situation and whether they have any practical suggestions as to what we could do in the present situation.

Barbero: It is clear that most things that have been worth while have tended to come down to the smallest unit on the spot. I was very bothered by Mr Salmon's discussion of management and how to bring it together in some way. In the educational area there is one place that it can transpose itself progressively to function. For example, in this meeting we have talked very little about role playing as it relates to understanding concepts of different functions, where they merge. How many institutions with whatever function bring their various people together at the middle or even the senior level? When I went to an institution to be a department chairman I had to sit on a hospital council. There was a great deal of talk about the features of care, much of it in relation to many other disciplines, not one of which was represented. In the educational area there is a great deal of talk about teamwork but little team action. One of our first functions on that council was to get the head nurse onto it. This was horrendous for the physician but soon it became apparent that a viable process might grow out of this beginning. At our meeting here Miss Hentsch, Miss Hockey and Miss Kisseih all said how pleased they were to have been invited, almost as if there were an inherent apology. This is where the teamwork really exists. Where is it at the senior level? Where is it at the middle level? How often does the student play the role of a nurse? We are experimenting in Philadelphia with students being nurses and they are all overwhelmed by this. Some of the things we have been talking about at the primary site level, in a small rural area, in a hospital, or in an out-patient clinic, all have common principles. How do we blend? How do people begin to trust each other and find that these roles are not rigidified, but that there is a valid and appropriate use for every individual? This may be different for each different setting, and the ability to tolerate this is part of the process of change. Where does a change process get its management?

Salmon: I do not know any easy solution to this problem of how one begins a change process, but I was involved in this requirement in my own business. We used social scientists to try to help us think out our own problems, to analyse what was wrong and how one could put it right, and to try to develop a new set of values. This is an agonizing and painful process because one is all the time looking at oneself as well as other people who are close to one. Any institution or organization which requires change cannot get it until it appreciates that it requires it and then sets about investigating the whole anatomy of the institution. I do not think it can be done from the bottom upwards. It has to start at the top, and the new thinking and the new change of attitude must come in right at the top level.

Ordoñez-Plaja: When Professor Dogramaci mentioned health sciences I was thinking on the same lines as Mr Salmon, but in terms of physiology, not anatomy. The schools of health sciences I have visited do not work as a team. They are an aggregate. We talk of the health sciences, but the average doctor is interested not in health but in disease. A nurse is interested in a patient more than in a disease. Most of the health professionals still look at disease as an entity, as something external—whether a devil or a microbe—that comes into the body. This is perhaps the place to remember one of the things Florence Nightingale said: "There are no specific diseases; there are only specific conditions that produce disease." We still look at disease and health as two separate entities. I do not know if it is only a problem of the Western world, but we tend to look at them as if they were black and white, good and evil. When does a disease start? Or does a disease ever start? Is it just that the conditions put a man in a situation in which he is going to get a disease anyhow? Isn't it time for us to start rethinking this and look at health and disease as a sort of thermometer on which zero on the Kelvin scale will be death? Nobody has discovered the exact moment at which they can say that someone is sick and he was healthy before that. That might sound too philosophical, but it has a practical implication, because if we do not reach an agreement about it we are never going to work as a team regarding health. Mr Salmon mentioned the social scientists; if we accept that health results from the possibility of adjusting to an ecological system, then everybody is a health professional. How are we to unify all those motivations, efforts, knowledge, and eventually wisdom to try to have a common goal and really work as a team for human welfare?

Dogramaci: We should accept that everything is relative. I shall long remember your comments earlier, Dr Ordoñez-Plaja, that the type of health described by WHO is enjoyed perhaps for only a few moments on honeymoon. Everything being relative, we should not concentrate on disease or even on conditions, but on human beings.

Bridger: Dr Barbero has referred to the need for trust and 'blending' as part of the process of change. The management of change could be said to be the growth of these capacities in a team. We need a degree of trust before expressing thoughts and ideas in a group. We also know that risking one's thoughts is necessary for engendering trust and building the team itself. It is equally true in terms of the value of our discussions and exchanges here. It also links up with what Dr de Kock van Leeuwen said about the use and opportunity for 'feedback' in communications between members of a group. Besides improving the general sum of knowledge and perhaps reaching nearer to a consensus or agreed viewpoint, conditions existing within the membership will have been affected by the way in which opportunities for speaking, listening and giving feedback are used. This is the 'management' aspect for which members as well as appointed leaders are responsible.

It is far from easy to communicate our *experience* of teamwork and health, as distinct from exchanging intellectual views and theories. In our efforts to do so we speak about *an* experience back home or elsewhere. When Dr Barbero wanted to communicate something of this order to us he gave us an actual experience of his own, as indeed did Dr Dogramaci and others. Thus, very often the most effective way that one can learn about the building of trust and 'blending' as a management job in a team is by exploring the degree of trust existing in the group one happens to be in, especially in any international situation; that is by seeing to what extent we are experiencing teamwork in the actual situation itself. Training for this 'management of change' could therefore be said to require the use of a task and team in real situations, where we can suspend business from time to time—or on an *ad hoc* basis—to study our mode of working and the kind of way we are reaching agreement or avoiding it. We need to be prepared to face a learning task of finding out the extent to which trust and teamwork are being built up in the actual team or conference situation.

I am spending much of my time in endeavours of this kind with people in industry, in health and educational fields where this approach is being developed. It is salutary to recognize that an international group or team can, in this way, develop better mutual understanding and more effective communication and action, internally and externally, than by concentrating on languages. This is not to suggest that speaking other languages is not important or helpful but rather that building cross-cultural as well as inter-personal trust adds a further dimension. At its simplest it means, for example, stating that one has not understood what someone else said, more especially when it was originally allowed to slip by without comment—not always easy to do. The 'suspending business' type of activity involves engaging a bit of our real selves in what we say and do—a better chance for building trust, and blending into a team, but also a higher risk in openness and commitment.

Hockey: I became uneasy when I had the feeling that the paramedical team of health workers was being considered as a matter of expediency because of lack of financial resources. We should look at the positive contribution of each member of this team. There should not be a lowering of standards but an increasing and enhancing of the standards of care because everyone is trained for their particular task, and is therefore able to do it better without causing frustration to any other member of the team. In this connexion I would like to mention education again, particularly the planning for education which several speakers have mentioned. This is one of the most fundamental issues of this symposium and I would make a plea for teamwork at that level. A multidisciplinary education planning panel for health work could perhaps be initiated.

Russell: Dr Dogramaci said that we should think of individual human beings, and of course this is the only possible way to look at everything, including medicine. We should really be taking an ecological approach to many of our problems, and in such an approach, of course, the doctor is not necessarily the most important member of the team. In fact he might well be driven back to his hospital, on a purely ecological approach.

Horn: Members of our symposium have not indicated any firm determination to break down the barriers that exist and that militate against the formation of a real health team. After Professor Fişek had pointed out that rural midwives had had a bigger effect in reducing infant mortality than a first-class hospital in Ankara, thereby underlining the value of rural midwives, someone asked for, and received, an assurance that these people were nurses who were allowed to carry out screening processes but who were not permitted to diagnose or prescribe. Nobody objected at the time, but we really ought to face up to this question. Several of us have spoken of the need to relate the concept of a team to the concrete realities that exist in large areas of the world today. That concrete reality is one that calls for a team which is not fragmented by craft prejudices which originated in the advanced countries hundreds of years ago. We should not accept a position where rural midwives who actually make a big contribution are allowed only to screen but not to diagnose or prescribe.

Miss Kisseih said that nurses want to be nurses, not something other than nurses, and somebody else pointed out that in one of the developing countries there was a much greater enrolment of doctors than of nurses, which seems wrong. Nursing as we know it in England originated with the Florence Nightingale tradition. It is not surprising to me that in certain countries there is not much interest in training such nurses, because nursing in the Florence Nightingale tradition is often thought of as nursing in hospitals, and in many African countries patients are nursed in hospitals by their relatives, just as they sometimes are in China, and they are also nursed by each other. Hospital nursing by trained nurses may appear to be an unnecessary luxury in many parts of the world. What then should nurses in these countries do? Their function should change. I do not think that we should cling tenaciously to a conception of nursing which was very good in its day, and which may still be very good in some parts of the world, but which in other parts should be superseded by a conception which greatly enlarges the scope of a nurse's work.

Kisseih: My reference to the need of the nurse to practise nursing is simply to clarify her position in the health team. The duties of the nurse depend on the availability of other health personnel and the prevailing health conditions in the country. These duties, therefore, vary from country to country.

Many European nurses are amazed at the scope of practice of the nurse in Africa where, because of the scarcity of other members of the health team, the nurse's duties in certain places overlap into medicine, pharmacy, catering, laundry and other areas. As I said earlier, all that the nursing statutory bodies insist upon is that the nurse must be given additional preparation for the performance of those functions which are outside her professional competence.

Wolstenholme: In a meeting at which we are commemorating the birth of Florence Nightingale, it seems hard that we are damning her as an originator of purely curative treatment by nurses in hospitals. She is the person who also inspired the district nursing service and rural health visiting. She said that she only used the word nursing for lack of a better, and that it meant putting us in the best condition to enjoy all the powers we have to use.

Fişek: All of us agree on having a team for health, and on thinking of the team in its largest sense. I am sure that Professor Hill is absolutely right to say that sometimes the most important man is the storekeeper or purchasing officer. Dr Ordoñez-Plaja said further that we must have a team and not an aggregate. That is the problem. In many places we have many staff but no team, no working together. Who the members of the team are and what their responsibilities are will change from place to place and from time to time. If in one community at a given time there is a shortage of medical doctors, nurses should do more than nursing and their responsibility should be extended to caring for, diagnosing or treating the most common diseases. Dr Horn mentioned that our rural midwives are not allowed to diagnose or treat: this is true. I am not against it in principle. They are not allowed because the circumstances in our area do not require it, since fully qualified medical doctors are available. I am sure that when they have enough qualified medical doctors in mainland China, the responsibility of peasant/doctors will be more limited. We should avoid giving a universal formula which is good for all countries, because the need and situation will be different from country to country and from time to time.

Hockey: But we must surely decide what tasks a nurse can do under all circumstances, and not say that a doctor should do it if a doctor is available. If we are quite certain that certain tasks can be assigned to a nurse, we should train nurses to perform those tasks and not have doctors to do them while we have an abundance of doctors. It is this that causes so much unhappiness, and I hope that this symposium will highlight this point.

Fişek: I think that what we teach a nurse in England, in Turkey, in China or in Malawi has to be different. We cannot give a general pattern

213

for nursing education and functions all over the world. In team work one member always completes the work of the others. If the number in the medical profession is limited, and if it is much easier to increase the number of nurses, then some responsibility of the medical profession has to go to the nursing profession, or the other way round. We should not have strict boundaries between professions in every country all the time.

Russell: One country that I visited very recently has 7700 doctors and 700 trained nurses. The result of this is to be seen in a medical college where the paediatric department has 42 cots, a professor, a reader, three lecturers and eight general doctors in the ward, mostly doing nursing duties.

Bridger: It has also become clear that leadership in teamwork is not the sole prerogative of the appointed leader. The latter is the formal leader and is accountable for the work of the team and the degree to which the objectives are attained. But all members may contribute by showing leadership in certain roles, functions or behaviour during the course of the work in hand. The opportunity for this wider form of leadership also depends on the attitude and values of the formal leader and his readiness to foster a climate in which trust and giving a lead can grow. In turn this emphasizes the importance of Dr Wolstenholme's suggestion (see p. 10) for a World Health Service which would provide active training and development for such leadership capability in addition to its primary purpose. WHO please note.

Christie: We have covered a great many areas in our discussions, but it is important that we should be aware of the areas in teamwork for world health that we have omitted. First, we have agreed that it is the general practitioner who is often the leader of the teams we are discussing, yet it is a world phenomenon that only 30–40 per cent of medical students want to go into general practice. I think the reason is that practice today, particularly in country areas, does not give them satisfaction, and everybody wants a career that will satisfy them. Why doesn't it give satisfaction? One reason is the absence of the kind of team help that we have been discussing. But I am sure that another—and this has not been mentioned—is that the doctor must have lines of communication to people from whom he can get advice. We have heard that the midwife must be able to get advice, if only by telephone. To get satisfaction in his work a general practitioner, who is a jack of all trades, must be able to get advice if he is in doubt. No one enjoys work when he is working in the dark. This can be organized, and in some countries it is organized. In Sweden for instance they have done a first-class job in this respect. In other countries they have paid no attention to it at all.

Another thing we have not discussed is group practice, which is team-work of a very high order. It is flourishing in certain parts of the world but has hardly started in others.

We have hardly discussed teamwork in hospitals. I have seen a great many hospitals in the last two years, and one finds that their organization is often based largely on political expediency, or on the ideas of some Minister of Health who was in office perhaps 10 or 15 years earlier.

Another area we have hardly touched on covers certain world trends in medical education. There is a trend, not only in China, but in America and Europe, to shorten the curriculum. One of the main tools of this shortening is by so-called systems teaching, to avoid duplication of effort for the student. Systems teaching starts preferably in the pre-clinical period and goes right through the medical course. This is team-work of a very high order, but it has to be organized with great care if it is to succeed.

Another world trend in education which is not confined to China is exposure of the student to community needs. In North America this is very widespread. Over 50 per cent of medical schools are making really strenuous efforts to expose their students to the local community, so that at an early stage they realize the significance of medicine, even though they haven't learnt it. It does not require very much skill to do this, and the students are immensely interested. This has been mentioned already with nurses but I do not think any reference has been made to medical students.

Another world trend is the stress on personal contact of teachers with the students, on group teaching and discussions. We are going back to the mediaeval days when students were taught by argument, discussion and disputation. This is happening in America, in Scandinavia, and elsewhere. It is curious how these changes seem to happen at the same time in various countries, though each rather prides itself on being the first.

These are some main points that I think we have omitted in our discussions. I am not saying this in any spirit of criticism, but so that we have a record of what might be discussed at a future date. Are there any other main areas of omission?

King: We shall have to leave a future Ciba Foundation symposium to consider the teamwork needed for the wealthy countries to assist those whom we have been prepared to consider as being economically unviable. How, through international teamwork, can the rich assist the poor, particularly the very poor, in the improvement of the world's health?

16: Teamwork for World Health: Personal Conclusions and Recommendations

F. G. YOUNG

THIS 124th major conference of the Ciba Foundation, the 10th of such meetings that have taken place outside Britain, relates to the 150th anniversary of the birth of Florence Nightingale on 12 May 1820, and it provides an opportunity to consider what lessons may still be learned from her example.

DEFINITIONS

Socrates said that if you wish to debate, you must first define your terms. We have spent a little time on definitions, and dictionaries have been quoted at times in our discussions; but we have, I think wisely, not spent too much time on such matters. Certainly definitions of a formal type are often sterile; indeed a dictionary is necessarily a vicious circle, defining words in terms of each other. Concepts are the things that matter. We found considerable difficulty in adopting a satisfactory definition of many words that are in common use in relation to health and to ancillary, auxiliary or paramedical workers, and indeed I think that we are not sure what ultimately we meant by the words 'doctor' or 'nurse'. This to my mind was satisfactory, since one can so easily be bemused by tidy categorization that obscures defective thinking. I am glad that we didn't attempt to hide our ignorance in this manner.

I thought that Dr Baker's table listing 'Health workers by income and type of practice' (p. 130) was the right pattern to consider in place of definitions. His categories related to the type of practice, to income and to length of education, and by this means he could include doctors, nurses, and all those we might otherwise call paramedical assistants, in a cellular pattern. I think that we were wise not to attempt to impose a cellular structure on this important pattern.

INTERNATIONAL DIVERSITY

The diversity of solutions to similar problems in the 13 countries represented among the 26 members of our symposium has been both confusing and stimulating. Dr M. Dadgar's description of the Iran

217

Health Corps was most exciting, and provided an excellent example of how the organizational capacity of an army could be employed for the promotion and dissemination of knowledge of health, and thus provide an outlet for energies that would otherwise be absorbed in peacetime military service. I suppose one can say that an army and its units provided an early example of teamwork in the evolution of human society. I noticed with interest that in Iran the institution of the Literacy Corps preceded that of the Health Corps. In my view you cannot effectively promote good health in the absence of general education: the two are inextricably joined. Now, the Iran Health Corps is a special solution to a problem, special to a country in which there is military service by conscription during peacetime, and such an example is not directly or simply applicable to countries in which no such peace-time conscription exists. Nevertheless, as mentioned here already, members of the armed forces of other countries can be, and are beginning to be, employed in ways not entirely unrelated to that in Iran.

Dr Horn's fascinating exposition of the experiments in which he has taken part in People's China in expanding the rural health services provided another special solution to a big problem, the results of which cannot be directly applied elsewhere. We did wonder if in time peasant/doctors would give way to practitioners with qualifications of a more ordinary type. I think this is very likely, but it is still a matter for the future. I was surprised that so little attention was given to nutrition in this symposium. But Dr Horn mentioned nutrition, and in the promotion of good nutrition, agriculture and medical care have a common field of interest. He emphasized the importance of agriculture in the activities of the peasant/doctors, who still remained peasants. We should have wasted time, in my view, if we had discussed whether a peasant as such, not in relation to doctoring but in relation to his agricultural activities, is to be regarded as an ancillary worker in the promotion of medical care and health, even though agriculture and the provision of food are, and can be, important factors in the maintenance of good health. The limits of the team that we wish to consider under the title of our symposium are to some extent completely arbitrary, and I am glad that we have, without worrying too much about precise definitions, accepted a team of moderately small size, based on the categories that Dr Baker gave in his pattern of service.

HEALTH SERVICE IN GREAT BRITAIN

Now I want to say something about the developments in medical care that are likely to occur in Great Britain between now and the end of the century. In a sense forecasts of this sort are like looking through a glass darkly; but if one wishes to forecast how many doctors will be required in a country such as Great Britain, then one must have some idea of what the doctors will be doing in the future. As a member of the Royal Commission on Medical Education, 1965 to 1968, I was concerned with attempting to look into the future to decide how many doctors would be needed by the end of the century. The production of doctors is a slow process and one must think clearly now, in 1970, about the training of the medical practitioners and teachers who will be active in 1995. Moreover the production of doctors is very expensive. As Professor Kenneth Hill[1] calculated some years ago, in Britain the figure is something like £10 000. The Royal Commission on Medical Education[2] came to a figure similar to Professor Hill's. Governments are naturally concerned about the cost of providing for the large number of doctors that one might calculate to be needed in the future, and wish to be assured that such needs as are predicted are reasonably based.

The Royal Commission on Medical Education came to the conclusion that in the last decade of this century the man who is ill in Great Britain and who needs treatment is most likely to receive it in a Health Centre with accommodation for up to 12 doctors, each with some degree of specialization but essentially and primarily general physicians. Those Health Centres will contain numerous ancillary staff (if I may use that expression), various diagnostic and other machines, and perhaps a bed or two for short stay. They will not be hospitals, though they will be in close association with hospitals, with the medical staff of the Health Centre holding joint appointments in a hospital. The Commission came to the conclusion that the patient will generally go to the Health Centre, and that the doctor will not go to the patient. This perhaps sounds inhuman, but the conclusion was reached that unless there were special humanitarian reasons to the contrary, there would be much advantage in bringing the patient to the Health Centre because of the facilities that would be available there and nowhere else. Therefore we thought that there would be little or no domiciliary medicine at that time. When the patient reached the Health Centre all possible chemical and physical tests and measurements would be performed by ancillary staff. Perhaps 95 per cent of the results would be irrelevant at the particular time, but it is much easier to do everything, when estimations are automatic and computerized, than it is to pick out what would at first sight seem to be desirable. But all the information obtained would be stored in one or two central computers, from which retrieval would quickly be possible at any future date at any Health Centre in Great Britain. As Dr Ordoñez-Plaja told us, the computer is not in any way a substitute for man. It is a valuable saver of human labour—as much as, or more indeed, than other electrical and mechanical devices can be—but with the aid of the human programmer who does the thinking.

The conclusion that the Commission came to suggested that in the year 1995 the patient will see a doctor only when all the information that

8*

can be made available through auxiliary services has been extracted. Then the doctor will decide whether or not the patient will be admitted to hospital, treated in the Health Centre or perhaps treated and sent home, or retained for observation. Today this situation may not seem very desirable, but we were trying to assess what is likely to happen rather than what we would wish to see, with our present eyes, come about at that time. In such a Health Centre of the future you will have a good example of the sort of teamwork which is beginning to develop in some countries now.

Despite all the ancillary services and the ancillary staff that should then be available, the Royal Commission on Medical Education calculated that the number of doctors required in Great Britain by the end of the century is such as to necessitate a doubling of the entry to the medical schools by that time. This is a very substantial increase and the Commission drew a curve showing the number of doctors in gainful employment, as extracted from the national censuses from 1911 to the present time, and extrapolated it to the end of the century. On this basis, over about 50 years from 1911 the curve was reasonably smooth, and the number of doctors for each million of the population was found to be increasing at about 1·25 per cent a year. Clearly this curve, which shows no sign of breaking in the range that was available, cannot go on indefinitely, because otherwise the whole of the population would become doctors in the course of time, but we found no reason to suppose that this extrapolation was not valid for the rest of the century. A comparable rate of increase is found in other countries, although the increase in the number of doctors for each million inhabitants is proceeding at rather different rates, ranging from 0·1 per cent per year in Switzerland to 5·3 per cent a year in Czechoslovakia, over a period from the early 1950s to the early 1960s. This increase in demand seems to me one of the reasons why developed countries can attract doctors from developing ones. The number of doctors per million of the population, that is the number of economically active ones, rises more rapidly than the population. So the Commission came to the conclusion that the use of paramedical auxiliaries will become increasingly important in Great Britain as in other countries.

THE BACKGROUND TO A NATIONAL HEALTH SERVICE

A national health service can plan the production of the number of doctors calculated to be necessary, but this is not a universal possibility and some countries do not proceed in this way. The background to the present state of the National Health Service in Great Britain which was set out earlier (pp. 95–101) provided an interesting picture. The evolution of the British National Health Service has a long historical background, to which I should like to allude in order to complete the picture that I see leading up to the end of the present century, and the future development of teamwork for medical care in Great Britain.

In Great Britain at the beginning of the last century, there developed a strong humanitarian movement. Many people thought that not only was the greatest happiness for the greatest numbers the objective of civilization, but that attempts towards its attainment were also an important motivating force in the evolution of the civilized community. In the early years of this movement, in fact in the later years of the eighteenth century, slavery was declared to be illegal in Great Britain, and then later, in the 1830s, in British possessions overseas. Men must be free, and men must have democratic rights; in Britain the suffrage Reform Bills of the 1830s and 1840s and later gave men the right to vote. Men must be educated, and the School Acts of the 1870s provided free elementary education for many children. Similar developments occurred in other communities around this time.

Men have the right to work and be paid for it, not to starve, and medical care must be available to all. Public assistance for those unable to fend for themselves, with care for those who are ill, was one of the objectives of this great humanitarian movement. And in the early years of this century, in 1910 and 1911, Insurance Acts were passed in Great Britain which provided a Health Service for those whose income was below a particular level. This development was introduced by Mr Lloyd George, who had based some of his ideas about health insurance on those of Bismarck in Prussia. The idea of extending health insurance to a wider section of the population was already being discussed by the British Medical Association in 1939, before the war of 1939–1945 came. The discussions continued during that war, with a coalition government in power in which the Minister of Health was a member of the Conservative Party; and after the war, in 1947, the idea of a National Health Service came to fruition under a Labour government. It was not a political act of one political party, but the natural outcome of 150 years of social development. This process seems not to have occurred by any conscious overall planning, but in retrospect can be related to a background of evolving political institutions and educational developments, based on humanitarian grounds. My point in emphasizing this background to the British National Health Service is that a big change of this sort was slowly generated by internal pressures. In Great Britain, the humanitarian warmth of the early years of the last century led, by the process I have sketched, to a situation in which, at present, one can visualize the perhaps chilly teamwork of 1995 in the Health Centres that I mentioned earlier. This type of development can be regarded as leading towards nationwide teamwork, with teams which include not only those who work for the improvement of health but also those who work for education and other attributes of a civilized community.

ASSISTANCE FROM WITHOUT

Miss Hentsch told us (p. 21) about the reluctance of some nations immediately to accept Red Cross aid offered in times of emergencies. Nations had sometimes to be persuaded to accept help. An emergency is a time when such external aid can be most acceptable, and indeed it is usually so, and international organizations like the Red Cross do magnificent work in this connexion. But is such external aid—"the provision of outside teams for world health"—likely to induce permanent changes in the pattern of medical care in the recipient countries? Or should we take note not only of the need to provide assistance in emergencies but also of the paramount importance of the induction of grass-root changes and developments, if I may borrow someone else's terminology? I believe that much does depend upon grass-root changes in our working towards health in the world as a whole—world health. We must expect resistance to change as natural, but persistence of a stimulus to change which acts over a long period of time can be most effective. There is a simple theorem in physical science which seems to be relevant to human affairs. I refer to Le Chatelier's theorem according to which, when a system is in stable equilibrium and the equilibrium is disturbed, then the components of the equilibrium rearrange themselves to minimize the effects of the disturbance. This is a physical law which underlies a law of thermodynamics, of which it is indeed an expression, but which seems to me to apply in large measure to human affairs.

A stable society must be expected to engender resistance to change because it is stable, and we should not be surprised if change of any sort, including obviously desirable assistance, may sometimes be reluctantly accepted. An external proposal for help or improvement is a disturbance that is imposed on a stable system, and the components of that stable system are, in terms of the theorem, likely to rearrange themselves to minimize the effectiveness of the disturbance. But the effectiveness of the disturbance will relate to the length of the time during which it operates. A long-term stimulus, but not a short-term acceptance of teams, may be needed. In that way the ideas that generated and sustained the external teams, and not only the teams themselves, can become acceptable. Helpfulness in an emergency must be offered, and is usually acceptable at the time. But one must seek longer-term effects in respect of the title of this meeting.

In my view evolution of human society depends to some extent on adaptive resistance to the effects of strain, and paradoxically one aim of civilized society seems to be to diminish the intensity of the process of evolution by which it came about. In our discussions of the nature of teams we did not decide about the maximum size of a team, and I wonder if, at the grass-roots, the nation as a whole is the team that works for the health of mankind, with the effectiveness of aids to health depending on the integrated action of the communities concerned, both donor and receiver. Small teams are important, but I think we should not ignore the bigger issues. An advantage of a small team is that the members will educate each other, so that those who knew little or nothing about the activities of some of the other members of that team will undergo the best sort of education in that subject. I certainly agree strongly, and Miss Kisseih emphasized it too (p. 150), that continuing education is of paramount importance in the developing and the developed countries alike.

TEAMS AND LEADERSHIP

The study of groups, as we have heard in our discussion, is really little more than 40 years old. The attributes of leadership and top-level management are being continually reviewed at present, and professional excellence is found not to be an indication of capacity for leadership, or not necessarily so, as was emphasized by Mr Salmon (p. 162) and others. In our discussions of teams for world health an ideal did not obviously emerge, nor did the means by which a leader of the team is to be found. Florence Nightingale exerted leadership over her nurses, cooperation with the doctors and later in her life leadership in the field of hygiene and sanitary reform. One can say reasonably that in her later years she enrolled cabinet ministers, doctors and army generals in her teams, exerting a remarkable leadership at a time when such qualities were not expected of women not of royal descent. If the medical profession had been open to Florence Nightingale, might she have become a doctor? Such speculation is not rewarding; but the fact that the structure of professions in developed countries in general, and indeed in all countries, has been erected by men for the benefit of men, without regard to the fact that women can be just as able as men in most of them, though they may need a period of absence for childbearing, is perhaps not irrelevant to the shortage of doctors and medical needs for the rest of this century.

Florence Nightingale's great opportunity emerged through the catastrophe of war. Periods of war, and of disaster in general, have proved to be the background for many important innovations, made possible perhaps by the loosening of those bonds which hold a stable society tightly together. She, having embraced the opportunity that offered under emergency conditions, became involved in her great work for life. Her emotional involvement, her personal involvement, in her great work perhaps led her to be somewhat unresponsive to the ideas of others, such as those of Pasteur about the transmission of infection by microorganisms, while her opposition to the State Registration of nurses was a related aspect of her character. Miss Nightingale's work was of the nature of an artist as well as that of a statistician, although she was indeed a first-class statistician and an innovator in that field. The creator of a work of art, emotionally involved at one stage, must disengage and step back to view the creation in an objective manner, in relation not only to the artist but to the world in general. Florence Nightingale was an outstandingly able administrator whose ideas about the necessity for clean water were of paramount importance in her time. And can we blame her for being sceptical about some of the new ideas which were then gaining ground but which were not accepted by doctors without a great deal of reluctance—ideas, for example, about the value of bacteriological methods for the examination and assessment of apparently clean water?

I said earlier that I was surprised that nutrition had not been considered more in our discussions, because the relationship of health and nutrition is clear, and often especially so in developing countries. Among the small numbers that make up this type of symposium not all aspects of the subject can possibly be covered. Administration has necessarily taken much of our attention, but youth today, the world over, is impatient of administrative structures. Youth tends to look for more direct human relationships. As Mr Dickson has so eloquently reminded us, the will to serve among youth is strong, but what can we do about it? I think we came to no clear conclusions, but we at least have stated problems that must be considered.

CONCLUSION

The title of my talk includes the words 'personal conclusions and recommendations'. I have given some personal ideas but I pause very much over recommendations. The members of this symposium as a team came to no final conclusions on which recommendations could be based, though we were much attracted by Dr Wolstenholme's idea about an international health service that might be so organized as "... to give to the young a practical outlet to their desire to remedy injustice and inequality". A junior WHO, in which nobody over 25 years of age would be allowed to take part, is an interesting, but perhaps not a realizable, idea. Dr Wolstenholme says that two obstacles to better health for mankind are lack of money and manpower. I would add a third: a natural reluctance of society to change from any form which seems to offer at that time a reasonable chance of stability. Perhaps a youthful WHO might do more to help in this respect than could be provided by those with a greater experience of stability than the young possess.

I venture to make two personal recommendations at the end of my talk: that we should all bring to the notice of governments and international organizations the book that will ultimately appear as a result of this conference, and that we promote the idea of another conference of this sort, in perhaps five years' time, with the object of reviewing progress.

SPEECH BY PROFESSOR S. ARTUNKAL

Professor of Pharmacology and Therapeutics, University of Istanbul
Guest of honour at the symposium

I AM deeply honoured by being the guest of honour at such a distinguished symposium. I must express my thanks to the Ciba Foundation for having created the opportunity to discuss this important subject of teamwork in the health services.

Teamwork itself is a very significant phenomenon of our scientific age. Its importance in medicine has been shown by the distinguished speakers of this symposium. We find teams engaged not only in laboratory research but also in the everyday care of the sick and the prevention of disease.

Florence Nightingale was the person who demonstrated the importance of helping the medical doctor in his duties. Her example has led to today's sophisticated teams of people with a different approach to the subject. It was the Crimean War which stimulated her activities, and maybe it would interest you to know that this war stimulated also another medical activity in Istanbul, that is, the foundation of a medical society, named the Ottoman Medical Society. This society was founded by medical doctors from different countries who had come to Istanbul in order to help. Their intention in founding this organization was to discuss the various health problems which arose because of the war. This organization is still operating today under the name of the Turkish Society of Medicine.

I hope that the expert ideas put forward at this gathering will lead to further progress in this field.

SPEECH BY PROFESSOR E. S. EGELI

Professor of Medicine, University of Istanbul
Former Rector of the University, and Chairman of the closing session of the symposium

People carry other people to
better days
NAZIM HIKMET

FLORENCE NIGHTINGALE is the perpetual symbol of love of humanity, the high value attached to human existence and the ideal of healing physical and spiritual wounds. Her efforts to realize these ideals during the Crimean War have gradually developed according to the needs of the day and have now reached their highest level.

The fact that the Ciba Foundation, in memory of the 150th anniversary of her birthday, has chosen the subject of public health, and made the very valuable decision to hold this meeting in Istanbul, where her efforts to realize this human ideal started, is to be appreciated. I would like to thank the organizers.

The main problem of our day is not to achieve social justice within a nation but to achieve it among the nations of the world. And without doubt the permanent missionaries of the humanist philosophy who can help in the realization of this ideal are doctors of medicine. If those in the field of politics attached to human value the necessary importance it receives within the ideology of medicine, human happiness would have been much more than it is today.

Lack of financial means and possibilities cannot be a detrimental factor to ideals heartily supported. In fact, the efforts of those who believe in this has made possible the wide range of opportunity today.

I hope the subjects covered in this symposium will help to open new horizons of happiness for humanity. However, there is one common danger now faced by humanity which I would like to touch upon. The youth movement which has embraced the whole world and is causing restlessness among all the civilized nations is something that should be considered as a mental disorder of humanity. Without doubt these movements, which are irrational and whose purpose is not clearly known, are potentially destructive in our civilization. The Foundation, through this symposium, should also search for measures to be taken against this irrational way of thinking and behaviour, which must be distinguished from the classical mental illnesses.

Istanbul has liked you a lot and benefited a lot from you. I hope that your short stay here has left you pleasant memories.

Hoping that you will be successful, patient and strong in your efforts to serve humanity and in your new studies, I salute you all sincerely.

226

Chairman's Closing Remarks

PROFESSOR R. V. CHRISTIE

THE Ciba Foundation made a very subtle choice when it dedicated this symposium to the memory of Florence Nightingale. When she arrived in Scutari she found a military hospital which was run by a carefully chosen team representing three government departments, trained along bureaucratic lines not to make trouble, not to spend money and never to risk responsibility. The regulations which this team obeyed to the letter were not designed to meet the situation, and the result was chaos.

In contrast, Florence Nightingale made lots of trouble, spent her own money when the need arose, never avoided responsibility and made her own rules to meet the situation. Before she left Scutari, hardly two years later, she had taught the British a lasting lesson on how teamwork should be conducted.

In this symposium we have not neglected to emphasize the hazards which can arise when teamwork becomes inflexible and uncritical. We have discussed the various areas where teamwork has proved profitable in the past, and have tried to define at least some of the important issues for the future. I believe it has been a very profitable symposium.

It could be said that discussions of this kind are meaningless without the cooperation and goodwill which are hardly apparent among our largest countries. But the truth is that the promotion of health commands universal interest and sympathy, and, as the Red Cross has shown with both China and Formosa among its members, and as we in Canada have found in our exchange professorship with Peking, medical overtures can succeed when others fail. The kind of effort which has been outlined by Dr Wolstenholme and Professor Young could well be the start of a new outlook on international understanding.

Bibliography

1: FLORENCE NIGHTINGALE—HANDMAID OF CIVILIZATION
G. E. W. WOLSTENHOLME

1. BISHOP, W. J. and GOLDIE, S. (1962) *A Bio-bibliography of Florence Nightingale.* London: Dawson.
2. GISH, O. (1969) *Britain and the Immigrant Doctor.* London: Institute of Race Relations.
3. PEARSON, L. B. (1970) *Partners in Development.* London: Pall Mall Press.
4. ROYAL COMMISSION ON MEDICAL EDUCATION (1968) *Report* (Chairman: Lord Todd). London: Her Majesty's Stationery Office, Cmnd. 3569.
5. WOLSTENHOLME, G. E. W. (1967) Outlines of a world health service as a step towards man's wellbeing and towards a world society. In *Ciba Foundation Symposium Health of Mankind*, pp. 254–261. London: Churchill.
6. WOLSTENHOLME, G. E. W. (1970) Florence Nightingale: new lamps for old. *Proceedings of the Royal Society of Medicine*, **64**, 1282–1288.

2: RESPONSE TO EMERGENCIES—NATIONAL AND INTERNATIONAL
Y. HENTSCH

1. BEER, H. (1967) *The League of Red Cross Societies in the Modern World.* Geneva: League of Red Cross Societies.
2. DUNANT, J. H. (1947) *A Memory of Solferino*, p. 57. London: Cassell.
3. GAGNEBIN, B. and GAZAY, M. (1963) *Encounter with Henry Dunant.* Geneva: Georg.
4. HUBER, M. (1930) In *The Red Cross—Principles and Problems*, p. 27. Geneva: Kundig.
5. INTERNATIONAL COMMITTEE OF THE RED CROSS (1969) *Rights and Duties of Nurses under the Geneva Conventions of August 12th 1949.* Geneva: International Committee of the Red Cross.
6. XXIst INTERNATIONAL CONFERENCE OF THE RED CROSS (1969) *Resolutions.* Istanbul: International Committee of the Red Cross and League of Red Cross Societies.
7. INTERNATIONAL COUNCIL OF NURSES (1969) *Statement on Nursing Education, Nursing Practice and Service and the Social and Economic Welfare of Nurses.* Basle: Karger.
8. LAMBERTSEN, E. C. (1953) *Nursing Team Organization and Functioning.* New York: Bureau of Publications, Teachers' College, Columbia University.
9. LEAGUE OF RED CROSS SOCIETIES (1970) *Disaster Relief.* Geneva: League of Red Cross Societies.
10. OFFICE OF PUBLIC INFORMATION, UNITED NATIONS (1968) *Everyman's United Nations*, 8th edn. New York: United Nations.
11. UNITED NATIONS ORGANIZATION (1968) *Assistance in Cases of Natural Disaster.* New York: United Nations, General Assembly Twenty-Third Regular Session, Resolution No. 2435 (XXIII).

229

BIBLIOGRAPHY

12. WAHI, P. N. (1970) *Education for the Health Professions—Regional Aspects of a Universal Problem.* Geneva: World Health Organization, Twenty-Third World Health Assembly, A23/Technical Discussions/4.
13. WORLD HEALTH ORGANIZATION (1946) In *Basic Documents,* 17th edn, p. 1. Geneva: World Health Organization.
14. WORLD HEALTH ORGANIZATION (1970) *Report of the Technical Discussions at the Twenty-Third World Assembly on Education for the Health Professions—Regional Aspects of a Universal Problem.* Geneva: World Health Organization, Twenty-Third World Health Assembly, A23/Technical Discussions/5.

3: THE NEW PRIORITIES IN TROPICAL MEDICINE
M. H. KING

1. KING, M. (1969) *The Development of Health Services in Malawi, 1970–1985.* Lusaka, Zambia: mimeographed document, Department of Social Medicine, University of Zambia.
2. PEARSON, L. B (1970) *Partners in Development.* London: Pall Mall Press.
3 REID, J. J. A. (1970) Gaps in medical care. *British Medical Journal* 1, 435.
4. UNITED NATIONS (1970) *United Nations Statistical Yearbook, 1969.* New York: United Nations.

Discussion

1. KING, M. (1966) *Medical Care in Developing Countries.* Nairobi: Oxford University Press.

5: AN EXAMPLE OF AN INTEGRATED APPROACH TO HEALTH CARE: TURKISH NATIONAL HEALTH SERVICES
N. H. FIŞEK

1. FIŞEK, N. H. (1962) The outline of national health services in Turkey [in Turkish]. *Planlama* 1, 55–65.
2. FIŞEK, N. H. (1968) Health planning in Turkey as an example of planning in developing countries. *Annales de la Société Belge de Médecine Tropicale* 381, 48.
3. FIŞEK, N. H. (1968) The design and evaluation of the health plan in Turkey. *Eighth International Congress of Tropical Medicine and Malaria,* Teheran.
4. FIŞEK, N. H. (1970) The factors hindering the development of health services in Turkey [in Turkish]. *Annual of the Turkish Medical Association.*
5. GOODMAN, N. M. (1964) Turkey's experiment in the "socialisation" of medicine. *Lancet* 1, 36–38.
6. HEPERKAN, Y. and CO-WORKERS (1967) *Vital Statistics from the Turkish Demographic Survey.* Ankara: School of Public Health.
7. INSTITUTE OF COMMUNITY MEDICINE (1970) *An Account of the Activities of the Etimesgut Rural Health District, 1967, 1968 and 1969.* Ankara: Hacettepe University Press.
8. MINISTRY OF HEALTH (1970) *Annual Budget Report* [in Turkish]. Ankara: The Ministry of Health, Government of Turkey.
9. ŞEHSUVAROĞLU, B. (1963) An outline of health services in Anatolia between the 13th and 19th centuries [in Turkish]. *Sağlik Dergisi* 37, 8–15.
10. TUNCA, Y. (1964) *Forty Years of Health Services in Turkey* [in Turkish]. Ankara: Sağlik ve Sosyal Yardim Bakanligi. Publications No. 303.

6: EXPERIMENTS IN EXPANDING THE RURAL HEALTH SERVICE IN PEOPLE'S CHINA
J. S. HORN

1. HORN, J. S. (1969) *Away with all Pests.* London: Paul Hamlyn.

7: BACKCLOTH TO THE NATIONAL HEALTH SERVICE IN ENGLAND AND WALES

1. CENTRAL OFFICE OF INFORMATION (1968) *Health Services in Britain.* London: Central Office of Information.

8: THE FAMILY CARE TEAM: PHILOSOPHY, PROBLEMS, POSSIBILITIES
LISBETH HOCKEY

1. ABEL, R. A. (1969) *Nursing Attachments to General Practice.* London: Her Majesty's Stationery Office.
2. AKESTER, J. M. and MACPHAIL, A. W. (1964) Health visiting and general practice. *Lancet* 2, 405–508.
3. ANDERSON, J. A. D. (1969) Health team in the community. *Lancet* 2, 679–681.
4. ANDERSON, J. A. D., DRAPER, P., AMBLER, M. and BLACK, J. M. (1967) The attachment of local authority staff to general practices. A follow-up study. *The Medical Officer* 118, 249–251.
5. ANDERSON, J. A. D., DRAPER, P. A., KINCAID, I. T. and AMBLER, M. C. (1970) Attachment of community nurses to general practices: a follow-up study. *British Medical Journal* 4, 103–105.
6. BODDY, F. A. (1969) General practitioners' view of the home nursing service. *British Medical Journal* 2, 438–441.
7. DEPARTMENT OF HEALTH AND SOCIAL SECURITY (1969) *Annual Report of the Department of Health and Social Security for the Year 1968.* London: Her Majesty's Stationery Office.
8. FLOYD, C. B. (1968) Car service in general practice: a two-year survey. *British Medical Journal* 2, 614–617.
9. GILHOOLEY, L. and SMITH, M. (1969) To diagnose. *District Nursing* 12, 8.
10. GORDON, I. (1967) Attachment of local authority nursing staff to general practitioners. *The Medical Officer* 118, 252.
11. HASLER, J. C., HEMPHILL, P. M. R., STEWART, T. I., BOYLE, N., HARRIS, A. and PALMER, E. (1968) Development of the nursing section of the community health team. *British Medical Journal* 3, 734–736.
12. HOCKEY, L. (1966) *Feeling the Pulse.* London: Queen's Inst. of District Nursing.
13. HOCKEY, L. (1968) *Care in the Balance.* London: Queen's Inst. of District Nursing.
14. KUENSSBERG, E. V. (1970) Influenza and the team in general practice. *Update* 2, 424–425.
15. MINISTRY OF HEALTH (1960) *Report of the Ministry of Health for the Year ended 31st December 1959.* London: Her Majesty's Stationery Office.
16. SMITH, J. WESTON (1967) Extended use of nursing services in general practice. *British Medical Journal* 4, 672–674.
17. WALKER, J. H. and MCCLURE, L. M. (1969) Community nurses view of general practice attachment. *British Medical Journal* 3, 584–587.
18. WARIN, J. F. (1968) General practitioners and nursing staff: a complete attachment scheme in retrospect and prospect. *British Medical Journal* 2, 41–45.

9: PAEDIATRICS AND THE COMMUNITY
GIULIO J. BARBERO

1. HENTSCH, Y. (1971) This volume, p. 14.
2. KISSEIH, D. A. N. (1971) This volume, p. 150.

Discussion

1. ORDOÑEZ-PLAJA, A. (1971) This volume, pp. 167–172.

10: PARAMEDICAL PARADOXES—CHALLENGES AND OPPORTUNITY
T. D. BAKER

1. AMERICAN DENTAL ASSOCIATION. BUREAU OF ECONOMIC RESEARCH AND STATISTICS (1965) Survey of Dentist Opinion, 1964. *Journal of the American Dental Association* **70** (February, March, April, May, and June) and **71** (July and September).
2. AMERICAN DENTAL ASSOCIATION (1965) *Reports of Offices and Councils. Section on Dental Education.* Chicago: American Dental Association.
3. AMERICAN DENTAL ASSOCIATION (1965) *Reports of Offices and Councils. Section on Dental Education*, pp. 37–47. Chicago: American Dental Association. [Cited by: Cassidy, J. E. (1968) *Maryland Dental Manpower Projection*, p. 53. Doctoral thesis, Johns Hopkins University, Baltimore, Maryland.]
4. BRYANT, J. (1969) *Health and the Developing World.* Ithaca, N.Y.: Cornell University Press.
5. CUNNINGHAM, N. (1969) An evaluation of an auxiliary-based child health service in rural Nigeria. *Journal of the Society of Health of Nigeria* **3**, 21–25.
6. FENDALL, N. R. E. (1968) The auxiliary in medicine. *Israel Journal of Medical Sciences* **4**, 614–628.
7. GLASSER, W. A. (1966) Nursing leadership and policy: some cross-national comparisons. In *The Nursing Profession—Five Sociological Essays*, ed. Davis, F. New York: John Wiley.
8. INTERNATIONAL COOPERATION ADMINISTRATION. OFFICE OF PUBLIC HEALTH. *Technical Assistance for Health.* No date. [Originally published in Part II— Health Exhibits from Official Sources—Appendix in Overseas Medical Research and Assistance—Hearings before the Subcommittee on Reorganization and International Organizations of the Committee on Government Operations, United States Senate, Eighty-sixth Congress, Second Session.]
9. MORLEY, D. (1963) A medical service for children under five years of age in West Africa. *Transactions of the Royal Society of Tropical Medicine and Hygiene* **57**, 79.
10. ROCKEFELLER FOUNDATION (1951) *Directory of Fellowship Awards for the Years 1917–1950.* New York: The Rockefeller Foundation.
11. ROSINSKI, E. F. (1969) Impact of technology and evolving health care systems on the training of allied health personnel. *Military Medicine* **134**, 383–385.
12. SENECAL, J. (1968) Training of paramedical personnel in the developing countries. *Israel Journal of Medical Sciences* **4**, 665–672.
13. SHOOK, D. C. (1969) Alaska native community health aide training. *Alaska Medicine* **11**, 62–63.
14. TINUBU, A. and CUNNINGHAM, N. (1968) *Gbaja Family Health Nurse Project— A Report on the First Year's Work.* Lagos, Nigeria: Institute of Child Health.
15. WORLD HEALTH ORGANIZATION (1963) *World Directory of Medical Schools.* Geneva: World Health Organization.

16. WORLD HEALTH ORGANIZATION (1967) *World Directory of Dental Schools.* Geneva: World Health Organization.
17. WORLD HEALTH ORGANIZATION (1968) *The Second Ten Years of the World Health Organization.* 1958–1967. Geneva: World Health Organization.

Discussion

1. COMMITTEE ON HIGHER EDUCATION (1963) *Report* (Chairman: Lord Robbins). London: Her Majesty's Stationery Office, Cmnd. 2154.
2. LEWIS, W. A. (1962) Education and economic development. *International Social Sciences Journal* 14, 685–699.
3. LEWIS, W. A. (1968) Personal communication.
4. ROYAL COMMISSION ON MEDICAL EDUCATION (1968) *Report* (Chairman: Lord Todd). London: Her Majesty's Stationery Office, Cmnd. 3569.

11: NEW CONCEPTS IN MEDICAL EDUCATION

E. BRAGA

1. BILLECOCQ, P. (1970) Address to the Ministers of National Education of French-speaking countries, Novakchott, Mauretania. Paris: *Le Monde* February 25.
2. CANDAU, M. G. (1967) Knowledge, the bridge to achievement. *WHO Chronicle* 21, 505–509.
3. KERR, C. (1969) In *The Modern University*, pp. 8–16, ed. Miescher, P.A. Stuttgart: Thieme.
4. PERKINS, J. A. (1970) The five crises of the university. *UNESCO Courrier*, June, pp. 28–32.
5. UNITED NATIONS EDUCATIONAL, SCIENTIFIC AND CULTURAL ORGANIZATION (1970) *La Planification de l'Education*, pp. 13–14. Paris: UNESCO.
6. WORLD HEALTH ORGANIZATION (1970) *Background Document of the Technical Discussions of the Twenty-Third World Health Assembly.* Geneva: World Health Organization, Twenty-Third World Health Assembly, A23/Technical Discussions/1.

Discussion

1. EXPERT COMMITTEE ON ENVIRONMENTAL HEALTH (1967) *The Education of Engineers in Environmental Health.* Geneva: World Health Organization, Technical Report Series, No. 376.
2. PEARL, A. and RIESSMAN, F. (1965) *New Careers for the Poor.* New York: Free Press; London: Macmillan.

12: PHILOSOPHY OF MANAGEMENT: THE PLACE OF THE PRO-FESSIONAL ADMINISTRATOR

B. L. SALMON

Discussion

1. COMMITTEE ON THE CIVIL SERVICE (1968) *Report*, vol. 1 (Chairman: Lord Fulton). London: Her Majesty's Stationery Office, Cmnd. 3638.
2. COMMITTEE ON SENIOR NURSING STAFF STRUCTURE (1966) *Report* (Chairman: B. L. Salmon). London: Her Majesty's Stationery Office, 32–533.
3. JOINT WORKING PARTY ON THE ORGANIZATION OF MEDICAL WORK IN HOSPITALS (1967) *First Report* (Chairman: Sir George Godber). London: Her Majesty's Stationery Office, 32–538.

14: MENTAL HEALTH CARE: A GROWING CONCERN TO COMMUNITIES
J. A. C. DE KOCK VAN LEEUWEN

1. LUFT, J. (1963) *Group Processes: an Introduction to Group Dynamics*, p. 10. Palo Alto, Cal.: National Press
2. TAYLOR, F. W. (1911) *The Principles of Scientific Management*. New York: Harper.

15: VOLUNTEERS—THEIR USE AND MISUSE
A. G. DICKSON

1. DICKSON, A. G. and DICKSON, M. (1969) *School in the Round*. London: Ward Lock.
2. SCHOOLS COUNCIL (1968) *Community Service and the Curriculum*. Working Paper No. 17. London: Her Majesty's Stationery Office.
3. SCOTT, P. (1967) The biological need to help. *New Society*, March 30.

Discussion

1. LEAGUE OF RED CROSS SOCIETIES (1965) *Guide for a Red Cross Welfare Service*. Geneva: League of Red Cross Societies.
2. WOLSTENHOLME, G. E. W. (1967) Outlines of a world health service, as a step towards man's well-being and towards a world society. In *Ciba Foundation Symposium Health of Mankind*, pp. 254–261. London: Churchill.

16: TEAMWORK FOR WORLD HEALTH: PERSONAL CONCLUSIONS AND RECOMMENDATIONS
F. G. YOUNG

1. HILL, K. R. (1964) Cost of undergraduate medical education in Britain. *British Medical Journal* 1, 300–302.
2. ROYAL COMMISSION ON MEDICAL EDUCATION (1968) *Report* (Chairman: Lord Todd). London: Her Majesty's Stationery Office, Cmnd. 3369.

INDEX OF AUTHORS*

Entries in bold type indicate a paper; other entries are contributions to the discussions.

* Author and Subject Indexes compiled by William Hill.

INDEX OF SUBJECTS

Printed by William Clowes & Sons Limited, London, Colchester and Beccles

DATE DUE

AYLORD | | | PRINTED IN U.S.A.